THE NEW WALLACE STEVENS STUDIES

The New Wallace Stevens Studies introduces a range of fresh voices and promising topics to the study of this great American poet. It is organized into three sections. The first explores concepts that have begun to emerge in Stevens criticism: imperialism and colonialism, his politics of utopia, his ideas about community building and audience, his secularism, and his transnationalism. The second section applies recent methodological and theoretical advances that have left a prominent mark on literary studies – from world literature and ecocriticism to urban studies, queer studies, intersectional thinking, and cognitive literary studies. Essays in the third section reassess issues that have long inspired critics. Here investigations include Stevens's reception by later poets, his attitude toward modern fiction, different modes of his poetic thinking, aspects of his rhetoric and style, and his lyrical ethics. This volume captures a cross-section of the most striking recent developments in Stevens criticism.

BART EECKHOUT is Professor of English and American Literature at the University of Antwerp. He has been Editor of *The Wallace Stevens Journal* since 2011 and authored *Wallace Stevens and the Limits of Reading and Writing* (2002). His edited books include *Wallace Stevens across the Atlantic* (2008); *Wallace Stevens, New York, and Modernism* (2012); and *Poetry and Poetics after Wallace Stevens* (2017).

GÜL BILGE HAN is a lecturer at the Department of English, Uppsala University. Her research lies at the intersection of modernist studies, world literature, aesthetic theory, and literary pedagogy. She is the author of *Wallace Stevens and the Poetics of Modernist Autonomy* (Cambridge University Press, 2019) and several essays on modernist aesthetics and poetry.

TWENTY-FIRST-CENTURY CRITICAL REVISIONS

This series addresses two main themes across a range of key authors, genres, and literary traditions. The first is the changing critical interpretations that have emerged since *c.* 2000. Radically new interpretations of writers, genres, and literary periods have emerged from the application of new critical approaches. Substantial scholarly shifts have occurred too, through the emergence of new editions, editions of letters, and competing biographical accounts. Books in this series collate and reflect this rich plurality of twenty-first-century literary critical energies, and wide varieties of revisionary scholarship, to summarize, analyze, and assess the impact of contemporary critical strategies. Designed to offer critical pathways and evaluations, and to establish new critical routes for research, this series collates and explains a dizzying array of criticism and scholarship in key areas of twenty-first-century literary studies.

RECENT TITLES IN THIS SERIES:

JENNIFER COOKE
The New Feminist Literary Studies
SUZANNE DEL GIZZO AND KIRK CURNUTT
The New Hemingway Studies
PAIGE REYNOLDS
The New Irish Studies
JENNIFER HAYTOCK AND LAURA RATTRAY
The New Edith Wharton Studies
MARK BYRON
The New Ezra Pound Studies

THE NEW WALLACE
STEVENS STUDIES

EDITED BY

BART EECKHOUT

University of Antwerp

GÜL BILGE HAN

Uppsala University

CAMBRIDGE
UNIVERSITY PRESS

University Printing House, Cambridge CB2 8BS, United Kingdom

One Liberty Plaza, 20th Floor, New York, NY 10006, USA

477 Williamstown Road, Port Melbourne, VIC 3207, Australia

314–321, 3rd Floor, Plot 3, Splendor Forum, Jasola District Centre,
New Delhi – 110025, India

79 Anson Road, #06–04/06, Singapore 079906

Cambridge University Press is part of the University of Cambridge.

It furthers the University's mission by disseminating knowledge in the pursuit of
education, learning, and research at the highest international levels of excellence.

www.cambridge.org
Information on this title: www.cambridge.org/9781108833295
DOI: 10.1017/9781108973946

First published 2021

A catalogue record for this publication is available from the British Library.

Library of Congress Cataloging-in-Publication Data
NAMES: Eeckhout, Bart, 1964- editor. | Han, Gül Bilge, 1984- editor.
TITLE: The new Wallace Stevens studies / edited by Bart Eeckhout, University of Antwerp,
Gül Bilge Han, Uppsala University.
DESCRIPTION: Cambridge ; New York : Cambridge University Press, 2021. |
Series: Twenty-first-century critical revisions | Includes bibliographical references and index.
IDENTIFIERS: LCCN 2020057998 (print) | LCCN 2020057999 (ebook) | ISBN 9781108833295
(hardback) | ISBN 9781108978286 (paperback) | ISBN 9781108973946 (ebook)
SUBJECTS: LCSH: Stevens, Wallace, 1879–955 – Criticism and interpretation.
CLASSIFICATION: LCC PS3537.T4753 Z693 2021 (print) | LCC PS3537.T4753 (ebook) |
DDC 811/.52–dc23
LC record available at https://lccn.loc.gov/2020057998
LC ebook record available at https://lccn.loc.gov/2020057999

ISBN 978-1-108-83329-5 Hardback

Contents

List of Contributors   *page* vii
List of Abbreviations   xi

Introduction
That Which Is Always Beginning   1
Bart Eeckhout and Gül Bilge Han

PART I EMERGING CONCEPTS IN STEVENS CRITICISM

1   Imperialism and Colonialism   17
    Lisa Siraganian

2   The Politics of Utopia   29
    Douglas Mao

3   Community and Audience   44
    Christopher Spaide

4   Secularism   58
    Matthew Mutter

5   Transnationalism   71
    Gül Bilge Han

PART II RECENT CRITICAL METHODS APPLIED TO STEVENS

6   World Literature   87
    Lee M. Jenkins

7   Ecological Poetics   100
    Cary Wolfe

8   Urban Studies   111
    Julia E. Daniel

v

9   Queer Studies   123
    Bart Eeckhout

10 Intersectional Studies   136
    Lisa M. Steinman

11 Cognitive Literary Studies   148
    G. Gabrielle Starr

PART III REVISIONARY READINGS OF STEVENS

12 Poetic Responses   159
    Andrew Epstein

13 Poetic Fiction   174
    Lisa Goldfarb

14 Poetic Thinking   186
    Charles Altieri

15 Constructive Disorderings   201
    Tom Eyers

16 Manner and Manners   213
    Zachary Finch

17 Lyrical Ethics   226
    Johanna Skibsrud

Index   237

Contributors

CHARLES ALTIERI teaches in the English Department at the University of California, Berkeley. He is on the editorial board of *The Wallace Stevens Journal* and has published many books, including *Painterly Abstraction in Modernist American Poetry* (1989), *Wallace Stevens and the Demands of Modernity: Toward a Phenomenology of Value* (2013), and *Reckoning with the Imagination: Wittgenstein and the Aesthetics of Literary Experience* (2015).

JULIA E. DANIEL is Associate Professor of Literature at Baylor University. Her research interests include urban ecocriticism, modern American poetry, and modern material culture, as seen in her book *Building Natures: Modern American Poetry, City Planning, and Landscape Architecture* (2017). Her work has appeared in *The Cambridge Companion to* The Waste Land, Wiley's *Companion to Modernist Poetry, Critical Quarterly*, and *Modern Drama*.

BART EECKHOUT is Professor of English and American Literature at the University of Antwerp. He has been editor of *The Wallace Stevens Journal* since 2011 and has published *Wallace Stevens and the Limits of Reading and Writing* (2002) besides four coedited volumes, *Wallace Stevens across the Atlantic* (2008); *Wallace Stevens, New York, and Modernism* (2012); *Poetry and Poetics after Wallace Stevens* (2017); and *Wallace Stevens, Poetry, and France* (2017).

ANDREW EPSTEIN is Professor of English at Florida State University. He is the author of *Attention Equals Life: The Pursuit of the Everyday in Contemporary Poetry and Culture* (2016) and *Beautiful Enemies: Friendship and Postwar American Poetry* (2006). His essays have appeared in *The Wallace Stevens Journal, Wallace Stevens in Context, Contemporary Literature, The Cambridge Companion to American Poets,* and many other publications. He maintains a blog about the New York School of poets called *Locus Solus*.

TOM EYERS is Associate Professor of Philosophy and Affiliated Faculty in English at Duquesne University. He is the author of three books: *Jacques Lacan and the Concept of the Real* (2012); *Post-Rationalism: Psychoanalysis, Epistemology, and Marxism in Postwar France* (2013); and *Speculative Formalism: Literature, Theory, and the Critical Present* (2017). His next book has the working title "Romantic Abstraction: Language, Nature, Historical Time."

ZACHARY FINCH teaches writing and literature at Massachusetts College of Liberal Arts (MCLA) in the northern Berkshires. He is a scholar of modern American poetry and poetics whose publications include articles on Sarah Piatt, Marianne Moore, William Carlos Williams, George Oppen, and Wallace Stevens, for which he won a John N. Serio Award in 2012. His poems and essays have appeared in journals including *American Letters & Commentary*, *Boston Review*, *Fence*, *Poetry*, and *Tin House*.

LISA GOLDFARB is Professor at New York University's Gallatin School, President of the Wallace Stevens Society, and Associate Editor of *The Wallace Stevens Journal*. She is the author of *The Figure Concealed: Wallace Stevens, Music, and Valéryan Echoes* (2011) and *Unexpected Affinities: Modern American Poetry and Symbolist Poetics* (2018), besides being coeditor of *Wallace Stevens, New York, and Modernism* (2012); *Poetry and Poetics after Wallace Stevens* (2017); and *Wallace Stevens, Poetry, and France* (2017).

GÜL BILGE HAN is a lecturer at the Department of English, Uppsala University. Her research lies at the intersection of modernist studies, world literature, aesthetic theory, and literary pedagogy. She is the author of *Wallace Stevens and the Poetics of Modernist Autonomy* (2019) and several articles and book chapters on twentieth-century poetry and modernist aesthetics. She is currently working on a comparative study that investigates poetic expressions of transnational solidarity in modernist and Global South responses to the rise of anticolonial struggles in the mid-twentieth century.

LEE M. JENKINS is Professor of English at University College Cork and a member of the editorial board of *The Wallace Stevens Journal*. She is the author of *Wallace Stevens: Rage for Order* (2000), *The Language of*

Caribbean Poetry (2004), and *The American Lawrence* (2015). With Alex Davis, she is editor of three Cambridge University Press collections, *The Locations of Literary Modernism* (2000), *The Cambridge Companion to Modernist Poetry* (2007), and *A History of Modernist Poetry* (2015).

DOUGLAS MAO is Russ Family Professor in the Humanities at Johns Hopkins University. He is the author of *Solid Objects: Modernism and the Test of Production* (1998); *Fateful Beauty: Aesthetic Environments, Juvenile Development, and Literature, 1860–1960* (2008); and *Inventions of Nemesis: Utopia, Indignation, and Justice* (2020). He is also the coeditor, with Rebecca Walkowitz, of *Bad Modernisms* (2006) and the editor of *The New Modernist Studies* (2021) as well as the Longman Cultural Edition of E. M. Forster's *Howards End* (2009). He currently serves as Series Editor of Hopkins Studies in Modernism.

MATTHEW MUTTER is Associate Professor of Literature at Bard College. His first book, *Restless Secularism: Modernism and the Religious Inheritance*, was published in 2017. His essays and reviews have appeared in *ELH*, *Twentieth Century Literature*, and *Arizona Quarterly*. His current book project explores the resistance of certain American novelists and poets to the hegemonic cultural authority of the social sciences in the twentieth century while examining the broader theoretical problems at the intersection of humanistic and social-scientific knowledge.

LISA SIRAGANIAN is the J. R. Herbert Boone Chair in Humanities, Associate Professor, and Chair of the Department of Comparative Thought and Literature at Johns Hopkins University. She is the author of *Modernism's Other Work: The Art Object's Political Life* (2012) and *Modernism and the Meaning of Corporate Persons* (2020); and the editor of *The Norton Anthology of American Poetry, volume D, 1914–1945* (2021).

JOHANNA SKIBSRUD is Assistant Professor of English at the University of Arizona, where she teaches modern poetry and poetics. She is the author of numerous books, including *The Sentimentalists* (2010; winner of the Scotiabank Giller Prize); a collection of critical essays, *"The Nothing That Is": Essays on Art, Literature and Being* (2019); and a critical monograph, *The Poetic Imperative: A Speculative Aesthetics* (2020).

CHRISTOPHER SPAIDE is a Junior Fellow in the Harvard Society of Fellows. His book project, "Lyric Togetherness," examines the plural pronouns and collective voices of American poetry from 1945 to today. His essays, reviews, and poems have appeared in *College Literature*, *Contemporary Literature*, *Harvard Review*, *Poetry*, and *The Yale Review*.

G. GABRIELLE STARR is Professor of English and Neuroscience at Pomona College. The author of two books, *Lyric Generations: Poetry and the Novel in the Long Eighteenth Century* (2004) and *Feeling Beauty: The Neuroscience of Aesthetic Experience* (2013), she has written extensively on aesthetics and cognition. She is also the president of Pomona College.

LISA M. STEINMAN, Kenan Professor of English and Humanities at Reed College, is the author of nine books, two of which include a focus on Stevens's work, and of numerous articles and book chapters on contemporary and modern poets. She has been a longtime editorial board member of *The Wallace Stevens Journal* and contributed to volumes such as *Poetry and Poetics after Wallace Stevens*; *Wallace Stevens in Context*; and *Wallace Stevens, Poetry, and France*.

CARY WOLFE holds the Bruce and Elizabeth Dunlevie Chair in English at Rice University, where he is also Founding Director of 3CT: The Center for Critical and Cultural Theory. His books include *Ecological Poetics; or, Wallace Stevens's Birds* (2020); *Animal Rites: American Culture, the Discourse of Species, and Posthumanist Theory* (2003); *What Is Posthumanism?* (2010); and *Before the Law: Humans and Other Animals in a Biopolitical Frame* (2012). He is Founding Editor of the series "Posthumanities" at the University of Minnesota Press.

Abbreviations

The following standard abbreviations for the works of Wallace Stevens are used throughout. As a rule, references to poems and prose are to the Library of America volume edited by Frank Kermode and Joan Richardson (abbreviated as *CPP*). Page references are provided for poems only when quotations from those poems are included in the discussion.

CPP   *Wallace Stevens: Collected Poetry and Prose.* Edited by Frank Kermode and Joan Richardson, Library of America, 1997.
L   *Letters of Wallace Stevens.* Edited by Holly Stevens, Alfred A. Knopf, 1966; reprint, University of California Press, 1996.

That Which Is Always Beginning

Bart Eeckhout and Gül Bilge Han

It is fitting to begin a collection of essays entitled *The New Wallace Stevens Studies* with an inquiry into what such newness might mean both for Stevens and for the purposes of the present volume. Perhaps no other poem captures the quintessentially Stevensian attitude toward newness as remarkably as his late lyric "St. Armorer's Church from the Outside." "In the air of newness" that surrounds the ruined, gutted chapel of St. Armorer's in that poem, the speaker comes upon

> an air of freshness, clearness, greenness, blueness,
> That which is always beginning because it is part
> Of that which is always beginning, over and over. (*CPP* 449)

The possibility of achieving newness and experiencing a sense of perennial beginning is to be found, unexpectedly perhaps, and certainly paradoxically, by meditating upon the architecture of an old chapel. Powered by the unlimited generativity of the imagination, the dilapidated chapel is seen in its "vivid element," as spreading out for a light, an influx of what the speaker calls the "*vif*," which, however slight, is capable of bringing forth the "dizzle-dazzle of being new." Such an influx is defined, furthermore, as a mode of constant "becoming" (*CPP* 449). New, vital forms arrive, Stevens seems to be saying, during moments of interaction with paradigms of the old, during confluences of what used to be there, what happens to be here, and what is in the process of becoming, rather than in simple negations of supposedly antiquated forms. Cycles of continuous innovation, transformation, and flux, contingent upon everything that has come before, underlie the creative impulse that seeks to satisfy the "need to be actual," which is the need to give "a new account of everything old" (*CPP* 448–49). *The New Wallace Stevens Studies* takes this Stevensian premise of perpetual renewal and remaking to heart. Our claim to newness is accurate insofar as asserting the new does not involve radically dispensing with the past

but building novel sets of approaches and accounts on aging foundations. The refreshing perspectives offered in the pages of this volume are
thus at the same time a continuation of the rich critical heritage
bequeathed by Stevens's most devoted readers – a heritage that, especially over the past few decades, has notably challenged and expanded
our understanding of his poetry and thought beyond what would have
been imaginable by the earliest critics striking out in the poet's wake.

If in many ways *The New Wallace Stevens Studies* draws on and
responds to the poet's critical afterlife in general, it positions itself
particularly in relation to two major edited volumes whose ambition it
has been to stake out most of the critical field. In its fourteen chapters,
John N. Serio's *The Cambridge Companion to Wallace Stevens* (2007) did
a wonderful job of introducing readers to the main topics that had
preoccupied Stevens specialists during the first half-century of critical
production: his biography; the various stages of his career; his attitudes
toward both contemporary poets and the Romantic tradition; the inspiration he drew from philosophy and the cycles of the seasons; how to come
to terms with the lyric speaker and a variety of linguistic features in his
verse; and the place of painting, figurations of the feminine, and belief
systems in his worldview. Ten years later, Glen MacLeod's more histori-
cist collection, *Wallace Stevens in Context* (2017), went to great lengths to
flesh out as many relevant contexts as possible. Its thirty-six chapters fell
into six organizing sections: the real and imagined places that played an
important part in Stevens's life; the two main natural contexts for his
poetry; a range of literary contexts; his relation to the other arts; some of
the main intellectual frameworks for his thinking; and an extensive series
of social, cultural, and political contexts. The two volumes together drew
on forty-three experts, nearly half of whom were former or current
editorial board members of *The Wallace Stevens Journal*. The latter is
itself in its forty-fifth year (at the time of publication, in 2021) and has
continued to publish scholarship twice a year without interruption,
increasingly in the form of thematic issues.

This might make it seem as if all bases had been covered. Yet with
a complex and elusive poet such as Stevens, there always appears to be
a surprising amount of space to present additional perspectives and
critical developments. What we are presenting in the current volume is
explicitly designed to complement the two previous Cambridge
University Press volumes by diversifying critical approaches and introducing a range of new voices and promising topics to the field. Although
a good many of our contributors are established scholars with an

impressive pedigree, the majority are early to mid-career critics. More importantly, the contributors whose work we showcase here have in recent years produced striking scholarship on Stevens, whether in leading journals or books of their own, that has sought to recalibrate and reorient critical responses to the poet. As a result, *The New Wallace Stevens Studies* is able to demonstrate the remarkable wealth of research recently initiated, often in the margins of what may be regarded as mainstream Stevens criticism (i.e., writings by the editorial board members of the Journal or contributors to the many panels and conferences organized by the Wallace Stevens Society), but just as frequently opening up new fields, cutting-edge theories, and untried methodologies rightly clamoring for our attention.

***

The division of this collection into three parts is meant to draw helpful through-lines and distinctions among contributions, since the essays range far and wide in their ambition. Part I starts from our observation that various accounts of Stevens over the past two decades have pushed forward a number of previously neglected or only recently theorized concepts that can help us analyze his work in greater depth. The writings collected under "Emerging Concepts in Stevens Criticism" thus include chapters on the relevance of imperialism and colonialism to the understanding of Stevens's poetics, the underestimated utopian nature of his thinking, his conception of an audience and how he saw his poetry as a form of community building, the kind of secularism his writings elaborate, and the precise quality of his transnational orientation.

Lisa Siraganian kicks off by mapping and extending the critical discussions of Stevens that have begun to tackle his engagement with questions of empire and Western colonial ideologies. Emerging as a global institution during the poet's lifetime, imperialism, especially in its cultural variety, intrigued and worried Stevens as a particular variation on the question of knowledge that fascinated him so much. As Siraganian reminds us, Stevens's views on the imperialist fantasies of his age – from Mussolini's colonial invasion of Ethiopia to the invention of modern warfare and the rise of totalitarian regimes – could be at times sympathetic. Yet in several poems, including "Anecdote of the Jar," "Owl's Clover," "Life on a Battleship," and "A Weak Mind in the Mountains," Stevens provides alternative and more complicated accounts that question and sometimes oppose colonizing modes of cultural domination. These are among the texts worth returning to and grappling with because they demand historical and ideological nuance. The contextualization of Stevens's poetry that Siraganian provides enables us to sort out his competing allegiances at a chaotic historical moment – allegiances not only to anti-imperialism but also to an embattled Western culture and ideology, and to a unifying world of art and poetry.

Stevens's response to the competing ideologies of his age takes on a different, if compatible, dimension in Douglas Mao's chapter, in which Mao identifies the utopian impulses of the poet's verse with a view to reevaluating his relation to the political. Stevens scholars have variously represented him as a crafter of poetic utopias, a skeptic of utopian thinking, and a champion of utopian material sufficiency. Mao's investigation adds to the picture by showing how, in his poetry of the late 1930s and early 1940s, Stevens situates leaders and movements impelled by visions of ideal futures within a conception of political life as an ongoing struggle for dominance between ideas. Reading several of Stevens's poems in dialogue with prominent cultural texts of the time – especially Karl Mannheim's *Ideology and Utopia* and Max Lerner's *Ideas Are Weapons* – Mao reveals how Stevens's view of history as an interplay of imagination and reality partook of important currents in interwar intellectual life. An examination of the particular utopian impulses in Stevens's verse thus prepares the ground for a more complete understanding of his vision of the relationship between the aesthetic and the ideological realms.

The third chapter complements the first two by expanding the terms of such politically oriented debates. Among the topics that have come into focus as a result of the increasing awareness of Stevens's worldliness are his figurations of collectivity and audience. These have posed challenges to the commonly received notion that Stevens's world is devoid of people. Though a prominent strand of Stevens criticism has argued that his poetry does not have a strong sense of either the interpersonal or an actual human audience, recent scholars are at last taking Stevens seriously as a poet of community. Christopher Spaide's engaging chapter illuminates how questions of community and audience have helped these scholars to reconceive both "the poem of the idea" and "the poem of the words": critics drawn to the former have focused on Stevens's historical and personal crises, political philosophy, aesthetics, place, and affect; those drawn to the latter have focused on his diction, genres, forms, speakers, and lyric pronouns. As Spaide demonstrates, community and audience, for Stevens, are never simply given but always counterbalanced by their others – individuality, impersonality, inhuman nature, and aesthetic autonomy. The poet's truest subject in this sense is neither community nor individuality but the never-settled contest between the two. Like Mao and Siraganian, Spaide adds conceptual rigor and precision to a discussion of the social and political contexts of Stevens's poetry. Such contexts continue to fuel critical debates about the writer's strategies for responding to the historical pressures of the actual world.

Another major and no less contested issue that has been leaving its imprint on analyses of Stevens's work is his stance toward secularism and religious faith. A polite but insistent critical struggle has been going on, especially in recent years, between scholars seeking to frame Stevens's poetry as fundamentally religious or spiritual in inspiration and those insisting on its twentieth-century expressions of secularist thinking. Matthew Mutter engages with and contributes to this debate by reassessing Stevens's understanding of secular modernity as a condition of both deprivation and liberation. He suggests that while Stevens was enticed by the secular model of the real as a domain of neutral, impersonal fact, as his career progressed he increasingly recognized that the very notion of a secular reality was itself an imaginative construction. This recognition is linked to Stevens's lifelong effort to rehabilitate, for what may be called his "secular anthropology," the imaginative human capacities that histor-ically generated religious ideas. A sense of play emerges in this context as central to Stevens's secularism: not only does it reconcile the secular values of freedom and sensuousness with the discordant necessity of the world, but it is also able to reveal an ongoing tension between the good of immanence and the need for transcendence.

While Mutter's chapter takes up the Stevensian imagination in its spiritual and secular guises, it is the geographical and cross-cultural range of the poet's imaginative vision that takes center stage in Gül Bilge Han's chapter on transnationalism. Drawing on recent theoretical appraisals of literary transnationalism and global modernism, Han examines how Stevens's desire to create new forms of interaction between distant geog-raphies and cultures constitutes a crucial component of his work. Her chapter argues that Stevens's poetry repeatedly interrogates both the possi-bilities and the limits of artistic mobility and travel beyond its local and national frameworks rather than simply proclaiming or celebrating the border-traversing capacities of poetic language and the imagination. In line with the opening chapters in this first part, Han views Stevens through a historically contextualizing lens, showing how his artistic impulse toward border-crossings is developed in dialogue with a range of cultural and political events, such as the rise of American nativism in the 1920s and subsequent developments of globalization and the Cold War.

***

Our second gathering of essays, which we have labeled "Recent Critical Methods Applied to Stevens," looks at a variety of methodological and theoretical advances that have made a prominent mark on literary studies in recent years – from world literature and ecocriticism to urban studies, queer studies, intersectional thinking, and cognitive literary studies. As several contributors to this part intimate, the methods and theories developed in such disciplines invite a renewed focus on Stevens's poetry, for they offer a variety of critical tools and thematic emphases that have not yet been fully integrated into studies on the poet.

Lee Jenkins's chapter, set up to be complementary with the preceding one on Stevens's transnationalism, assesses the poet's relationship and relevance to the study of world literature. Jenkins undertakes her multifaceted investigation by activating Pascale Casanova's rubric of the "two orders" – the political and the aesthetic – that together constitute the "world literary space." Stevens's involvement in the global cultural marketplace and his defense of poetic autonomy – his projection of his poetry as a world in itself – present seemingly incompatible yet mutually constitutive positions that inform his specific relationship to world literature. By way of illustration, Jenkins explores not only Stevens's Orientalism but also his global reception and readership in a surprising diversity of world-literary contexts: from contemporary Chinese poetry and the Anglophone world poetries of Kashmiri American and Iranian American poets Agha Shahid Ali and Roger Sedarat to a contemporary Italian poet such as Valerio Magrelli, as well as postwar British and Irish poetry.

The idea of a "world" for Stevens was able to encompass more, however, than the literary and poetic universe of letters; neither was it limited to the external events and pressures of his cultural and political surroundings. It also meant, to an important measure, his natural surroundings and what we now call the environment. Cary Wolfe's chapter proposes that we reconsider Stevens as an ecological poet as well. To do so, we should begin to see his cultural significance as radically different from the emphasis in previous accounts on the philosophical resonances of his poetic "mundo" – a universe structured by seasonal cycles – or his lyrical depiction of natural phenomena. Instead, Wolfe deploys a concept of environment that is more scientifically up-to-date, as highlighted in the contemporary biology of perception and cognition found in the writings of Humberto Maturana and Francisco Varela. Illuminated by their theories, the ecological significance of the poet's work may well be located in how Stevens's poetics manages to enact the very "operating program," with all its attendant paradoxes, of autopoietic living systems, rather than engaging in a merely representational relationship to what we used to call "nature."

If Wolfe presents us with a fresh sense of Stevens's nonrepresentational ecological poetics, Julia Daniel's chapter pursues another underexplored aspect of the poet's relationship to his environment, this time from a more cultural-material angle that takes into account the presence of urban spaces and experiences in his writings. As Daniel reminds us, Stevens was profoundly influenced by modern urbanization during his formative years in New York City, and he often turns to understated cityscapes for his exploration of the ideal aesthetic relationship between reality and the imagination. Daniel identifies two major modes of urbanization that are palpable throughout Stevens's works: a "dark," antipoetic variety in which city architectures prevent contact with nature and community, thereby also precluding the production of a vibrant poetry, and an organic, aesthetic urbanization where cities may be held up as sites of poetic inspiration and surprising connection with the more-than-human world. Stevens's recurrent vacillation between these two modes proves to be characteristic of the multiform, often ambivalent ways he engaged with the modern urbanism he witnessed up close.

To further diversify types of scholarship, Bart Eeckhout's chapter on queer studies tilts more heavily toward the biographical than other chapters do. With the knowledge and insights gained from queer studies and relevant biographical and historical scholarship, Eeckhout proposes to resituate Stevens not only within the aesthetic circles that may be drawn around his work but also and especially within the social circles in which he moved during his lifetime, and the poetic circles of those who have been attracted to his writings. From the new modernist studies, his investigation derives an interest in social networks at the expense of a narrow focus on self-reliant individuals; from queer studies, it borrows a fundamentally querying spirit about sexual identities and desires. Eeckhout offers a bird's-eye survey of Stevens's most significant queer precursors, contemporaries, and heirs, paying particular attention to the final two categories. As case studies, he singles out Stevens's friendships with George Santayana and José Rodríguez Feo, in which not-knowing played a central role, and the attractiveness of Stevens's licensing the fictive imagination to poets such as James Merrill and Richard Howard.

Eeckhout's account offers an example of criticism that reads Stevens in relation to the social categories informing so much academic work today – from sexuality to gender, race, ethnicity, class, or nationality. *Wallace Stevens in Context*, for instance, included individual chapters on "Race" and "The Feminine." So far, however, very few applications to Stevens have attempted to explore the confluences and possible conflicts between such critical perspectives. To address this shortcoming, Lisa Steinman reflects on the ways in which previous critical work informed by questions of race, class, and gender in Stevens's poetry might be refigured in light of the complicating analyses put forward by intersectional thinkers. Steinman offers, as an example of the merits and drawbacks of reading Stevens intersectionally, a rich discussion of "The Virgin Carrying a Lantern," from *Harmonium*. She sets her reading against a description of how contemporary writers of color have responded more to Stevens's style than to his representations of others – an emphasis that has allowed such writers to voice a deep ambivalence and reposition their own work (as well as Stevens's) within the African American literary tradition. Steinman convincingly demonstrates that the voices of these poets open up new possibilities for intersectional studies of Stevens.

Perhaps more than any of his contemporaries, Stevens has long been famous for being a poet of the mind. In his poetry and prose, he draws parallels between lyrical composition and the mind "in the act of finding / What will suffice," realizing at the same time that such a search is forever ongoing, because "It can never be satisfied, the mind, never" (*CPP* 218, 224). These qualities, as Gabrielle Starr's chapter shows, make Stevens's writings an excellent candidate for the interdisciplinary field of cognitive literary studies, which involves an exchange and cross-fertilization among the disciplines of neuroscience; cognitive linguistics; stylistics; literary criticism; and theories of embodiment, enactivism, and the extended mind. Such investigations have the potential to deepen our insight into various aspects of Stevens's writings: his way of disorienting readers through the use of imagery; his enactment of visual perception as a dynamic interplay between brain and world; his strategic use of rhyme and experimental sonic strategies; or his surprising patterns of phonemic, syllabic, and syntactic structuring. On this occasion, Starr offers a cognitive analysis of two powerful aesthetic modes in Stevens's poetry. The first of these is disruption, in which Stevens violates metrical expectations or creates perceptual or cognitive disorientation. The second involves the manipulation of pleasure (either represented in the poem or generated in readers) to call attention to certain formal aspects of a poem, and at times to help new formal features emerge from a disorderly formal background.

***

Taken together, the contributors to Part II demonstrate the implications, for the study of Stevens, of major theoretical and methodological interventions that have been reshaping the literary field. In a manner that responds more immediately to the long pedigree of Stevens criticism and its typical interests, the essays in our third and final part, gathered under the umbrella of "Revisionary Readings of Stevens," seek to reassess and deepen our understanding of issues that have long inspired critics. Here the collected topics include the reception of his work by subsequent generations of poets, his attitude toward modern fiction, various modes of his relation to philosophical thinking, aspects of his rhetoric and style, and finally the ethical dimension of his lyrical engagement.

One of the most productive formats in Stevens criticism for many years has been the juxtaposition with other poets, from earlier inspirational figures to contemporary writers and successors keeping up a dialogue with his work. Synoptic views of twentieth-century American poetry sometimes pitted writers in the Stevens tradition against a Poundian avant-garde. Such an opposition, however, has had difficulty integrating the significance of Stevens's heritage – its characteristic idiom, poetics, philosophical concerns – with certain strands in postwar poetry, particularly the experimental movement known as the New York School. In Andrew Epstein's chapter, the case of these poets is developed as an instructive example of the complexity and riches of poetic responses to Stevens. Epstein challenges the tendency to overlook Stevens as an important precursor, arguing that such neglect causes problems in both directions: it unnecessarily limits our sense of the New York School poetry while reinforcing the distorted image of Stevens as a backward-looking aesthete devoted solely to abstraction and imagination. For all their differences, Epstein proposes, Stevens and the New York School poets share a number of vital interests: an obsession with painting and a passion for all things French; a delight in wordplay and the sensuous surfaces of language; an anti-foundational skepticism toward fixity in self, language, or idea; and, most crucially, an embrace of the imagination and deep attraction to the surreal combined with a devotion to the ordinary and everyday.

Apart from three early experiments in playwriting and the nonfictional prose of his essays and letters, Stevens was – and wanted very much to be – a poet. As a result, scholars of modernist fiction have most often ignored him as a relevant contemporary writer, and vice versa, in criticism on the poet, the art of the contemporary novel has been receiving short shrift. Yet as Lisa Goldfarb's chapter elucidates, the fact that Stevens positioned himself so adamantly in the realm of poetry and kept away from the art of the novel does not mean he did not ponder questions of aesthetic affinity. In a 1948 letter, for instance, he commented on Marcel Proust as follows: "The only really interesting thing about Proust that I have seen recently is something that concerned him as a poet. It seems like a revelation, but it is quite possible to say that that is exactly what he was and perhaps all that he was" (*L* 575). Starting from a wider consideration of Stevens's relation to modernist fiction, Goldfarb amplifies Proust's presence in Stevens in segments that probe the poet's insight into Proust's writing style and the Proustian echoes in his own verse – particularly, the interlacing themes of the senses, time, and memory in shorter poems selected from various stages of Stevens's writing life.

The next two chapters swing to what might be called the other end of the scale of juxtapositions with non-poetic genres. If there is a topic that has garnered most sustained attention from Stevens scholars over the years, it is the relation between his poetry and philosophy. Though critics have used countless, often conflicting theoretical frameworks to discuss Stevens's philosophical leanings – from phenomenology and deconstruction to American pragmatism, to name but a few – there is something about which such heterogeneous approaches tend to agree: Stevens's work is deeply invested in articulating reflective states of mind that stage the processes of, and conditions for, poetic thinking. In recent years, critics have grown increasingly wary of mistaking the thinking that occurs in Stevens's verse for illustrations of external schools of thought. The two chapters dedicated to philosophy in *Wallace Stevens in Context* symptomatically share a skepticism toward the idea that Stevens's idiosyncratic thinking can be explained by importing insights from philosophy – even as both chapters outline the ways in which Stevens may be taken to engage with various philosophical traditions and issues. Taking this skeptical stance about imported theories as its point of departure, Charles Altieri's authoritative chapter focuses on the vital role Stevens attributes to the imagination for enacting modes of poetic thinking. As a culmination to decades of reflection and writing on the matter, Altieri identifies four distinct modes and trajectories of thought that may be said to build the larger arc of Stevens's oeuvre. He reveals how the poetry evolves from trying out various modes of thinking against generalization (in *Harmonium*) to valuing how poetic thinking can become central to ordinary life (in *Ideas of Order*), then to blending the unreal of fiction with the work of realization (conceived in the manner of Paul Cézanne), and finally by the time of *The Rock*, to a mode of poetic thinking that values the artifice present in even the most elemental of experiences.

Tying in with Altieri's wariness of theoretical reduction, Tom Eyers approaches Stevens with the purpose of examining how the writer's thought experiments undercut established notions of historical time. Eyers argues that Stevens subtly eludes our most common ways of treating literature. Where many scholars today adopt a historicizing and contextualizing approach to literary texts, Stevens, in Eyers's reading, moves in a more uncanny and challenging direction. Eyers locates in Stevens's verse repeated scenes of historical-temporal "afterwardsness," whereby what would seem to have come first in fact came later, and what one would have expected to follow on is instead shown to have been there all along. Far from resulting in mere disorder, such instances, when read closely and associatively, bring into being a singular poetic logic of historical time, and they invite a radical rerouting of our expectations about modernism. Stevens's "constructive disorderings," according to Eyers, resist collation into a theory and are inseparable from the literary techniques that make us notice them.

This emphasis on literary technique returns us to the precise workings of Stevens's language, which has been a consistent focus of critical attention since at least Helen Vendler's award-winning *On Extended Wings* (1969). But perspectives on the poet's idiomatic language continue to evolve as the topic inspires some of the best scholarship in the field. A chapter that testifies to this rich strand is indispensable, then, to a volume presenting recent evolutions in Stevens criticism, the more so since questions of language and style were not among the more worldly issues covered in *Wallace Stevens in Context*. For the present volume, Zachary Finch proposes that the rhetorical artifice in Stevens's poetry may be best understood through the concept of "manner." In contrast with style, a notion that seeks to define the personal signature of a writer's work, manner refers to the more social, public aspects of a writer's rhetorical bearing. Drawing on a range of thinkers and writers who have theorized aesthetic manner and the politics of manners – from Pierre Bourdieu to Giorgio Agamben, Henry James, and Lionel Trilling – Finch allows Stevens's interest in textiles and clothing, in figurations of nobility, and in the mannerist syntax of repetition to emerge not as neutral aesthetic traits but as expressions of a sensibility tied to social categories such as class and race.

Johanna Skibsrud's concluding chapter reactivates ethical questions in a spirit that should leave the reader wondering about the underestimated value of Stevens's aesthetic investments in the lyric as a mode of sharing pleasures between writer and reader. Considering how the "ethical turn" in literary criticism that was trumpeted for some time in the 1990s has had only a ripple effect in Stevens scholarship, the question of the poetry's ethical dimensions has been far from exhausted. Skibsrud builds on the work of scholars like Derek Attridge, William Waters, Rachel Cole, Mara Scanlon, and others to argue for the lyric as an actual, rather than a virtual, extension of subjectivity beyond a linear narrative frame. She emphasizes Stevens's wish to present poetry as an opportunity for engagement and interpretation, while taking seriously his emphasis on the impasse of language and subjective perception. With its close readings of several poems taken from different moments in Stevens's career, this beautiful final investigation acts both as testament to and argument for the capacity of lyric to express the nonlinear, fundamentally poetic relation between language and truth, self and other.

***

Although each individual chapter in *The New Wallace Stevens Studies* is designed to pursue a specific angle that contributes to the generous spread of topics overall, we have sought to keep the division between chapters sufficiently porous to allow also for critical dialogue and exchange. As our summary has already suggested, several chapters build clusters in pointing toward interlocking issues and approaches. Thus, the three opening contributions about imperialism/colonialism, the politics of utopia, and community/audience refocus critical attention on the social and political relevance of Stevens's verse. The subject of the poet's preoccupation with foreign geographies and cultures inspires a second cluster on transnationalism and world literature, with both chapters sharing an interest in Stevens's poetic expansions and resonance beyond his national borders. Other clusters explore the eco-urban and queer-intersectional implications of Stevens's verse, thereby situating it in relation to questions of environment and cultural identity formation, and we finish with two clusters that elaborate on the poetry's resistance to philosophical assimilation and its ideologies of aesthetic form.

We are very pleased to record here, at the tail end of this introduction, how delighted we have been throughout with the quality of the incoming work we commissioned for this volume and the professionalism of our contributors. We are convinced that, as a result of so much individual and collective effort and care, *The New Wallace Stevens Studies* manages to bring to the study of this poet a wide spectrum of refreshing, frequently surprising, but always engagingly formulated perspectives that have been evolved in constant dialogue with contemporary critical theories and approaches. Thanks to the gifted writers assembled in the following pages, this volume is able not only to build on and add significantly to state-of-the-art scholarship on the poet but also to stake out several uncharted territories for future studies. With its selection of multifaceted topics and its launching of perhaps less-familiar critical voices, *The New Wallace Stevens Studies* should be able to spark new debates on the place in contemporary literary criticism, as well as the wider cultural significance, of a writer whose work continues to occupy one of the most prominent positions in twentieth-century poetry.

WORKS CITED

MacLeod, Glen, editor. *Wallace Stevens in Context*. Cambridge UP, 2017.
Serio, John N., editor. *The Cambridge Companion to Wallace Stevens*. Cambridge UP, 2007.
Stevens, Wallace. *Letters of Wallace Stevens*. Edited by Holly Stevens, U of California P, 1996.
　Wallace Stevens: Collected Poetry and Prose. Edited by Frank Kermode and Joan Richardson, Library of America, 1997.
Vendler, Helen. *On Extended Wings: Wallace Stevens' Longer Poems*. Harvard UP, 1969.

PART I

Emerging Concepts in Stevens Criticism

CHAPTER I

Imperialism and Colonialism

Lisa Siraganian

During Wallace Stevens's lifetime, imperialism – "the practice, the theory, and the attitudes of a dominating metropolitan center ruling a distant territory" (Said 9) – was already a global institution. But imperialism also was becoming a more nebulous institution. Maintaining a distant empire seemed to be requiring less conquering and brutal control of subject peoples (whether the British ruling over India or the French over North and West Africa) and more developing of complex ideological, cultural, and social practices, all operating within the matrix of global capitalism. Or as Stevens put it in "Owl's Clover," "the books / For sale in Vienna and Zurich to people in Maine, / Ontario, Canton" (*CPP* 576). By the 1960s, scholars gave this evolving phenomenon of imposed cultural representation and ideological soft coercion a name: "cultural imperialism" (Tomlinson 2). Since the publication of Fredric Jameson's seminal "Modernism and Imperialism" (1988), a growing number of critics have examined the ways in which modernist culture was a persistent yet suppressed part of the story of cultural imperialism.[1] Literary and artistic practices, they argued, were inflected by the historical conditions of empire, imperialism, and colonialism experienced worldwide during the first half of the twentieth century. Critics such as Frank Lentricchia and Aldon Lynn Nielsen observed that Stevens's poetry, in particular, embraced or at least condoned certain tropes of imperial and racial domination. Even Jameson saw Stevens's work as an example of the phenomenon. The poet often absorbed "Third World material" as part of his art's systematic operation, explained Jameson: cultural objects marked as exotic were transformed "back into Nature and virtual landscape" in his poetry ("Stevens" 15).

Parsing Stevens's relationship to imperialism was never an entirely transparent procedure, however, as critics such as John Carlos Rowe, Angus Cleghorn, James Longenbach, Edward Marx, and Gül Bilge Han have explored.[2] This chapter expands on this line of inquiry by exploring imperialism and colonialism in Stevens through brief readings of some key poems. Stevens's poetry rarely invokes concepts like empire directly or mimetically, preferring a composite psychological and philosophical inquiry into the topic. He writes not about "A Colony" but, as one section title of "The Comedian as the Letter C" reads, about "*The Idea of a Colony*" (*CPP* 29; emphasis added). Moreover, as many critics have observed, his poems are resolutely intended as "imaginative constructions" (Burt 325) rather than as literal recordings of the few places he had traveled to outside of the United States, or of the people and events he might have witnessed there.[3] Yet Stevens was also an avid reader of two daily newspapers (*The New York Times* and *The Hartford Times*); his letters are filled with references to locales and news stories far and wide, as he closely followed geopolitical events including the invention of modern warfare and the rise of totalitarian regimes. Italy's October 1935 invasion and attempted imperial conquest of Ethiopia became daily reading, mentioned often in his letters (*L* 289–90, 295, 300). Shortly thereafter, he wrote the long poem "Owl's Clover" with the self-proclaimed aim of applying his "own sort of poetry" to "What one reads in the papers" (*L* 308). "Owl's Clover" was a more topical example than most, but the method he followed there was not wholly anomalous in his oeuvre. As Alan Filreis persuasively argues, Stevens's poetic composition depended on comprehensively exploring the media of his day for what he called "*materia poetica*" (xvii) – the matter of poetry.

Reading contextually, with a view to some of Stevens's patterns of composition (which could involve removing the more obvious or literal allusions to world events), provides a new perspective on his poetry and its "*materia*" of the news of empire. While his views on the imperialist fantasies of his age were at times sympathetic, poems like "Anecdote of the Jar," "Owl's Clover," and "A Weak Mind in the Mountains" also provide more complicated accounts that question and sometimes oppose colonizing modes of cultural domination. Stevens was invested in the problem of imperialism – to the extent that he was – because imperialism entailed a belief system that so obviously produced very real and consequential world actions and events. Those actions included brutal, disturbing, and distant events, like Mussolini's invasion of Ethiopia, yet also deliciously personal and rewarding occasions for a rich cosmopolitan like Stevens, who frequently received (at his request) material such as art prints, tea, and jade figurines from his far-flung correspondents all over the world. In turn, these various manifestations of imperialism in action, whether the result of invading countries or importing exotic goods, produced more (or different) beliefs and worldly effects, ad infinitum. It was this powerful circuit of belief-cause, to reality-effect, to new belief-cause, and so on that intrigued Stevens. Imagination "is always attaching itself to a new reality, and adhering to it," he writes in "The Noble Rider and the Sound of Words" (*CPP* 656). For just that reason, the "new reality" of modern imperialism, whether in its militaristic, political, or cultural guise, could not be ignored. Modern poetry was already attached to the reality of imperialism via Stevens's "adhering" imagination.

Take "Anecdote of the Jar," an important early poem that offers in allusive miniature a range of ambivalent responses toward empire – responses that Stevens would continue to explore throughout his life (*CPP* 60–61). On a certain level, we can read the poem as a straightforward tale of cultural imperialism (as past critics have done): the primitive colony is tamed and subjugated to Western ideas merely by introducing a Western manufactured object into it. But the poem is not entirely clear on how to assess that scenario – if, indeed, that situation is what is intended. The first line begins by recounting a deliberate action in the first person – "I placed a jar in Tennessee" – that alters, either by invisible violence or ideological conquest, the wild "hill" on which the jar was placed. The jar, in its manufactured roundness, "made the slovenly wilderness / Surround that hill," where before nature spread over and composed the hill. The "wilderness" then becomes "sprawled around, no longer wild," as the jar "took dominion everywhere."

The sense here is of "slovenly wilderness" fighting a losing battle (being dominated by the imposing jar), yet we cannot be sure whose side in that war we are being asked to take. When meadow weeds are tamed as grass lawn, is that a good or bad development? Good for elevating the neighborhood's property values and creating an imagined pastoral landscape in one's backyard, bad for fighting climate change or ensuring biodiversity. Although Stevens obviously did not intend that particular reading, it captures something of the ambiguity toward primitive wilderness and colonial domination to which the poem does allude. The lines also simultaneously invoke the majesty and command of a modern art object ("tall and of a port in air") along with something very different: modernity's ubiquitous Western commodities, "gray and bare," sterile and unnatural. The jar "did not give of bird or bush, / Like nothing else in Tennessee." The jar's "tall" height – an odd attribute for a household item one would find in the cupboard – suggests an object arrogating its place in the world. It seems to be seizing a role for itself that might not have been deserved.

"Of a port in air" is also an unusual and awkward phrase, suggesting an ambivalence toward the jar's intended function. An open jar might collect matter from the atmosphere (rainwater, insects, leaves) and thus be likened to a "port," but that word has more obvious commercial connotations. As apertures of empire, ports are the literal entry and exit points of people and commercial goods. They are also the places where a cultural production is unmistakably rendered as or transformed into a commodity – where a Chinese artist's jade carving becomes an exotic figurine, whatever else it might have been prior to that moment. Again, is that type of transformation (from weeds to lawn, from foreign creation to exotic commodity) one that the poem is asking us to celebrate or to decry? The language connotes appraisal without nudging us toward a final verdict one way or another. Finally, that the "port" is "in air" seems to allude to a word – airport – that was only a few decades old when the poem was written. Airports were already changing the global landscape and world imagination during Stevens's time, as planes and other aircraft were used by multiple militaries during the First World War.

It would be a mistake to read this "anecdote," these twelve lines about placing a jar on a Tennessee hillock, as a fully fleshed-out *allegory* of empire. These allusions to imperialism and colonialism linger for the reader mostly as evocative allusions, and often faint or deliberately ambiguous ones at that. But a poem like "Anecdote" helps us see how imperialism, especially in its cultural variety, intrigued and concerned Stevens as a particular variation on the question of knowing that continually fascinated him. Cultural imperialism was one of the engines driving far-off places into becoming their new realities. It produced situations like the one he describes: the most ordinary and familiar of objects could turn a distant world into a place hazily envisioned in an imagined personal anecdote. On the one hand, this was an exciting prospect: the distant world was becoming more ubiquitous in his imagination. On the other, it could be perilous: the world's sprawling places were becoming harder to know or, more seriously, to evaluate fully.[4] This predicament presents a serious difficulty because it fundamentally challenges his conception of art. A poem's effectiveness demands the interpersonal recognitions that are deeply contingent on one's current place and its conditions: in "Of Modern Poetry," Stevens proclaims that poetry "has to be living, to learn the speech of the place" (*CPP* 218). The practices and theory of a metropole dominating a distant territory (i.e., the jar dominating the wilderness) would seem, almost by definition, to create a situation that distorts or impedes any form of intimate "living" and listening. If truly learning a place's speech (rather than imposing a speech on a place) is a necessary requirement for poetry, then the reality of imperialism seems to produce a situation threatening the possibility of poetry.

Of course, to say that Stevens understood imperialism as just another species of a larger family of problems for modern poetry looks at best insensitive, and at worst like a paradigmatic example of Western elitism and racial ordering. Invoking Chinua Achebe's judgment on Joseph Conrad's *Heart of Darkness*, Edward Marx observes that "there is something equally troubling and exploitative in Stevens's use of the exotic and primitive as signposts to the near-breakup and reconstruction of the mind" (161). What could be more symptomatic of the colonialist imagination than to see other people's fraught struggle for existence and self-determination as a tribulation for your (second) career as a poet? Stevens never entirely resolved this contradiction, and his work exhibited many of the racial and cultural prejudices of his time. But neither was he blind to his failings. He frequently examined, particularly in the 1930s and later, how and why it was so difficult to keep these spheres of art, ethics, and politics resolutely distinct and separate. Many of his poems work through the various ways in which ideas – or symbols, or art generally – can fail to be convincing for a reader or a writer, and he was especially cognizant that poverty and ideology, along with divergent cultural frameworks, were frequent causes of that failure.

Stevens considers many of the intricacies of this argument in the aforementioned "Noble Rider" essay. The poet's function, he writes, is "to make his imagination" his readers' and "he fulfills himself only as he sees his imagination become the light in the minds of others" (*CPP* 660–61). But what happens when empire makes the whole world feel more insistently the poet's own, yet his imagination cannot expand to those parameters without invariably distorting what he sees? Will he see the light in others' minds? Writing that essay during Hitler's invasion and attempted conquest of North Africa (part of Nazi Germany's violent and imperial ambitions), Stevens puts it thus: "We are close together in every way. We lie in bed and listen to a broadcast from Cairo, and so on. There is no distance. We are intimate with people we have never seen and, unhappily, they are intimate with us" (*CPP* 653). In Stevens's rendering, the more than six thousand miles separating Hartford and Cairo have shrunk ("There is no distance"), but imagination struggles to integrate this new "pressure of reality" (*CPP* 654). The "unhappily" is key, for it implies that radio broadcasts do not produce true connection with others, unlike the listening represented in "Of Modern Poetry." We are not in Hartford lying contentedly in bed next to a person in Cairo who, perhaps, will attempt in the morning to combat the Nazi offensive. Instead, the radio show from Egypt produces the false guise of intimacy without the accompanying deep feeling and knowledge of Egyptian people, or them of us. Scenarios like this one, Stevens fears, invoke an imaginative, partial presence of a place and the people there: deceptive proximity without true understanding.

In various poems, Stevens represents this sense of difficulty and struggle due to the collapse of distance brought on by empire's acts and effects. "A Weak Mind in the Mountains" offers an imagined current scene in the here and now, immediately followed by a distant one, all combined in one developing thought process. As in "Noble Rider," this poem combines the experience of an immediate present perception in the first stanza ("the blood / Spurted from between the [butcher's] fingers / And fell to the floor") with an illusory experience of combined far-off lands in the second: "The wind of Iceland and / The wind of Ceylon, / Meeting, gripped my mind, / Gripped it and grappled my thoughts." In the third stanza, the results of this composite meditation fail to coalesce in the poet's "weak mind," at least this time around, and seem only to lead to exhaustion: "The blood of the mind fell / To the floor. I slept" (*CPP* 192). But the last, fourth stanza envisions another possibility that might occur on some other occasion: "Yet there was a man within me / Could have risen to the clouds, / Could have touched these winds" (*CPP* 192–93). The reiterated past modals ("Could have") imagine different hypothetical outcomes at an alternative moment, when the speaker could have touched the winds of Iceland and Ceylon (Sri Lanka) as he did apparently effortlessly with the blood between the butcher's fingers.

The works discussed thus far reveal Stevens exploring the problem of imperialism in a fairly abstract register, with subtlety and ambivalence. A poem like "A Weak Mind" depicts a poet carefully inching toward a better, coalescing result the next time around, and possibly attaining it in an iteration of future poems.[5] But sometimes both his aesthetic refinement and optimism waver. The poems considered next take a more direct and often satirical dive into the problem, with mixed results. "The Comedian as the Letter C," for example, does produce an allegory of empire, albeit a poetic empire. As Marx explains, in the poem's fourth section, "The Idea of a Colony," Stevens explicitly creates "an allegory based on the similarity between the development of a poetic world" and the colonization process (155). The emigrating poet who leaves France for Mexico, and eventually the Carolinas, has grand ambitions: "Crispin in one laconic phrase laid bare / His cloudy drift and planned a colony" (*CPP* 29). The colonial reach of his poetic dominion would be vast, for he "Projected a colony that should extend / To the dusk of a whistling south below the south, / A comprehensive island hemisphere" (*CPP* 30–31). But, as Gül Bilge Han observes, a poetics that could combine very different imagery and symbolism into a single universal poetry risks reproducing a "colonial logic," effectively generating an "undifferentiated and homogenizing globalized vision" (121). Crispin's vision might not be "weak" in precisely the way the poet-speaker's "weak mind in the mountains" fails to touch the distant winds, but Crispin's grand poetic aims are clearly being set up for failure – and mockery.

Stevens composed "Comedian" in Hartford in 1921, when many American poets of his generation were traveling to and living in Western Europe with relative ease and delight. But a very different situation developed in Europe in the 1930s, and Stevens's letters (written at home in Connecticut) registered the social, economic, and political upheaval he read about. He seemed especially uneasy about Mussolini's invasion and attempted colonial conquest of Ethiopia. Mussolini aimed to colonize the African nation quickly; instead, his invasion provoked several years of violent insurgency as tens of thousands of Ethiopians died in Italian-led pogroms and massacres (Marcus 147–50). When Italy declared war on the Allies in June 1940, the exiled Ethiopian government found its fortunes reversed and exiled Ethiopian Emperor Haile Selassie (originally Ras Tafari Makonnen) returned home in 1942. The late, colonial power grab to create Mussolini's "Ethiopian Italian Empire" ended in failure.

This regular news from Africa seemed particularly to bother Stevens because it resembled America's founding tale of discovery, conquest, and colonization. Invoking his mixed feelings toward Mussolini, Stevens poses the following question in late 1935 to the editor Ronald Lane Latimer:

> [O]ught I, as a matter of reason, to have sympathized with the Indians as against the Colonists in this country? A man would have to be very thick-skinned not to be conscious of the pathos of Ethiopia or China, or one of these days, if we are not careful, of this country. (*L* 295)

Despite the hazard of imperialism coming home to America, Stevens's skin remains thick and he cannot quite bring himself to "sympathize." The next line continues: "But that Mussolini is right, practically, has certainly a great deal to be said for it" (*L* 295). Presumably, Stevens means that his own legal and political standing as an American, both a literal and symbolic colonial heir many times over, obliges him to affirm Mussolini's dubious rightness. In a sense, his poems of the second half of the 1930s keep posing versions of this dilemma in a variety of ways: could there be an anti-imperialist, American alternative to sympathizing (or rationally identifying) with the colonized, thereby avoiding whatever political implications such sympathizing might entail?

The interwar years offered no shortage of demagogues he might have considered, but Stevens tended to target Mussolini to satirize his imperial plans. In "Life on a Battleship," for instance, the captain at the world's center appoints himself "imperator," an archaic, specifically Roman term for an absolute ruler (*CPP* 199). Like Crispin, this dictatorial captain (on his aptly named ship, *The Masculine*) plans to commandeer resources: he will build one single, massive boat, "a cloud on the sea, the largest / Possible machine, a divinity of steel" (*CPP* 198). From these new headquarters he will draft the world's rules according to his whims. Just as Mussolini launched his career as a socialist agitator before attempting Italy's inter-national domination, the battleship captain's campaign commences after "The rape of the bourgeoisie [was] accomplished" (*CPP* 198). He is a contemporary Captain Ahab – hyper-masculine, fascistic, and treacher-ous. He might possess the heroic poet's aspiration to transcendental power, but he lacks any judiciousness and succumbs to human delusions.

Stevens's most topical and unusual (for him) attempt at conceptualizing imperialism and the subsequent problems it generates was "The Greenest Continent" section of "Owl's Clover," written during the height of Mussolini's empire building.[6] Stevens's overruled title for "Owl's Clover" was "APHORISMS ON SOCIETY" (*L* 311), a phrase that more explicitly captures the sequence's episodic quality. Throughout the five discrete poems, Stevens envisions a sculpture of horses in various situations of misrecognition by the spectators who come across it. Each poem of the five reveals the distinct ways in which the material and ideological conditions of modernity can transform a statue into something misunderstood, com-modified, or simply discarded. In the third section, his self-described "poem about Africa" (*L* 305), eventually titled "The Greenest Continent" but referred to in his letters as "the STATUE IN AFRICA" (*L* 307), he grapples extensively with Western imperialism by imagining a war between African "bushmen" and avaricious "angels," the latter with "Leonardo"-like trum-pets (*CPP* 578). He tries to envision a poet like himself, yet one unmarked by imperialism and absent a mass culture that efficiently and, from Stevens's perspective in 1936, dangerously spreads Western culture abroad.

Throughout the poem, Stevens blends his political satire with the broader and more ambiguous cultural description of a symbolic world, primitive and lush, with African warm greens next to the Western statue's cold white. Satirizing invading soldiers as buffoonish angels, these images of combat turn into high-handed burlesque. As Angus Cleghorn points out, the battle also invokes a mock-heroic treatment of Milton's war with Satan (89–90). In the process, the poem combines Europe's Christian missionary past with Mussolini's plans to dominate Ethiopia. At times, these iconic binaries (warm vs. cold, green vs. white) risk undermining the political allusions. And by depicting the Italian regime's Ethiopian invasion as a melodramatic battle, Stevens risks "trivializing . . . the stakes of the war" for the Africans fighting in it (Nielsen 64), or merely satirizing Mussolini's fascist propaganda for its puffery.

Despite the crude allusions to the Ethiopian invasion – whether intended symbolically, satirically, or in some combination – readers would have grasped the poem's implied anti-imperialism. But the poem's central illustration of attempted and failed cultural conquest presents a more complicated anxiety about Western culture's fate. The West tries to coerce an African culture to submit to its supposed colonial destiny by accepting and deferring to a statue of horses:

> But could the statue stand in Africa?
> The marble was imagined in the cold.
> . . . .
> Its surfaces came from distant fire; and it
> Was meant to stand, not in a tumbling green,
> Intensified and grandiose, but among
> The common-places of which it formed a part. . . . (*CPP* 579)

For this speaker, the statue was not designed for the intensely warm, "tumbling green" of the African landscape but for the cold urban parks, the "common-places" of the West. Thus, the statue symbolizes differently in Africa than in New York City or Hartford. Acknowledging these cultural differences generates more serious doubts. The speaker begins to question the ontological status of the statue *as* public art object, exploring the material choices that the sculptor made and whether they would signify similarly in a different place: "Could marble still / Be marble after the drenching reds, the dark / And drenching crimsons, or endure?" (*CPP* 579). He fears, in other words, that marble does not signify prosperity and permanence in Africa; the rock's affluent standing is jeopardized. If so, this sculpture heroically representing Western man may have sunk in value or meaning. Eventually, concerns about the effects of cultural objects in Africa lead the speaker to question the very premise of imperialism and the spread of Western culture. If Western statues don't belong in Africa, do Western ideas and Western armies belong there either?

Stevens embeds his anti-imperialism within a longer poem to ask what happens to displaced Western cultural objects when their value drops. Modernity's material and ideological conditions leave Western art objects misunderstood and discarded or commodified and sold. The beginning of "The Greenest Continent" specifically links imperialism's dangers to European cultural commodification. As a portable, commodified art object, the horse statue may have failed in Africa, yet it is only one among a myriad of similar pieces sold on the global market during Europe's fire sale, as empty German castles were gutted, their libraries sold to the distant (colonial) states, "to people in Maine, / Ontario, Canton." Europe's infrastructure remains, while portable cultural objects, such as "armorial books" with symbols of royal heraldry, flood markets along with European cuisine and café culture (*CPP* 576). Even Europe's musical heritage is sold on cheap gramophone records. The poem's marble equestrian monuments are just one more marketable European product to be purchased at the right price. Not only does Europe force militaristic imperialism on Africa, but Western culture is also simultaneously commodified and sold to Africa and to anyone else with the means to purchase it. Africa's markets open wide, linked to global commodity flows.

Yet "The Greenest Continent" also represents Western culture's commodification and exportation as equally dangerous to the militaristic imperialism of Mussolini. Rowe describes the ideology of "free-trade imperialism" in similar terms to suggest how Western cultural objects colonize people who purchase Western things (xi). Thus, when a Pacific Islander buys a bottle of Coca-Cola, she feels the force of US free-trade imperialism whether or not a Coca-Cola executive ever appears in her village. Stevens's grievance in this poem is counterintuitive and different. He worries that commodification and global sales devastate the cultural value of these objects *themselves*. Cultural imperialism makes a Western sculpture less meaningful to everyone, even to its creators. Indeed, in "The Greenest Continent," the trouble he locates in cultural imperialism is not how it colonizes another people and decimates their culture, but how it makes Western culture less valuable, because it becomes less monolithic and domineering. Foreign consumers alter the nature of Western products – whether adapting royal heraldry for their own monarchical lines; or, more recently, transforming clothes hangers and cans into toys in Zimbabwe; or Twittering on cell phones to coordinate demonstrations in Iran – inventing ways of using them unimagined by their producers.

By challenging Mussolini's imperialism, Stevens's topical poem tackles specific, late-1930s world events and political debates to secure Western culture. In subsequent years, his preoccupations often focused on unresolved problems in "Owl's Clover." The "Canonica" poems (his 1938 sequence of object-poems) explicitly reject militaristic imperialism yet remain preoccupied with how the poet can make unifying sense of a scattered world. "Parochial Theme," the first poem of "Canonica," is a case in point, counseling against the temptations of nation building through ideology or conquest: "Piece the world together, boys, but not with your hands" (*CPP* 177). The speaker distinguishes between aesthetic collaging and a more coercive ordering by imperialists whose "boys" attempt to "piece the world together" with guns, just as Mussolini's Ethiopian Italian Empire violently forces national blending. Other poems in the sequence play on this theme: "Idiom of the Hero" flatly rejects – in singsong couplets – the possible "blend[ing]" of radically opposed nations or ideologies (*CPP* 184), while "Prelude to Objects" dismisses "the Louvre" as a repository for imperial collecting (looting) in favor of commonly found objects (*CPP* 179). Arguably, "Canonica" extends Stevens's politically infused, anti-imperialist poetics of "Owl's Clover" by enacting a strategic, consumerist relation to foreign objects.

On the topic of imperialism, as on so many issues, Stevens continued to argue, resolve, dispute, and reconsider. His dialectical predisposition observed in longer poems such as "Owl's Clover" reappears in his shuttling between positions from one poem to the next, each entertaining a different prospective solution. When we are faced with these divergent experiments, contextualization helps us to sort out Stevens's competing allegiances at a chaotic historical moment: to anti-imperialism, to an embattled Western culture and ideology, to a unifying world of art and poetry. Perhaps the more surprising takeaway of this exploration is how contemporary many of Stevens's dilemmas appear. One can glimpse, with his pensive remarks on radio as a medium, a kind of critic of social media *avant la lettre*, condemning the false intimacy of his moment's technology. More clearly than most poets of his generation, he saw globalization as the existential problem it would become by the turn of the twenty-first century, leading to irreconcilable scenarios of competing plural values.

Notes

1 Balthaser argues that cultural anti-imperialism was a widespread component of American modernism during the 1930s (4). See also Rowe.
2 Parts of this chapter are adapted from my earlier article; see Siraganian. See also Ragg and Redding.
3 See Costello and Matterson.
4 On value in Stevens, see Altieri.
5 On Stevens's poetry as experimentally iterative, see Kotin 94.
6 See Longenbach 182 and Nielsen 63–64.

WORKS CITED

Altieri, Charles. *Wallace Stevens and the Demands of Modernity: Toward a Phenomenology of Value.* Cornell UP, 2013.

Balthaser, Benjamin. *Anti-Imperialist Modernism: Race and Transnational Radical Culture from the Great Depression to the Cold War.* U of Michigan P, 2015.

Burt, Stephanie. "Wallace Stevens: Where He Lived." *ELH*, vol. 77, no. 2, Summer 2010, pp. 325–52.

Cleghorn, Angus J. *Wallace Stevens' Poetics: The Neglected Rhetoric.* Palgrave, 2000.

Costello, Bonnie. "Traveling with Stevens." *The Wallace Stevens Journal*, vol. 38, no. 1, Spring 2014, pp. 15–26.

Filreis, Alan. *Wallace Stevens and the Actual World.* Princeton UP, 1991.

Han, Gül Bilge. *Wallace Stevens and the Poetics of Modernist Autonomy.* Cambridge UP, 2019.

Jameson, Fredric. "Modernism and Imperialism." 1988. *Nationalism, Colonialism, and Literature*, by Terry Eagleton, Fredric Jameson, and Edward W. Said, U of Minnesota P, 1990, pp. 43–68.

"Wallace Stevens." *New Orleans Review*, vol. 11, no. 1, Spring 1984, pp. 10–19.

Kotin, Joshua. *Utopias of One.* Princeton UP, 2018.

Lentricchia, Frank. *Ariel and the Police: Michel Foucault, William James, Wallace Stevens.* U of Wisconsin P, 1988.

Longenbach, James. *Wallace Stevens: The Plain Sense of Things.* Oxford UP, 1991.

Marcus, Harold G. *A History of Ethiopia.* U of California P, 1994.

Marx, Edward. *The Idea of a Colony: Cross-Culturalism in Modern Poetry.* U of Toronto P, 2004.

Matterson, Stephen. "'The Whole Habit of the Mind': Stevens, Americanness, and the Use of Elsewhere." *The Wallace Stevens Journal*, vol. 25, no. 2, Fall 2001, pp. 111–21.

Nielsen, Aldon Lynn. *Reading Race: White American Poets and the Racial Discourse in the Twentieth Century.* U of Georgia P, 1988.

Ragg, Edward. "The Orient." *Wallace Stevens in Context*, edited by Glen MacLeod, Cambridge UP, 2017, pp. 55–64.

Redding, Patrick. "Politics." *Wallace Stevens in Context*, edited by Glen MacLeod, Cambridge UP, 2017, pp. 267–76.

Rowe, John Carlos. *Literary Culture and U.S. Imperialism: From the Revolution to World War II.* Oxford UP, 2000.

Said, Edward W. *Culture and Imperialism.* Random House, 1993.

Siraganian, Lisa. "Wallace Stevens's Fascist Dilemmas and Free Market Resolutions." *American Literary History*, vol. 23, no. 2, Summer 2011, pp. 337–61.

Stevens, Wallace. *Letters of Wallace Stevens.* Edited by Holly Stevens, U of California P, 1996.

Wallace Stevens: Collected Poetry and Prose. Edited by Frank Kermode and Joan Richardson, Library of America, 1997.

Tomlinson, John. *Cultural Imperialism: A Critical Introduction.* Johns Hopkins UP, 1991.

CHAPTER 2

The Politics of Utopia

Douglas Mao

I

Why should Wallace Stevens be thought of as a poet of utopia? In many ways, he would seem an inapt choice for the role. Known in the decades after his death, and not unreasonably, as a writer obsessed with the confrontation between the individual imagination and the reality that encircles it, he evinced little interest in the question of what institutional arrangements or cultural priorities might prevail in an ideal society. He did not engage visibly with the tradition of fictional utopias running (in the West) from Plato and Thomas More through Edward Bellamy's best-selling *Looking Backward* of 1888 and its early twentieth-century successors. And where prominent con-temporaries such as Ezra Pound and T. S. Eliot took it upon themselves to offer recipes, or at least guidelines, for the renovation of social, political, and economic life, Stevens seemed content to recur to the question of how an inhabitant of the twentieth century, or at the furthest a public-minded poet, might navigate perplexities of the modern world. How could a writer apparently so little attracted by speculation on the ways a perfected society might distribute goods or assign labor, nurture culture or address inequality, come to be credited with utopian insight?

The answer is straightforward – if also, at a minimum, tripartite. First, Stevens's explorations of the modern subject's predicaments were grounded in a rejection of belief in a heavenly afterlife, and this as a matter of both metaphysical truth and historical tendency. In his break-through poem of 1915, "Sunday Morning," he suggested not only that we must "find in comforts of the sun" and "any balm or beauty of the earth, / Things to be cherished like the thought of heaven" but also that when the earth comes to "Seem all of paradise that we shall know," the "sky will be much friendlier then than now, / A part of labor and a part of pain," not "this dividing and indifferent blue" (*CPP* 53–54). Second, he was by no means averse to commenting on political movements that promised ideal futures. Efforts to replace faith in heaven with utopian projects very much drew his attention when they took the form of programs inspiring people in great numbers and obviously reshaping the world. Third, Stevens returned frequently to the question of whether and on what terms human beings could enjoy sustained happiness or fulfillment. That poetry could help lend savor to life was clear, but how far did its bounty extend? What might its limitations, if any, teach us about pleasure and meaning in general? How could people live without – and how could they live meaningfully within – conditions of security and material provision such as utopia is ordinarily thought to imply?

Interpreters of Stevens over the years have illuminated an array of utopian manifestations in his writing. In a 1984 essay, Fredric Jameson discerned in Stevens's poems a paradox according to which the Symbolic Order – whose space is that "of the images, ideas and names of 'things as they are'" – is both "ideological and Utopian, both a simple reflexion or projection of the real with all its contradictions, and a small-scale model or Utopian microcosm of the real in which the latter can be changed or modified" (188). Four years later, Frank Lentricchia would note a fleeting "utopian urge toward classless society" in a 1904 journal entry (145) as well as a persistent, if usually repressed, suspicion that the version of the good life Stevens generally adopted (one centrally defined by bourgeois satisfactions) might be historically parochial and deeply *un*satisfying (198, 204). In 2002, Bart Eeckhout would observe relatedly that maintaining utopias of sensuous hedonism, as Stevens seems to recommend in poems like "Landscape with Boat," requires that the "sociopolitical world of conflict and potential violence . . . be hummed away into oblivion" (182–83).

Other scholars have shown how Stevens's attention to the pleasures of daily experience could be understood, by himself and by those who read him, either as opposing anti-utopian astringency or as critiquing utopian planning's subjugation to a distant future. In *Wallace Stevens and the Literary Canons* (1992), John Timberman Newcomb noted how late-1950s critics such as Irving Howe preferred Stevens's evident affirmation of the possibilities of "self-renewal" over a literature of endless crisis associated with Eliot and Pound: "Stevens's combination of utopian and quotidian emphases offered a great deal" to "a literary world sated on the transcendent anti-utopianism of Eliotic high modernism" (192). In *Wallace Stevens: The Plain Sense of Things* (1991), James Longenbach identified in "Owl's Clover" (1936) and other poems an attention to "the virtues of ordinary experience, . . . in which historical decline is measured soberly and the possibility of progress is not forgotten in apocalyptic or utopian fantasies" (181). In his 1994 book *Modernism from Right to Left*, Alan Filreis showed similarly how for a contemporary such as Marianne Moore, Stevens around 1937 "was just the right poet for refuting utopian claims because he had an ear sharp enough to quote the left's basic *lack* of hope back to itself," though by the end of "The Man with the Blue Guitar" he finds it "no longer necessary to exaggerate the utopianism of his detractors" (178, 279).

Scholars of more recent years have detected other utopian inflections in Stevens's addresses to the poetic monad and celebrations of ordinary experience. In *Redeeming Words and the Promise of Happiness* (2012), Richard Kleinberg-Levin proposes that if in its content Stevens's poetry "argues for a happiness to be found right here, revealed in the very ordinariness of this world" (5), its form itself, its richness of verbal play, contains its own "utopian promise of happiness" (2), a version of the *promesse du bonheur* that was named by Stendhal and invoked as lodestar by Theodor Adorno (6). In *Utopias of One* (2018), Joshua Kotin limns a Stevens for whom the political catastrophes of the early twentieth century demonstrated the failure of humanism, and whose response was eventually to create (in "The Auroras of Autumn") a poetic utopia only he could inhabit, one from which even his readers were essentially excluded.[1] I myself argued across a few articles (2000, 2005, 2012) that in his recourse to the unfailing generativity of the imagination, Stevens counters the anti-utopian assertion that unimperiled material stability would condemn its beneficiaries to meaninglessness and boredom. Under this view, not only the faith in quotidian plenitude highlighted by Longenbach, Filreis, and others but also something like the dissatisfaction detected by Lentricchia counters axiologies that would tether profundity to deprivation and existential validity to pain.

At stake in treatments of the politics of utopia in Stevens, then, have been questions about the autonomy of the work of art in and after high modernism, about poets' relations to political programs, about the legitimacy of social and political optimism, about the foundations and resilience of happiness. All of these are linked, it would seem, by Stevens's ongoing concern with the possibilities of the imagination – source of poems and of utopias, implement and overlord of poets as of revolutionists, fount of the pleasures of ordinary existence. Yet there remains a dimension of the imagination-utopia connection that has not yet been brought out as strongly as it deserves, and whose illumination may help us place Stevens still more precisely among secretaries of utopia and within the intellectual life of his time.

II

The temporal span of Stevens's poetic career coincided with a long dry spell in the publication of influential utopian fictions, at least in English-language writing. Over most of this period, there were few significant utopias of the kind made familiar by More and Bellamy – that is, narratives in which an emissary from something like the real world of the reader visits an ideal society and learns how its social arrangements conduce to happiness, justice, and peace. The publication year of "Sunday Morning," 1915, was also that of Charlotte Perkins Gilman's *Herland*, arguably the last major utopia of the post-Bellamy boom; among novels of radical social engineering in the next three decades, the one that would prove a touchstone was not a utopia proper but Aldous Huxley's stridently anti-utopian *Brave New World* (1932), which suggested the perils, for both freedom and human dignity, of a society built on exhaustive behavioral conditioning. In *Dark Princess* (1928) and the "Black Empire" tales (1936–38), W. E. B. Du Bois and George Schuyler, respectively, imagined emancipatory regimes for people of color, yet Du Bois's novel does not depict a utopian totality and Schuyler's envelops in irony its representation of an Africa reclaimed by and for Black people.[2] It was not until 1948 that a durably resonant, unapologetically utopian riposte to Huxley would appear, in the form of B. F. Skinner's *Walden Two*. And it was arguably not until the 1970s that utopian fiction would again exhibit the capaciousness of invention that had made its late nineteenth-century efflorescence so crucial a forum for rethinking the possibilities of human social organization.

If the interwar and Second World War years were not propitious for English-language utopian fiction as such, part of the reason was surely that programs for radical social transformation were so resoundingly operative in non-literary reality. Communist organizing and the Roosevelt administration in the United States; the Bolshevik government of the Soviet Union; fascist regimes in Germany, Italy, and Spain: all were legible as utopian experiments unfolding in real time. And as a number of scholars have noted, Stevens responded to these exercises of the applied imagination with a poetry at once appreciative of their historical importance and largely unimpressed by their claims to social truth. In the fourth canto of "A Duck for Dinner" (itself the fourth part of "Owl's Clover"), he posits that "the future" may depend upon "an orator, / Some pebble-chewer practiced in Tyrian speech, / An apparition, twanging instruments / Within us hitherto unknown" (*CPP* 584); in canto VI, he reflects that while for ordinary people the "future . . . is always the deepest dome, / The darkest blue of the dome and the wings around / The giant Phosphor of their earliest prayers," there has been a "diverting of the dream / Of heaven from heaven to the future, as a god" (*CPP* 586). Thus is the divinity within ourselves directed into channels not foreseen in "Sunday Morning." But "Duck" IV also wonders what will happen if, "instead of failing, it never comes, / This future" (*CPP* 584), and "Duck" VI represents the "tempo . . . of this complicated shift" as a "leaden ticking circular in width" (*CPP* 586).

"Owl's Clover" was not the only analysis of the utopian imagination to come before English-language readers in 1936. Another was Karl Mannheim's *Ideology and Utopia: An Introduction to the Sociology of Knowledge*, which combined a translation of that sociologist's *Ideologie und Utopie* of 1929 with new material written specifically for the English edition. There, Mannheim identifies as the "principal thesis of the sociology of knowledge" that "there are modes of thought which cannot be adequately understood as long as their social origins are obscured" (2) and argues that it "is not men in general who think, or even isolated individuals who do the thinking, but men in certain groups who have developed a particular style of thought in an endless series of responses to certain typical situations characterizing their common position" (3). His project, then, is to uncover the social wellsprings of "ideology," wherein "ruling groups . . . become so intensively interest-bound to a situation that they are simply no longer able to see certain facts which would undermine their sense of domination," and of ideology's opposite number, "*utopian* thinking," wherein "certain oppressed groups are intellectually so strongly interested in the destruction and transformation of a given condition of society that they unwittingly see only those elements in the situation which tend to negate it" (40).

One of the lasting contributions of Mannheim's book lay in its very construction of the utopia-ideology binary. But a perhaps no less noteworthy feature is its picture of a world shaped by ongoing combat between ideas. "Men living in groups," he observes, "do not confront the objects of the world from the abstract levels of a contemplating mind as such"; rather, "they act with and against one another in diversely organized groups, and while doing so they think with and against one another" (3–4). Unlike "academic discussion," then, "Political discussion . . . seeks not only to be in the right but also to demolish the basis of its opponent's social and intellectual existence" (38); it "is the tearing off of disguises – the unmasking of those unconscious motives which bind the group existence to its cultural aspirations and its theoretical arguments" (39). We might say, therefore, that political adversaries perform a version of the work undertaken by the sociologist of knowledge, attempting to seal the fate of opposing views by exposing how they emerged from particular configurations of interests.

The American (or ex-American) poet with whom Mannheim was most prominently associated by the end of the 1930s was T. S. Eliot: both were members of The Moot, a discussion group of mainly Christian thinkers founded in 1938 that included, among others, Reinhold Niebuhr, Paul Tillich, and John Middleton Murry. I know of no evidence that Stevens specifically read Mannheim. Yet given the latter's recognition among American intellectuals of the time, it seems hard to imagine that the author of "Owl's Clover" was not acquainted in some measure with Mannheim on ideology and utopia. And it seems still less likely that Stevens would have been unaware of a 1939 book that explicitly picks up on Mannheim's analysis of political contestation: Max Lerner's *Ideas Are Weapons*. An influential liberal columnist and political commentator, Lerner often wrote for the *New Republic*; indeed, *Ideas Are Weapons* includes a dozen pieces that appeared in that leftist magazine between 1935 and 1939. The importance of the *New Republic* to Stevens has been well demonstrated, scholars having affirmed that he was "a regular reader" (Longenbach 149), charted his changing political views in relation to its reportage (Brogan throughout), and elucidated the significance of his placement of three poems there in 1935 (Filreis 180–87).

Lerner begins the title essay of his collection (whose subtitle is *The History and Uses of Ideas*) by recalling something said to him by the legal scholar Hermann Kantorowicz: "Men possess thoughts but ideas possess men" (3). For Lerner, there are two "phases" in the realm of ideas, a rational one in which ideas are tools (and thus more or less possessed by people) and an irrational one in which people are possessed by "big sweeping ideas like racism, individualism, Nazism, communism, democracy" (3). It is "the recognition and exploitation of this possessive power of ideas that makes the genius of our age" (3), according to Lerner, and coming to terms with the fact that "the rational right-thinking man has . . . ceased to be regarded as the center of our intellectual system" means, among other things, enlarging our approach to intellectual history. What is required is an exploration of "the history of ideas as the expression of broad social and class forces," what "Karl Mannheim, in his *Ideology and Utopia*, has called the 'unmasking' of ideologies" (5). And this not because we ought to "surrender . . . to the force of the irrational" (7) but rather so that we can "be clear about the meaning of democratic ideas, . . . make those ideas persuasive, and . . . above everything make them an integral part of our daily lives" (10).

That Stevens knew at least of the title of Lerner's book is suggested by the funny-not-funny conceit governing the fifth of his "Extracts from Addresses to the Academy of Fine Ideas," published two years later:

> The law of chaos is the law of ideas,
> Of improvisations and seasons of belief.
>
> Ideas are men. The mass of meaning and
> The mass of men are one. Chaos is not
>
> The mass of meaning. It is three or four
> Ideas or, say, five men or, possibly, six.
>
> In the end, these philosophic assassins pull
> Revolvers and shoot each other. One remains.
>
> The mass of meaning becomes composed again.
> He that remains plays on an instrument
>
> A good agreement between himself and night,
> A chord between the mass of men and himself,
>
> Far, far beyond the putative canzones
> Of love and summer. The assassin sings
>
> In chaos and his song is a consolation.
> It is the music of the mass of meaning. (*CPP* 230–31)

Whether or not Stevens was familiar with Mannheim and Lerner, this canto reads as an evocation, and also a partial amendment, of their theses. Stevens here reproduces their sketch of a world in which political ideas battle it out for dominance, but he also gives a far more prominent role to ideas' individual generators. While Mannheim acknowledges that "the dominant utopia" often "first arises as the wish-fantasy of a single individual," he also stresses that "It is the task of sociology always to show . . . that the first stirrings of what is new . . . are in fact oriented towards the existing order and that the existing order itself is rooted in the alignment and tension of the forces of social life" (206–07). Stevens's aim, transverse or lateral to Mannheim's, is to counter the myth that ideas bubble up organically from the masses as a whole. Beginning his second couplet with "Ideas are men," he might be taken to be saying that ideas come from people in the mass – from many "men." Yet the succeeding lines decisively, though circuitously, assert that ideas originate with individuals or, at the furthest, with parties or groups constituting a subset of the people as a whole. The "mass of meaning and / The mass of men are one," but chaos "is not / The mass of meaning"; hence, chaos would seem not to be the "mass of men." And therefore if "The law of chaos is the law of ideas," then the law of the mass of men is not the law of ideas, which means that the idea is not the mass of men. Rather, the idea emerges from some person or faction that uses persuasion, propaganda, or violence, presumably, to eliminate all opponents and secure the idea's mass acceptance: "He that remains plays on an instrument // A good agreement between himself and night, / A chord between the mass of men and himself."

The twisty logic the reader has to follow out to obtain this moral seems eminently suitable, of course, to an address to an Academy of Fine Ideas. But it also recapitulates the difficulty of keeping hold of the point that political ideas are not organic upwellings of the masses' desire. The surviving assassin, in Stevens's construction, plays a chord between the mass of men and himself, but he does not sing or play a song the masses invent. This is not quite to contest Mannheim's central claim that we can and should trace ideologies and utopias to the social matrices that generate them, but it is to reposition the emphasis so far as *almost* to make an opposing argument. Stevens implies that while it may be worthwhile to excavate how a given political position is rooted in the interests of a given social fraction, it's perilous to ignore the individuals or parties who author those positions (whether or not we choose to conceive of those authors as channels or conduits of larger social forces). To ignore them is to fall prey to precisely the kind of mystification that demagogues and party vanguards exploit.

This tableau of the individual player or singer responding to, but not emerging from, the people *en masse* had already served Stevens in "The Man with the Blue Guitar" of 1937. In that poetic sequence, the one who addresses the general public is less the politician than the poet; yet near its close, Stevens suggests how utopia might prove a temptation for any wielder of imagination. Poem XXVI, home to the sole appearance of "utopia" per se in Stevens's verse, runs as follows:

> The world washed in his imagination,
> The world was a shore, whether sound or form
>
> Or light, the relic of farewells,
> Rock, of valedictory echoings,
>
> To which his imagination returned,
> From which it sped, a bar in space,

Sand heaped in the clouds, giant that fought
Against the murderous alphabet:

The swarm of thoughts, the swarm of dreams
Of inaccessible Utopia.

A mountainous music always seemed
To be falling and to be passing away. (*CPP* 146–47)

On close inspection, this poem proves a sort of anticipatory structural complement to "Extracts" V. For where the later canto will assert the individual imagination's role in the production of political futures, "Man" XXVI limns utopia's position within the individual imagination. It does not appear to treat the utopian impulse kindly. "The Man with the Blue Guitar" as a whole is devoted to the interplay of reality and imagination; in this late episode, the former is figured not just as a shore lapped by the latter but also as something that defends the latter against one of its own worst tendencies. Setting bounds to the imagination, reality in its eminent solidity becomes a giant doing battle with the "murderous alphabet" of "inaccessible Utopia" – in other words, with the imagination's propensity to turn from benign tide into sinister "swarm." This last noun, twice repeated in a single line, clearly evokes the German term *Schwärmerei*, which reads more positively in "It Must Be Abstract" VIII (from "Notes Toward a Supreme Fiction") but whose specter here suggests dangerously over-the-top belief in one's own visions, fanaticism as uncontrollable frenzy.

Yet the poem's final couplet muddies the waters. "A mountainous music always seemed / To be falling and to be passing away": does this music belong to the inaccessible utopia or to the world-shore of "Sand heaped in the clouds"? Are the falling and passing away a good thing or a bad? And is it in fact possible to keep utopia and the reality-world-shore from changing places, or even merging? Reconsidered in light of these closing lines, the shore heaped in the clouds may seem to partake more of cloudiness than to resist it, and the figuration of the world as "a bar in space" may imply not sturdiness against an ambient atmosphere but a liability to float adrift amid mental currents. The closing couplet doesn't free the swarm of utopian ideas from murderousness, then, but it does intimate the possible mis-guidedness of thinking that reality can be clung to in an effort to keep such ideas at bay. And in truth this is something we should have grasped from the first couplet, since if the world is a shore, the imagination-ocean is not just bounded by it but also sculpts it, continuously transforming the thing that sets its limits. By the end of the canto, what seems mad is not to deny that utopian vision can change the world but to believe that the world-shore could, any more than Yeats's Cuchulain in his own battle with the sea, claim some final victory over the imagination's waves.

By the mid-1940s, a Cold War Stevens (much in line with the one construed by Howe) would be prepared to proclaim a cleaner victory, or at least a cleaner moral victory, of immediate reality over revolutionary vision. Canto XIV of "Esthétique du Mal" (1944) presents Konstantinov, an ardent communist who in the 1920s came paranoically to believe that Lenin's New Economic Policy was a bourgeois plot (Macdonald 177), as "the lunatic of one idea / In a world of ideas, who would have all the people / Live, work, suffer and die in that idea / In a world of ideas." Konstantinov "would not be aware of the lake" by which he walked, would "not be aware of the clouds, /. . . / His extreme of logic would be illogical." This observation then leads to a summa often quoted as a distillation of Stevens's values: "The greatest poverty is not to live / In a physical world, to feel that one's desire / Is too difficult to tell from despair" (*CPP* 286).

In the closely related fourth canto of "Description Without Place" of the following year, Stevens moves, to similar effect, from the "sun of Nietzsche . . . gildering the swarm-like manias / In perpetual revolution, round and round," to "Lenin on a bench beside a lake" (*CPP* 299) – presumably Lake Geneva, mentioned in "Esthétique" XIV and by which Lenin did walk during his Swiss exile. Stevens's Lenin takes "bread from his pocket, scatter[s] it," but in so doing repels rather than attracts some nearby swans, who fly away, perhaps sensing that the revolutionary is in the grip of a vision in which "All chariots were drowned" (*CPP* 300, 299). No matter: to Lenin, the

> distances of space and time
> Were one and swans far off were swans to come.
>
> The eye of Lenin kept the far-off shapes.
> His mind raised up, down-drowned, the chariots.
>
> And reaches, beaches, tomorrow's regions became
> One thinking of apocalyptic legions. (*CPP* 300)

"[N]ot the man for swans," Lenin seems, like Konstantinov, to fail to live in the physical world (*CPP* 299). But of course the reader of "Description" V may object that the visions swarming for Lenin in Geneva did end up transforming Russia and indeed the world as a whole, his imagination thus proving by no means lunatic respecting what is and what isn't possible. It would seem, then, that Stevens's brief against the projects of utopian visionaries rests not on some failure of theirs to impinge on reality but on their tendency to be divorced from ordinary experience at their origin. To adopt the famous dyad of "It Must Give Pleasure" VII: the problem might be that their orders are imposed rather than discovered.

Yet if this characterization serves well enough in accounting for the mid-1940s poems, it seems somewhat short of adequate to those of the preceding years, when Stevens often leavened his anxieties about utopian visionaries with hints of admiration. In "Lytton Strachey, Also, Enters into Heaven" (1935), the ventriloquized Strachey worries that in the "apologetic air" of the beyond, where the famous might be observed "without their passions" and stripped of their mythologies, "one well / Might muff the mighty spirit of Lenin" (*CPP* 564–65). In the final stanza of "The Blue Buildings in the Summer Air" (1938), the speaker urges a mouse, apparently representing ordinary hungry life, to "nibble at Lenin in his tomb. / Are you not le plus pur, you ancient one?" (*CPP* 196). The mouse may be the *plus pur* representative of the masses, but it's also still a mouse, and Stevens leaves unclear whether the contrast between *la souris moyenne sensuelle* and the big-dreamed revolutionary is to the former's or to the latter's advantage. "Sad Strains of a Gay Waltz" (1935, one of Stevens's *New Republic* poems) forecasts that "Some harmonious skeptic soon in a skeptical music // Will unite these figures of men and their shapes / Will glisten again with motion" (*CPP* 101); "A Duck for Dinner" mitigates derision of the pebble-chewer with the acknowledgment that "to think of the future is a genius, / To think of the future is a thing and he / That thinks of it is inscribed on walls and stands / Complete in bronze on enormous pedestals" (*CPP* 585). Even "Extracts" V, with its late date of 1941, follows the previously quoted lines with the qualification "And yet it is a singular romance, / This warmth in the blood-world for the pure idea, // This inability to find a sound, / That clings to the mind like that right sound, that song // Of the assassin that remains and sings / In the high imagination, triumphantly" (*CPP* 231).

One reason Stevens had to be attracted to the utopian visionary was that utopian imagination, whatever its failings and even dangers, was still imagination: the future-dreamer whose projects shape the world (Lenin, if not Konstantinov) confirms imagination's power to act upon the real, which Stevens could never wholly wish to see denied. A second reason for his appreciation was surely that this large figure, like the figure of the hero, spoke to that yearning for the noble, the lofty, and the great that Stevens sometimes saw as a component of human desire left conspicuously unsatisfied by a knowing, anti-Romantic twentieth century. But there was perhaps a third reason for Stevens's ambivalent admiration, less Yeatsian-Poundian and more Mannheimian.

As we've seen, one of the key claims of *Ideology and Utopia* is that the war between ideas increasingly plays out as a war of competing demystifications. "[D]ifferent coexistent forms of utopian mentality," Mannheim writes, "are destroying one another" in a "reciprocal conflict" whose "modern form" is "clearly perceptible in the way the socialists have gone about unmasking the ideologies of their antagonists. We do not hold up to the adversary that he is worshipping false gods; rather we destroy the intensity of his idea by showing that it is historically and socially determined" (250). Given that Mannheim's own project was one of revealing historical and social determinations, we might expect him to celebrate such work unreservedly. Yet at the end of his lengthy taxonomy of the forms of "the utopian mentality," he observes that for all its abstract virtues, the war of unmaskings might prove a costly one. "We approach," he remarks, "a situation in which the utopian element, through its many divergent forms, has completely (in politics, at least) annihilated itself" (250), and this "complete disappearance of the utopian element from human thought and action" implies "a static state of affairs in which man himself becomes no more than a thing." Deprived of utopia, man, "who has achieved the highest degree of rational mastery of existence," would be "left without any ideals" and become "a mere creature of impulses. . . . [J]ust at the highest stage of awareness, . . . with the relinquishment of utopias, man would lose his will to shape history and therewith his ability to understand it" (262–63). Herein, we might say, lies Mannheim's variation on the Frankfurt School theme of reason bringing on the end of reason.

For the Stevens of the late 1930s and early 1940s, as for Mannheim, utopia as it affects the real was fundamentally the idea of utopia and as such was embedded in an ongoing history of ideas in conflict. Key moments in Stevens's poems suggest, moreover, that for him as for Mannheim "the relinquishment of utopias" might – again notwithstanding the faultiness of any given utopian vision – constitute a loss for humankind. The observation in "Sad Strains of a Gay Waltz" that the "epic of disbelief / Blares oftener and soon, will soon be constant" (*CPP* 101) reads, in context, not as coolly evaluative but as wary and mournful, a prospection of the loss of something more particular than belief in general or the play of imagination broadly conceived. Yet where Mannheim marks as all too imminently possible the "disappearance of the utopian element from human thought and action," Stevens suggests that anxiety on this score is ultimately misplaced. To be sure, he does at times limn an authoritarian future where dissent would be so fully suppressed that new ideas would have no room to emerge: "Extracts" V might be understood in this fashion. And yet that canto's opening couplet – "The law of chaos is the law of ideas, / Of improvisations and seasons of belief" – makes clear that what Stevens will depict in the succeeding lines is one cycle of a recurring process: the surviving assassin will preside not forever but only until a new configuration unleashes a new war of ideas. The end of "Sad Strains" similarly looks forward to a resolution of the epic of disbelief at the hands of the "harmonious skeptic," deviser of a form of the unbelieving belief that Stevens would go on to pursue in his explorations of the hero and the supreme fiction. Soon, "Sad Strains" assures us, "these figures of men and their shapes / Will glisten again with motion, the music / Will be motion and full of shadows" (*CPP* 101).

This figure of the possessor of singular imagination musically bringing the masses to order materializes also, as we've seen, in "The Man with the Blue Guitar" and "Extracts" V. Clearly, this figure is serviceable to Stevens's purposes because it links harmoniousness in general with the capacity of the one to marshal the many, with modulation between sensuous experience and social need, and with the demagogue's ability to enchant and enthrall. What our present discussion suggests, however, is that another important feature of the musical performance, for Stevens's figural purposes, is its limited duration. What matters in these poems isn't so much that music is a temporally unfolding art per se as that any dance or song or other piece will end, with another following on its heels. Where for Mannheim utopias' ever-augmenting proficiency at destroying other utopias portends a loss of human "will to shape history and . . . to understand it," Stevens seems to envisage little prospect of such a dissolution. There's no more chance of reaching an end to the contest of utopian programs than of reaching the end of imagination tout court.

Of course, this cycling of seasons of belief may appear condemned to trivialness by virtue of its very cyclicality: considered from a certain vantage of Olympian weariness, the spectacle of ideas as weapons shooting each other endlessly may seem not just meaningless in itself but an affirmation of the meaninglessness of everything. This is certainly one of the feelings that "Extracts" V evokes. Yet Stevens never suggests that the turns of the cycle repeat each other qualitatively: on the contrary, he affirms that new ideas will differ from old, so that whether or not their succession looks valueless *sub specie aeternitatis*, it does prove the actuality of change. We may say, then, that if Stevens draws hope from the imagination's changefulness when trying to understand how life in utopia might retain its meaning and savor, as suggested earlier, he draws comfort from the same place when considering whether the life of utopian ideas could ever (as Mannheim worries) come to an end. For better or for worse, but on balance for better, the imagination goes on. A mountainous music always seems to be falling and to be passing away.

Notes

1 Kotin remarks a different strain in late poems such as "The Course of a Particular." Here, Stevens models for readers "a practice of receptivity and acceptance" of the things of the world and insists that "the desire for transcendence inhibits receptivity" (107).
2 The extent of Stevens's own attention to the possibility of racial emancipation as a component of utopia may be gauged by "The Greenest Continent," the stunningly regressive third section of "Owl's Clover." Though Stevens there responds to Mussolini's invasion of Ethiopia by denying that (post-)Christian Europe can subjugate Africa in some abstractly complete sense, he also represents Africa as a realm of jungles, snakes, and primitive magic inhabited by "jaguar-men," "lion-men," and "the flicking serpent-kin / In flowery nations" (*CPP* 577).

WORKS CITED

Brogan, Jacqueline Vaught. *The Violence Within / The Violence Without: Wallace Stevens and the Emergence of a Revolutionary Poetics*. U of Georgia P, 2003.
Eeckhout, Bart. *Wallace Stevens and the Limits of Reading and Writing*. U of Missouri P, 2002.
Filreis, Alan. *Modernism from Right to Left: Wallace Stevens, the Thirties, and Literary Radicalism*. Cambridge UP, 1994.
Jameson, Fredric. "Wallace Stevens." *Critical Essays on Wallace Stevens*, edited by Steven Gould Axelrod and Helen Deese, G. K. Hall, 1988, pp. 176–91.
Kleinberg-Levin, Richard. *Redeeming Words and the Promise of Happiness: A Critical Theory Approach to Wallace Stevens and Vladimir Nabokov*. Lexington Books, 2012.
Kotin, Joshua. *Utopias of One*. Princeton UP, 2018.
Lentricchia, Frank. *Ariel and the Police: Michel Foucault, William James, Wallace Stevens*. U of Wisconsin P, 1988.
Lerner, Max. *Ideas Are Weapons: The History and Uses of Ideas*. Transaction, 1991.
Longenbach, James. *Wallace Stevens: The Plain Sense of Things*. Oxford UP, 1991.
Macdonald, D. L. "Wallace Stevens and Victor Serge." *Dalhousie Review*, vol. 66, nos. 1–2, Spring-Summer 1986, pp. 174–80.
Mannheim, Karl. *Ideology and Utopia: An Introduction to the Sociology of Knowledge*. Translated by Louis Wirth and Edward Shils, Harvest, 1985.

Mao, Douglas. "Privative Synecdoches." *The Wallace Stevens Journal*, vol. 29, no. 1, Spring 2005, pp. 56–61.

"The Unseen Side of Things: Eliot and Stevens." *Utopian Spaces of Modernism: British Literature and Culture, 1885–1945*, edited by Rosalyn Gregory and Benjamin Kohlmann, Palgrave, 2012, pp. 194–213.

"Wallace Stevens for the Millennium: The Spectacle of Enjoyment." *The Southwest Review*, vol. 85, no. 1, Jan. 2000, pp. 10–33.

Newcomb, John Timberman. *Wallace Stevens and the Literary Canons*. UP of Mississippi, 1992.

Stevens, Wallace. *Wallace Stevens: Collected Poetry and Prose*. Edited by Frank Kermode and Joan Richardson, Library of America, 1997.

CHAPTER 3

Community and Audience

Christopher Spaide

Follow a prominent strand of Wallace Stevens studies over a half-century in the making, and you might expect a chapter on "Community and Audience" in his poetry to amount to something between a brief interlude and a blank page: there is neither a sense of community nor any actual human audience to speak of. Or else a chapter titled "Community and Audience" might focus, paradoxically, on Stevens's idiosyncrasy and alienation, his self-address and private languages. In the eyes of this critical community (better populated, apparently, than any community in Stevens's own poetry), Stevens wrote for an audience of one, Americanizing the royal "we," speaking for others only as a matter of elaborate stagecraft – the impersonation and costumery of his one-man show. In a 1951 review, Randall Jarrell diagnosed in Stevens's *The Auroras of Autumn* "the weakness . . . of thinking of particulars as primarily illustrations of general truths, or else as aesthetic, abstracted objects, simply there to be contemplated; he often treats things or lives so that they seem no more than generalizations of an unprecedentedly low order." In Jarrell's depiction of Stevens's mathematical mind, the lives of "us poor, dishonest people" were nothing but abstracted plot-points, "no more than data to be manipulated": "It is the lack of immediate contact with lives that hurts his poetry more than anything else" (140–41). Later twentieth-century critics found even less than "immediate contact with lives." Hugh Kenner found Stevens's world "empty of people," his poems "not populated, except by cartoon-like wisps" (75, 83); Mark Halliday, titling a study *Stevens and the Interpersonal* (1991), beheld nothing there: "Stevens' poetry largely tries to ignore or deny all aspects of life that center on or are inseparable from interpersonal relations" (3). Stevens's legacy as modern poetry's strictest solitary – in art, in life, in lasting sensibility – persists pervasively among postwar and contemporary poets, whether avowing their indebtedness (Louise Glück, in her 1996 collection *Meadowlands*: "If you're so desperate / for precedent, try / Stevens. Stevens / never traveled; that doesn't mean / he

44

didn't know pleasure" [311]) or mingling fondness and fury. "No one living a snowed-in life / can sleep without a blindfold": that Stevensian axiom opens Terrance Hayes's "Snow for Wallace Stevens" (2009), which sympathetically adopts the tones of a fellow solitary while pushing back at a modernist forerunner "with pipes of winter / lining his cognition," insulated from others inside his own chilly disposition (57).

Follow, instead, a nascent strand of Stevens criticism, and you can find many of these critical assessments and poetic reactions recited in opening paragraphs and dutifully itemized in footnotes.[1] But rather than wholeheartedly accept their categorical truisms, twenty-first-century critics cite these proponents of a solipsistic Stevens only to correct them or contradict them outright, presenting instead the Stevens who preemptively insisted, in a 1940 letter to Hi Simons, "I don't agree with the people who say that I live in a world of my own" (*L* 352). Buoyed in part by late-twentieth-century studies that helped to bring Stevens out of his mind and into the social and political world, in part by a renewed theoretical curiosity about lyric and its powers of address and identification, a critical mass is at last taking Stevens seriously as a poet of *community* – a key word in recent work by Bonnie Costello, Gül Bilge Han, Joshua Kotin, J. Hillis Miller, Jason Puskar, and Justin Quinn, and a peripheral or secret subject in countless other studies. If, as Stevens writes in his "Adagia," "Every poem is a poem within a poem: the poem of the idea within the poem of the words" (*CPP* 912), then these critics reconceive both the "poem" and the "poem within a poem." Those drawn to "the poem of the idea" have explored historical and personal crises, political philosophy and aesthetics, place and affect; critics drawn first to "the poem of the words" have reconsidered Stevens's diction, genres, forms, speakers, and even his decisions on the minute level of lyric pronouns – what Stevens meant when he wrote "I" or "he," spoke to "you" or for "us." Of course, any alteration to "the poem of the idea" alters "the poem of the words," and vice versa, especially for this poet who proposed that "A change of style is a change of subject" (*CPP* 910): resourcefully contextual and keenly formalist approaches alike have led critics to the same questions concerning community and audience, and often to the very same poems.

The largest contingent of critics of "the poem of the idea" – those most explicitly concerned with "community," and perhaps the most divisive – has followed Stevens through time, reexamining the sequential developments of his career and unraveling its entanglement with political and social timelines. Nearly all these critics concentrate on Stevens's long, kaleidoscopic sequences, which enact community's multiplicity with their antiphonies of voice, persona, and perspective. Recently, no sequence has been reread more, and more variously, than "Owl's Clover" (1936), which has undergone a critical about-face: no longer seen as simply an interesting failure (by Stevens's critics) or a failure to be interesting (by Stevens himself), the sequence now stands out as the testing ground of Stevens's 1930s poetry, an unrepeatable experiment in depicting community. But what kind of community? For Joel Nickels, it is the spontaneous and self-organizing collective subject of the *multitude*, in the sense elaborated by the contemporary political philosophers Michael Hardt and Antonio Negri. That term appears in the sequence's closing lines, as Stevens weighs if we conceal the "passion to fling the cloak, / Adorned for a multitude," the passion to choose the continuities and conformities of being "The medium man among other medium men" (*CPP* 591). The multitude's value is precisely that it lets those men disagree: in Nickels's reading, a multitude "can accommodate negativity without degenerating into an aggregation of competing grouplets," inviting even an imagination as potent as Stevens's into a "permanent, collective debate, shot through with negativity and possessing delicately counterbalanced forces and actors" (39, 185). Hardt and Negri appear also in Jason Puskar's divergent reading of Stevens's "drastic community" (*CPP* 574), which is grounded less in political theory than in the history of finance. Reading "Owl's Clover" in light of Stevens's work in corporate surety bonds (securities of good conduct, forfeited upon broken contracts), Puskar finds a 1930s social order "knit together not from bonds of trust, but from a distrust so pervasive that it justified an abstract and far more impersonal conglomeration of mutually reinforcing hedges" (182). Though "the birds / Of chaos" of "Mr. Burnshaw and the Statue," amassing into "spectacular flocks," offer one optimistic figure for a nonhierarchical "mighty flight of men" (*CPP* 573–74), Puskar finds a "counter-metaphor" for community in the monstrous social body of the Bulgar (194). Frankensteined from essentialized immigrant features ("these hands from Sweden," "These English noses and edged, Italian eyes"), the Bulgar's patchwork anatomy prompts Stevens's most skeptical inquisition of collectivity: "Is each man thinking his separate thoughts or, for once, / Are all men thinking together as one, thinking / Each other's thoughts, thinking a single thought . . . ?" (*CPP* 582–83).

Another divisive portrait of community comes a decade later, in the backward glance of the postwar sequence "The Auroras of Autumn" (1948). Who "we were" once, what "we were" together, which catastrophe dissolved our fraternal community – these questions remain unanswered even by the nostalgic reminiscences and mesmerized tones of canto IX:

We were as Danes in Denmark all day long
And knew each other well, hale-hearted landsmen,
For whom the outlandish was another day

Of the week, queerer than Sunday. We thought alike
And that made brothers of us in a home
In which we fed on being brothers, fed

And fattened as on a decorous honeycomb.
This drama that we live – We lay sticky with sleep. (*CPP* 361–62)

The first time J. Hillis Miller used these lines as an epigraph, in *Poets of Reality* (1965), he found Stevens reflecting on a prelapsarian moment of clannish brotherhood before "The vanishing of the gods" – "the basis of all Stevens' thought and poetry" (219). Forty-six years later, Miller framed the same lines with, in Jean-Luc Nancy's phrase, the modern world's "conflagration of community," at once an allusion to the historical crux of the Holocaust and an unsparing figure for the dissolution of what Miller calls "indigenous community" (*Conflagration* 7). According to that myth of essential togetherness, Danes live among Danes, reveling in an experience distinctly Danish; "hale-hearted landsmen," they trace a common origin to Denmark, a homeland barring anything "outlandish" and "queer"; knowing each other well and thinking alike, they are cozily at home even in language, resting "sticky with sleep" within a bounded, patterned, "honeycomb"-like community. As Stevens's farewell to this idea of community – "Simply to name all the features of an indigenous community, even in a lyric poem so celebratory of its idea as this one is, is to destroy it by bringing it self-consciously into the light" (Miller, *Conflagration* 11) – "The Auroras" makes room for Nancy's alternative idea, an inessential community of singularities with nothing in common. In Joshua Kotin's more pessimistic reading, the same sequence suggests that Stevens, after decades of approaching "the problem of value as a problem of community formation," solved it by bidding farewell to "the idea of community altogether" (55). Fended off by the sequence's impenetrable difficulty, private associations, and ambiguity of reference ("Does Stevens's 'we' include us? We cannot be certain"), Kotin concludes, "The Auroras" succeeds as "an attempt to construct a community of one – a community in which relative judgments of value are absolute judgments of value. The poem's success hinges on its inaccessibility" (63, 65).[2]

To time Stevens's thinking to books or landmark poetic sequences can usefully sync it with world history (or a publication schedule). But it has drawbacks: it might suggest Stevens dwelt on community as a passing fad to work through and leave behind, and it overlooks his own rueful self-assessments about the place of people in his work. Or the place of place: "Life is an affair of people not of places. But for me life is an affair of places and that is the trouble" (*CPP* 901). Stephanie Burt's earliest Stevens criticism explores how Charles Baxter, August Kleinzahler, and Adrienne Rich answer that "trouble" by resocializing their modernist precursor and repopulating his places. Reworking the Stevensian "poem of the empty landscape," each postwar poet "revises Stevens' poems of American deprivation by infusing them with historical particulars and by trying to bring in the perspectives of precisely the other people Stevens fails to reach" ("Charles Baxter" 115–16). More recently, Burt has introduced us to a Stevens far more socialized than we assume: the late Stevens who assiduously wrote his adopted state of Connecticut, its folklore and local history (from pre-colonial times to the modern era), and its ecologies and environments (rural and urban), into poetry. This is not simply the Stevens of "Farewell to Florida," who claimed membership in "My North," a New England that "lies in a wintry slime / Both of men and clouds, a slime of men in crowds" (*CPP* 98). Rather, Burt argues, the late Stevens submerged state-specific allusions most easily apprehensible to Connecticut's local audiences. For Hartford residents, for example, the deteriorating structures, "great pond," and garden lilies of "The Plain Sense of Things" (*CPP* 428) might recall Stevens's beloved Elizabeth Park: "This little park is almost all there is in Hartford," he wrote to Barbara Church in 1952, "and I like it especially on Sundays when people go there" (*L* 761). Stevens's special affection for this place at its most peopled may account for the collective life prevalent in the Elizabeth Park poems: the nuns in "Nuns Painting Water-Lilies," the "men" in "The Plain Sense of Things," the "birds" making "intelligible twittering" and the "lucent children" of ducklings in "The Hermitage at the Center" (*CPP* 456, 428, 430). It might even frame these late, local poems not only as solitary meditations but also as democratic environments. "The Elizabeth Park poems," Burt writes, "suggest that Stevens calls into being for himself and for any imagined readers a kind of figurative urban park, ... a space designed (like all successful city parks, and in contradistinction to private houses) for multiple simultaneous uses, by people of different ages and tastes" ("Wallace Stevens" 331).

   To call Stevens a regional poet is not quite to nominate him as Connecticut's poet laureate, speaking for its people, bursting with state pride. In Stevens's poems of riverbanks, roads, shores, and other "geographic transitional space," Burt detects a parallel boundary, "the line between a mostly solitary inner life and the resonances it seeks in outward space" ("Wallace Stevens" 342). Even Stevens's poem about Hartford's public transportation, "On the Way to the Bus" (1954), testifies not to modernity's anonymous vehicular communities (as in Elizabeth Bishop's "The Moose") but to one "journalist," a word humming resonantly with "journeying" in public, private "journaling," and – via the French *jour* – to daily routine. Commuting through "light snow," this "Transparent man" encounters afresh his region's reinvigorations, first sensory and emotive ("A refreshment of cold air"), then cognitive and imagistic ("a clearness emerging / From cold"), finally linguistic if quietly personal ("A way of pronouncing the word inside of one's tongue") (*CPP* 472). But other, more social poems register Connecticut's landscapes and monuments, display almanac-grade attention to seasons and microclimates, and transcribe a regionally common knowledge and intersubjective spirit that we might call "folk-lore" (from "The River of Rivers in Connecticut" [*CPP* 451]) or "mythology." The latter word appears in a late fragment, "A mythology reflects its region," the rare poem that both names and speaks for Stevens's adopted state: "Here / In Connecticut, we never lived in a time / When mythology was possible. . . ." Our secular time arrived too late for "mythology," so Connecticut's stony spirit will have to rest on a disillusioned plain sense, on literal bedrock and the materials we hew and quarry from the terrain ("Wood of his forests and stone out of his fields"), and on our "increased, / Heightened," and "freshened" sense once we become rooted there (*CPP* 476). Stevens's scrutiny of the routine, intangible, intersubjective binds between his fellow New Englanders may explain his appeal to Kathleen Stewart in her theory of "ordinary affects," "the varied, surging capacities to affect and to be affected that give everyday life the quality of a continual motion of relations, scenes, contingencies, and emergences" (1–2). Quoting the first and last lines of "July Mountain,"

> We live in a constellation
> Of patches and of pitches,
> Not in a single world,
> . . . .
> The way, when we climb a mountain,
> Vermont throws itself together (*CPP* 476),

Stewart surmises that everything we and Stevens telegraphically mean by "Vermont" is not any "single" phenomenon but a "constellation" of partial potentials turned kinetic all at once. Vermontness exists "in the differences and repetitions of a grab bag of qualities and technologies that can be thrown together into an event and a sensation," among them "fall colors, maple syrup, tourist brochures, calendars, snow, country stores; liberalism and yet the fight over gay marriage; racial homogeneity and yet everywhere white lesbian couples with babies of color," and so on (29–30). Surely some of these "qualities and technologies" would be news to Stevens, but they testify to a communal experience that only his patchwork sense of place, of local significances and "an always incipient cosmos," could throw together (*CPP* 476).

The Connecticut poems – with a verbal austerity suited to New England winters, a lexicon of place-names and local flora, a marshalling of communities into a city- or state-sized "we" – demonstrate that Stevens's sense of community affects not only "the poem of the idea" but also "the poem of the words." As his earliest and latest critics have noted, disparaged, or defended, diction alone can welcome or repulse entire classes of readers. "An air of preciousness bathes the mind of the casual reader" of *Harmonium*, R. P. Blackmur admitted, when such uncommon vocabulary as "fubbed" and "ructive" and "funest" (among other *OED* deep cuts) crops up, but to decipher Stevens's originality "you have only to know the meanings of the words and to submit to the conditions of the poem." (In the case of "funest," Blackmur had to confess, "Small dictionaries do not stock it" [71–73].) Recently, Harris Feinsod has reconsidered Stevens's eclectic diction, especially his mid-century penchant for Romance languages and macaronic play, as one American poet's bequest to a hemispheric "xenoglossary," "a shared auxiliary lexicon open to poets across the Americas" (98). Reframing Stevens's "Latinization of American English" not as a verbal garnish or dash of exotica but "an effort to entangle US poetry with a hemispheric linguistic fabric," Feinsod argues that we should understand Stevens "as richly multilingual, a poet bent on 'the beau language without a drop of blood,' the 'palabra of a common man,' the 'fluent mundo,' a poet whose xenoglosses are microcosms of the global auxiliary language he calls 'lingua franca et jocundissima'" (98, 107).

If the minute scale and idiosyncratic palate of Stevens's diction offer one new vantage on "the poem of the words," the zoomed-out, transhistoric scale of genre provides another. By a curious paradox, as Stevens's critics have branched radially outward to consider each of his favored genres – poems of modern love and marriage, landscape and still life, aphorisms and *adagia* – they tend to return to questions of audience and community, to whom and for whom Stevens speaks.[3] Few genres complicate those questions more than elegy, as it addresses a dead or transfigured audience, congregates a community of mourners, and imaginatively aligns nature's untroubled recurrence and human mortality. As Jahan Ramazani has shown, Stevens began as a mock elegist, cloaking "a deep nostalgia for meaningful social and poetic rites of mourning" behind mockery for "the cultural codes governing grief" and especially "burial practices and elegiac conventions" (90). Among the conventions Stevens mocked or ignored outright are elegy's social dimensions: apostrophes to divinities or the deceased, the call to mourners, and the funeral procession. (The only communal mourners in *Harmonium* are death's inhuman delegates, "The Worms at Heaven's Gate," who speak chorally: "Out of the tomb, we bring Badroulbadour, / Within our bellies, we her chariot" [*CPP* 40].) Certainly some of Stevens's elegies and self-elegies glimpse him at his most solitary, bereft of others and alone in dying, or cast him as nearer to skeletonkind than humankind, "A countryman of all the bones in the world" (*CPP* 598). But other elegies reunite Stevens with communities of various proportions: the preemptively posthumous generation of "A Postcard from the Volcano" (who imagine "Children picking up our bones"); the ghosts, craving feeling, who surround the "Large Red Man Reading" ("There were ghosts that returned to earth to hear his phrases"); and the universal club of all of us mortals, which Stevens could invoke forebodingly, as in "The Owl in the Sarcophagus" ("This is that figure stationed at our end"), or flippantly, as in "Table Talk" ("Granted, we die for good") (*CPP* 128, 365, 373, 566). When Stevens takes, in Helen Vendler's genre-coining phrase, his "last looks" – sustaining a binocular vision that keeps both life and death in focus – he can write poems like "The Rock," which in Vendler's reading begins as his "most nihilistic" poem in its curt denials of existence ("It is an illusion that we were ever alive") and ends its first section "with a participatory reprise" of erotic desire, generational integrity, and universal belonging: "The blooming and the musk / Were being alive, an incessant being alive, / A particular of being, that gross universe" (*Last* 44–45; *CPP* 445). Stevens's binocular style respects "both the aridity of age and the elasticity of regained vitality," Vendler concludes. "This last look can hold at its interface both contempt and joy" (*Last* 46).

At once the most blatant and shiftily elusive way "the poem of the words" can invoke a community is to give it voice, forgoing the expected lyric "I" for a plural pronoun, an elastic "we." In "Collecting Ourselves: 'We' in Wallace Stevens" (2018), Bonnie Costello surveys the plural pronoun's overtones across all stages of Stevens's poetry and prose, finding "evidence throughout of Stevens's active imagining of the collective, not only within the voice of solitude, but as a granulated and as a choral presence" (1068).[4] Stevens could even reimagine that presence over the course of a single poem, as in "The Idea of Order at Key West," where Costello discerns "a situational first-person plural without an antecedent," a pronoun whose scope is as tidal as the sea (1076). First a "we" of humankind – "aspectual rather than collective," distinguishing "us" from the enigmatic singing "she" – Stevens's "we" soon "implies particular listeners in time" (1077), then narrative framers ("we said," "we knew"), then the "pluralized perspective" of social beings who "must submit our world-making to the *polis*," framed by Key West and the multitude of "glassy lights" over the harbor (1079; *CPP* 105–06). Even when Stevens apparently grounds that "we" in an "abrupt and even comically disjunctive present-tense address to Ramon Fernandez," the borders of the assembled community remain hazy: does Stevens's "we" *include* Fernandez as a corroborating witness, or *exclude* him at first, inviting him "to step in now as an outsider" (1079)? Costello's conclusion about this poem's shape-shifting pronoun applies to Stevens's "we" generally: it is "neither a static abstraction in the poem, nor a fully localized group in a story, but a dynamic presence, a 'we' variously erotic, filial, communal, humanistic, and textual, in that the reader can feel hailed, and that the keen sounds of the poem bring the song into our ears and mouths." Far from a grammatical tic or stylistic quirk to leave on the page, Stevens's "we" welcomes his audiences and grants them the cry of the poem's occasion: "It is not ideas that gather this faceted human 'spirit,' but the saying of ourselves, in which the question of 'origins' dissolves into effects we intuit" (1080).

As Costello amply demonstrates in her field-forming study *The Plural of Us* (2017), which centers on W. H. Auden and includes examples from W. B. Yeats, T. S. Eliot, Marianne Moore, and countless English-language poets before and since, Stevens was not the sole modernist to speak for "us." But among his peers Stevens may be unique in one tendency: he gravitates toward an inclusive or universal "we" precisely when his poems appear to call for an "I" – that is, in poems of alienation, estrangement, and privacy; in moments of epiphany, anagnorisis, or confessed limitation; in singular articulations of desire, embodiment, whim, and whimsy; and in meditations on the philosophical problem of other minds or the political question of personal liberty.[5] "Did we expect to live in other lives?"; "There is so little that is close and warm. / It is as if we were never children"; "You know then that it is not the reason / That makes us happy or unhappy" (*CPP* 289, 295, 477). This tendency becomes brightly obvious in the "Adagia": though many forgo personal pronouns, among the rest "we" far outweighs "I": "We live in the mind"; "We have to step boldly into man's interior world or not at all"; "The poet represents the mind in the act of defending us against itself" (*CPP* 904, 909, 911). There is something solecistic, even spell-check-able, about these sentences, as though Stevens had mismatched his singulars ("the mind," "man's interior world") with his plurals ("we," "us"). One solution to this pronominal conundrum is to treat Stevens's plural pronoun as a royal "we," mentally supplying the errata: *for "we," read "I."* (A common pedagogical recommendation for new readers of Stevens is to mind his peculiar pronouns and their variance from the lyric "I," and even to provisionally swap in that more common pronoun.)[6] A more perplexing solution would be to recognize the generally unspoken and still unrecognized axiom underlying much of Stevens: that anybody's experience, the poet's included, is nothing special, nothing wholly alien to anyone else, and therefore something that can be extended universally. That axiom permits a different pronominal substitution, from singular to plural: if "I," then "we."[7] In a 1943 letter to Hi Simons clarifying two lines from "Notes Toward a Supreme Fiction," Stevens himself demonstrates this universalizing logic:

> If "I am a stranger in the land," it follows that the whole race is a stranger. We live in a place that is not our own and, much more, not ourselves. The first idea, then, was not our own. It is not the individual alone that indulges himself in the pathetic fallacy. It is the race. (*L* 444)[8]

If a critical pendulum has swung from Stevens the "individual," too often cast as a congenital "stranger," to his concern for the condition of "the whole race," what might be the equilibrium position? My opening quotations from Jarrell, Kenner, and Halliday may overstate their cases, but are those cases wholly incorrect? And where do they originate in our understanding (or misunderstanding) of Stevens's poetry? What does it say about Stevens's eccentric sense of community that so many of our best readers have such trouble locating it? What should we conclude, not only about the state of Stevens studies but the carnivalesque variety of the poems themselves, if the same poetic sequence can strike one reader as an occasion to rethink community entirely, another reader as a solipsistic "community of one"?

Perhaps the sturdiest footing for future Stevens studies to start on is this: community and audience, for Stevens, are always counterbalanced by their others – individuality, impersonality, inhuman nature, aesthetic autonomy.[9] As his poems unfold, *one* will come to stand for *many*, or *many* fix their attentions on *one*. Where "Sunday Morning" and "The Idea of Order at Key West" pivot from singular female presences to a collective "we," the posthumous generation penning "A Postcard from the Volcano" fixates finally on what "he that lived there left behind" (*CPP* 128). Where "The Man with the Blue Guitar" ponders picking "A million people on one string" (*CPP* 136), the "major man" of "Notes Toward a Supreme Fiction" is deemed not a superheroic "exception" but another "part, // Though an heroic part, of the commonal" (*CPP* 336). In these and other poems, Stevens's truest subject is not community, not individuality, but the never-settled contest between the two. And often that contest, less an intellectual contradiction to be definitively puzzled out than a dramatic conflict played out anew in poem after poem, gives Stevens not only a subject but also a structure, a stylistic challenge, and an inciting set of poetic and political stakes.

Consider an uncollected poem, a late poem meditating on lateness and too-lateness in their various guises: "The Sick Man" (1950), published five years before Stevens's death. That title sets us up for a character study of a solitary man, sick in health, pushed to society's margins, even placed in quarantine. Instead, the poem's first two sentences, each encompassing one sonorous tercet, depict two antiphonal forms of a distinctly American artistic collectivity. As though listening in stereo, the first sentence picks up "Bands of black men" – marching bands, instrumental bands playing "mouth-organs" and "guitars," moving "In the South" on the migratory scale of "thousands" – and the second, tuning in "Here in the North," hears "Voices in chorus, singing without words." Tracing geographical, racial, and cultural differences, these same six lines find hints of commonality, grounds for new unity: both melodies are playing "late" and "in the night"; both emanate from "long movements," musical and demographic; and both are "drifting," not yet set to any memorable, mutually meaningful words. Finding the apt "words of winter" is the duty of the titular sick man, listening to "drifting" tunes and literal "movements" from a bedridden, solitary remove (*CPP* 455). And yet Stevens's third, last sentence, sustained across three tercets, concerns not only that individual but also the two communities – white and Black, North and South, vocal and instrumental – that "will come together" in imaginary lyrics:

> And in a bed in one room, alone, a listener
> Waits for the unison of the music of the drifting bands
> And the dissolving chorals, waits for it and imagines
>
> The words of winter in which these two will come together,
> In the ceiling of the distant room, in which he lies,
> The listener, listening to the shadows, seeing them,

Choosing out of himself, out of everything within him,
Speech for the quiet, good hail of himself, good hail, good hail,
The peaceful, blissful words, well-tuned, well-sung, well-spoken. (*CPP* 455)

In a Stevensian sleight of hand, racial and national harmony becomes as achievable as a musical "unison," an exact identity in pitch; the individual's role within the community is figured as the lyricist's gift to the wordless playing of both band and chorus. Sounding out that triple unison of Black bands, white voices, and sick man, Stevens sings everything in threes: the three tercets united by this third and last sentence, the thrice-repeated salutation "good hail," and the anaphoric triplet of compound adjectives – "well-tuned" instrumentation, "well-sung" choral performance, "well-spoken" lyric utterance – that Stevens strings together in his last line's stately hexameter. Is it any accident that the same lines imagining an anthem for a hypothetically "peaceful, blissful" society echo the most impersonal S-Man in Stevens's oeuvre, "the listener, who listens in the snow," of "The Snow Man" (*CPP* 8)? Call it not a correction but a retrospective reminder: all along, this listener has listened to the manifold sounds of his neighboring people and places, "well-tuned, well-sung, well-spoken."

Notes

1 For a recent response to Halliday that finds Stevens's "central preoccupation with the self to be balanced and qualified by a recurrent orientation toward the other," see Gilbert (335).
2 For a dissenting reading that argues "The Auroras" moves "towards a communal vision" achieved by "the imagination of the community, not some Emersonian transparent eyeball," see Quinn (79).
3 On modern love and marriage, see Selinger 95–100; on landscape and still life, see Costello, *Shifting* 53–85 and *Planets* 26–47; on aphorisms and *adagia*, see Perloff.
4 Two invaluable precedents for Costello's study of Stevens's pronouns are Blasing 133–48 and Vendler, "Stevens."
5 Even in the late work's "scenes of private meditation and intense interiority," Costello observes, "the first-person plural remains the dominant pronoun of subjectivity" (1085).
6 See, e.g., Cook 319, 328–30; Serio xii; and Vendler, *Wallace Stevens* 44.
7 Apparently, no feeling was exempt from Stevens's universalizing substitutions – not even feelings of the utmost abnormality: "I don't think we should insist that the poet is normal or, for that matter, that anybody is" (*CPP* 906).
8 Though Stevens's letter specifies lines 8–9 of canto IV of "It Must Be Abstract," here he collages from and un-versifies line 1 ("The first idea was not our own") and lines 13–14 ("we live in a place / That is not our own and, much more, not

ourselves") (*CPP* 331–32). The quoted clause recalls Exodus 2:22 ("I have been a stranger in a strange land") and Psalm 119:19 ("I am a stranger in the earth").
9 On aesthetic autonomy not as an escape from community but "as a necessary condition for poetic engagement," see Han (4 and esp. 94–138).

WORKS CITED

Blackmur, R. P. "Examples of Wallace Stevens." 1931. *Selected Essays of R. P. Blackmur*, edited by Denis Donoghue, Ecco, 1986, pp. 71–100.

Blasing, Mutlu Konuk. *Lyric Poetry: The Pain and Pleasure of Words.* Princeton UP, 2006.

Burt, Stephanie. "Charles Baxter, August Kleinzahler, Adrienne Rich: Contemporary Stevensians and the Problem of 'Other Lives.'" *The Wallace Stevens Journal*, vol. 24, no. 2, Fall 2000, pp. 115–34.

"Wallace Stevens: Where He Lived." *ELH*, vol. 77, no. 2, Summer 2010, pp. 325–52.

Cook, Eleanor. *A Reader's Guide to Wallace Stevens.* Princeton UP, 2007.

Costello, Bonnie. "Collecting Ourselves: 'We' in Wallace Stevens." *ELH*, vol. 85, no. 4, Winter 2018, pp. 1065–92.

Planets on Tables: Poetry, Still Life, and the Turning World. Cornell UP, 2008.

The Plural of Us: Poetry and Community in Auden and Others. Princeton UP, 2017.

Shifting Ground: Reinventing Landscape in Modern American Poetry. Harvard UP, 2003.

Feinsod, Harris. *The Poetry of the Americas: From Good Neighbors to Countercultures.* Oxford UP, 2017.

Gilbert, Roger. "The (Inter)personal." *Wallace Stevens in Context*, edited by Glen MacLeod, Cambridge UP, 2017, pp. 335–43.

Glück, Louise. *Poems 1962–2012.* Farrar, Straus and Giroux, 2012.

Halliday, Mark. *Stevens and the Interpersonal.* Princeton UP, 1991.

Han, Gül Bilge. *Wallace Stevens and the Poetics of Modernist Autonomy.* Cambridge UP, 2019.

Hayes, Terrance. *Lighthead.* Penguin, 2010.

Jarrell, Randall. *Poetry and the Age.* Expanded ed., UP of Florida, 2001.

Kenner, Hugh. *A Homemade World: The American Modernist Writers.* Alfred A. Knopf, 1975.

Kotin, Joshua. "Wallace Stevens's Point of View." *PMLA*, vol. 130, no. 1, Jan. 2015, pp. 54–68.

Miller, J. Hillis. *The Conflagration of Community: Fiction before and after Auschwitz.* U of Chicago P, 2011.

Poets of Reality: Six Twentieth-Century Writers. Harvard UP, 1965.

Nickels, Joel. *The Poetry of the Possible: Spontaneity, Modernism, and the Multitude.* U of Minnesota P, 2012.

Perloff, Marjorie. "Beyond 'Adagia': Eccentric Design in Stevens' Poetry." *The Wallace Stevens Journal*, vol. 35, no. 1, Spring 2011, pp. 16–32.

Puskar, Jason. "Wallace Stevens's 'Drastic Community': Credit, Suretyship and the Society of Distrust." *Incredible Modernism: Literature, Trust and Deception*, edited by John Attridge and Rod Rosenquist, Ashgate, 2013, pp. 181–98.

Quinn, Justin. *Gathered Beneath the Storm: Wallace Stevens, Nature and Community*. U College Dublin P, 2002.

Ramazani, Jahan. *Poetry of Mourning: The Modern Elegy from Hardy to Heaney*. U of Chicago P, 1994.

Selinger, Eric Murphy. *What Is It Then between Us? Traditions of Love in American Poetry*. Cornell UP, 1998.

Serio, John N. Introduction. *Wallace Stevens: Selected Poems*, edited by John N. Serio, Alfred A. Knopf, 2009, pp. xi–xxii.

Stevens, Wallace. *Letters of Wallace Stevens*. Edited by Holly Stevens, U of California P, 1996.

Wallace Stevens: Collected Poetry and Prose. Edited by Frank Kermode and Joan Richardson, Library of America, 1997.

Stewart, Kathleen. *Ordinary Affects*. Duke UP, 2007.

Vendler, Helen. *Last Looks, Last Books: Stevens, Plath, Lowell, Bishop, Merrill*. Princeton UP, 2010.

"Stevens and the Lyric Speaker." *The Cambridge Companion to Wallace Stevens*, edited by John N. Serio, Cambridge UP, 2007, pp. 133–48.

Wallace Stevens: Words Chosen Out of Desire. U of Tennessee P, 1984.

CHAPTER 4

Secularism

Matthew Mutter

Readers of Wallace Stevens encounter an intricate and copious lexicon. They also discover certain elemental words. Some of these – "blue," "fiction," "shadow" – are idiosyncratic hieroglyphics by which Stevens condenses his abiding poetic themes. He experiments with their sense, resonance, and implication as they reappear from poem to poem. Many such elemental words – "the earth," "reality," "inhuman," "enough" – serve as coordinates by which Stevens plots his world. They elaborate this world as distinctly secular. Stevens wanted to write "the great poem of the earth" over against the poetry "of heaven and hell" (*CPP* 730) and to replace "The search for god" with "The search / For reality" (*CPP* 410). He sought dimensions of the human that were "part of the inhuman more" (*CPP* 467) – of the expansive world divested of spirit. Perhaps the fundamental project of his poetry is to affirm the immanent world as a fitting home for the human. "It seems / As if the health of the world might be enough" (*CPP* 278): this is Stevens's invitation to a viable secularity. But the hesitation in these same lines – "seems," "as if," "might" – suggests that his affirmation is complex and troubled.

Stevens accepted many features of the secular model of reality that emerged in Western modernity: that God or the gods had died, that nature had been neutralized or depersonalized, and that human meaning was an ontological anomaly. The history of religion was a history of projecting this "anthropomorphic" meaning onto the cosmos. Looking back from modern eyes, such projections are understood as consoling fictions of desire, unaware of their own fictionality. It follows that secularity is characterized as an amplified state of human self-consciousness that discovers, as William James put it, "the trail of the human serpent . . . over everything" (33). The secular poet views the religious past – indeed, the totality of premodern history – as a time "Before we were wholly human and knew ourselves" (*CPP* 280). In the twentieth century, even Stevens's most penetrating critics tended to share his view of secularity. Those who accepted

Stevens's diagnosis of the secular condition tacitly understood secularism as a "subtraction story," in which the modern mind gradually purged its illusions to approach the neutral, unencumbered reality that had been masked by religion.[1] Those who emphasized Stevens's spirituality, whether construed as Gnostic, Nietzschean, or humanist, typically assumed that it was a "substitute" for or "naturalization" of the obsolete ethos of religion.[2] "Little of what we have believed has been true," Stevens wrote in 1941 (*CPP* 655). We know, now, that the cosmos is neutral materiality, not meaning, that the gods were illusions, not revelations, and that human experience is ontologically marginal, not central. Stevens takes this knowledge to be inevitable; it is the unpalatable but inexorable truth about the real. Both epistemic responsibility and human dignity demand that we resist nostalgia for the gods: "no man ever muttered a petition in his heart for the restoration of those unreal shapes" (*CPP* 842).

Stevens construed secular modernity as a condition of both deprivation and liberation. On the one hand, it is a state of dispossession. The meanings elaborated by the religious imagination were, despite their illusory status, "a part of the glory of the earth," for they gave life style and depth (*CPP* 842). The mechanical, disenchanted world now appears "bare," "desolate," "empty," and "flat" – as a "vacancy" that chills "the shaken realist" (*CPP* 282). If this is the "true" world, it seems inadequate to human desire. In "Esthétique du Mal," he asks, "What place in which to be is not enough / To be?" (*CPP* 282). The stark secularity of existence (the material substrate of human being) does not seem to support the distinctly human ways in which we flourish (our spiritual being). On the other hand, the emptiness of secular reality is celebrated as a space of pure possibility. If we "live in an old chaos of the sun," there is no cosmic order or authority to which our lives must conform. This is the exhilaration of being "unsponsored, free" (*CPP* 56). The imagination is now autonomous and unconstrained.

That Stevens thinks of secularity in terms of deprivation and liberation suggests something further: it is above all a crisis concerning value. It is a crisis, as the title of one of Stevens's poems suggests, about "How to Live. What to Do." This is why Stevens can celebrate reality as the ultimate value and speak, at the same time, of the "disaster of reality" (*L* 386). He sees secular modernity as a "general transition to reality," but the reality that remains after the progressive shedding of metaphysical illusion is ruinously barren: it is all fact and no value (*CPP* 657). Stevens's poetry is perpetually saying farewell to ideas and feelings that are linked to the "death of God," for it is construed not as an isolated event but as an ongoing series of negations. "Esthétique du Mal" confronts, for instance, not only the death of God but also the death of Satan. Why was "The death of Satan ... a tragedy / For the imagination" (*CPP* 281)? It is because "Satan" is the name for a set of imaginative resources for dealing with – for dramatizing – the force and significance of evil in human experience. Satan's disappearance is another secular negation – "A capital / Negation destroyed him in his tenement" (*CPP* 281–82). Along the same lines, secular negations counsel against transfiguring pain and suffering into value – giving them a plus sign – because this would make the world "presence" rather than brute "force." As the "Back-Ache" wryly says in the poem "Saint John and the Back-Ache," "Presence is *Kinder-Scenen*," or a childish nostalgia that the mature secularist must resist (*CPP* 375).

When suffering is linked to the figure of Satan, Stevens suggests, it takes on an impermissibly moral – and thus human – aspect. But there are new resources for value, "Esthétique" suggests, if we imagine secularization itself as theater. The death of Satan was a tragedy – in the everyday sense of an unfortunate event – that must be superseded by a higher mode of tragedy, which, the poem proposes, "may have begun, / Again, in the imagination's new beginning" (*CPP* 282). "[U]nder every" secular "no," Stevens insists, "Lay a passion for yes that had never been broken" (*CPP* 282). This "yes" is an affirmation of the material world in its sheer givenness. To say "yes" is to convert all of life into ennobling tragedy. "Merely ... living as and where we live" becomes "an adventure to be endured" (*CPP* 287, 285). For Stevens, in other words, the appeal of secularism is profoundly dramatic, for it involves an awakening from error, a trial of dispossession, and a heroic image of the metaphysically abandoned self, facing reality with dignity and resourcefulness. The loss of religious meaning is an opportunity to test one's imaginative mettle. Indeed, Stevens explicitly configures modernity as "theatre" in "Of Modern Poetry." In this poem, the secular poet must "construct a new stage" and write a new "script" – and must do so with shoddy equipment (his "instrument" is a "wiry string") and no lighting crew (he is "A metaphysician in the dark") (*CPP* 218–19).

The secular world of fragmented, violent fact is what Stevens calls a "chaos." In his poetry, the responsibilities of the secular poet toward this chaotic reality vary in ambition. In "Of Modern Poetry," for instance, the besieged dramatist is content to articulate "sudden rightnesses" (*CPP* 219). Elsewhere he calls for a "harmonious skeptic" who might produce a comprehensive new "order," a "skeptical music" (*CPP* 100–01). Whether small and provisional ("sudden rightnesses") or far-reaching ("supreme fictions"), the secular poet is able to elaborate value through a revised understanding of an old faculty: the imagination. The challenge for secularism is that reality is the domain of fact, and fact has been segregated from value. For Stevens (especially the later Stevens), the imagination is the faculty that identifies or creates value. If reality is "things as they are," the imagination is "the power of the mind over the possibilities of things" (*CPP* 135, 726). New readers of Stevens are quickly acquainted with the dialectic in his poetry between the poles of reality and the imagination. But Stevens increasingly came to view the distinction – which reproduces the secular empiricist opposition between fact and value – as untenable. Indeed, one of the historical ironies of this distinction is that it is difficult to untangle the epistemic claims of secularism (facts pitted against illusions) from the ethos of secularism (the values it affirms, the states it admires). The very epistemic stance of secular reason – its cool detachment from the clamor for human mean- ing, its refusal to render brute facts comfortable – is itself replete with meanings. It "radiates" certain values – in particular, "the sense of freedom, power, control, invulnerability, dignity" (Taylor 286). There is a treacherous circularity: a fact is exemplified by its value-neutrality, yet the less a fact accommodates prevailing human values, the more unpalatable it becomes. Eventually, reverence for unpalatable facts becomes the exemplary disposition of honest, tough-minded, secular rationality.

This mood is pervasive in the earlier Stevens. Many poems display an exhilaration in confronting the inhuman factuality of the real. Stevens often figures the secular world as "rock" or "stone": "The earth is not earth but a stone" (*CPP* 142). In "How to Live. What to Do," a poem that Stevens said "so definitely represents my way of thinking" (*L* 293), the "rock / Impure" becomes a metonym for "a world unpurged," that is, a world whose moral inhospitality to the human is both confronted and celebrated (*CPP* 102). The poem composes a scene that is superficially desolate: a cold wind blows on a "tufted rock." The wind, however, is not desolate: it falls "upon them / In many majesties of sound." Indeed, the sound is "heroic," precisely because "There was neither voice nor crested image, / No chorister, nor priest" (*CPP* 103). The heroism and dignity of the unadorned world are assimilated to the mind insofar as the mind can countenance this barrenness. The poem establishes implicit analogies among metaphysical barrenness (no organic life, no "crested image"), inhumanity (no "voice"), and emancipation from religious tradition (no "priest"). The very valuelessness of this world becomes the poet's presiding value. Reality becomes the ultimate value insofar as it no longer houses value. The bare fact is the noble fact.

Poems like "How to Live" make it evident that the Stevensian imagination, far from standing opposite reality, is intimately involved in the delineation of reality as secular. As Stevens writes in a later poem, "The Plain Sense of Things," "the absence of the imagination had / Itself to be imagined" (*CPP* 428). The construal of the real as inhuman thrills the imagination. It provides an opportunity for a heroic renunciation of metaphysical meaning and for the autonomous work of self-creation. Stevens stages an agonistic struggle between the human self, which still craves meaning and joy, and the recalcitrant stone of the world: "That I may reduce the monster to / Myself, and then may be myself // In face of the monster, be more than part / Of it" (*CPP* 143). Stevens worried that the values of heroism and nobility had atrophied in secular modernity; the real as "monster" offers a new stage for heroic struggle. The poet must face its secular monstrosity and subdue ("reduce") it to the needs of desire. He must be "part / Of it" and so renounce religious otherworldliness but also be "more than part / Of it."

Beginning in the 1940s, Stevens's poetry began to acknowledge that his reality was an active construction of his secular imagination. In the parodic self-consciousness of "Landscape with Boat," to dispatch "the colossal illusion of heaven" is to inaugurate a (comically) endless activity of stripping down reality to an ostensibly "neutral centre" (*CPP* 220). The pursuit of this reality entangles him in the same austere, mystical dispositions that accompanied the most fervent religious asceticism: "He wanted the eye to see / And not be touched by blue. He wanted to know, / A naked man who regarded himself in the glass / Of air. . . ." This desire makes him "An anti-master-man, floribund ascetic" (*CPP* 220). To adopt the idiom of "How to Live," the "world unpurged" – the material world reclaimed from the religious disappointment in its imperfection – can only be accessed by purgation. The nakedness of the "neutral centre" demands his own extreme nakedness; he becomes a no-one looking at nothing. The poem closes by resisting the secular ambition to remove "truth" from the orbit of human need. It imagines instead a symmetry between the speaker's own expressive needs and the world outside: "'The thing I hum appears to be / The rhythm of this celestial pantomime'" (*CPP* 221).

Stevens could never shake the authority of that mode of secularism exemplified in scientific empiricism. In one of his last essays, he insisted that Max Planck rather than Blaise Pascal "was a much truer symbol of ourselves" (*CPP* 866). But Stevens began to test his own view of reality against the (would-be) scientific prophets of secularity. In "The Noble Rider," he registers a profound skepticism, for instance, about Freud's version of the "voice of the realist": "His conclusion is that man must venture at last into the hostile world and that this may be called education to reality" (*CPP* 651). Stevens recognizes that Freud's view of the real as unremittingly hostile to human flourishing is a kind of mythmaking: as Paul Ricoeur has written, Freud's concept of "Ananke" (the Greek word for "necessity") "is a symbol of a world view" characterized by a "wisdom that dares to face the harshness of life" (328).[3] Stevens himself used the ancient allegorical figure of "Ananke," but he called it a "god" – a "final god" or a "common god" (*CPP* 581, 580) – for "Ananke" is an interpretation of empirical reality, not empirical reality as such. Stevens realized, perhaps, that he had been overly seduced by the image, pervasive in Freud and others, of the real as violence; his later poetry struggles to characterize the real as "innocent" rather than as hostile (cf. *CPP* 360–62). And "The Noble Rider" takes another crucial step when Stevens begins to describe "reality" not as "solid, static objects" or an "external scene" available for neutral description but rather as "the life that is lived in the scene that it composes" (*CPP* 658). Stevens's later poetry aimed to plot the secular coordinates of that "life," yet his secularity becomes more flexible and conversant with the religious imagination that it ostensibly displaced.

Once the secular is seen as a new imaginary rather than the self-evident testimony of "things as they are," the question arises as to what relation a secular ethos and aesthetics bears to the religious. A knotty question for Stevens was whether his secular poetics demanded a radical break with the religious traditions that preceded it or whether it involved translations and substitutions of the concepts and values found in those traditions. In *Restless Secularism*, I have argued that Stevens's affirmations of immanence, combined with the theoretical histories he took from the early anthropology of religion, put him in a poetic bind. Stevens's poetry is constructed on a view of the world as inhuman and impersonal. Skeptical anthropology of religion (combined with empiricist philosophy) proposed that the origins of religion lay in the anthropomorphic imagination, through which, in Stevens's idiom, "Eve made air the mirror of herself" (*CPP* 331). Giambattista Vico and others taught him that this personifying and divinizing imagination was necessary for the development of a distinctly *human* consciousness. Language irresistibly created divinity, and poetry was inseparable from religious consciousness. "The Pure Good of Theory," for instance, revises the biblical creation story such that "Adam" becomes its author rather than witness: Adam's "mind malformed" the world in anthropomorphic "metaphor." Metaphor's job is to carry across; here, it alienates Adam from the very abundance of the sensory world by removing it to an inaccessible "paradise" that houses our "divine" parent (*CPP* 291).

In "Notes Toward a Supreme Fiction," we read, "From this the poem springs: that we live in a place / That is not our own and, much more, not ourselves" (*CPP* 332). It's important to recognize that this human condition has not changed in secular modernity: it was just this condition, as in Vico's history, that drove Eve and Adam to elaborate their metaphysically promiscuous metaphors. The distinctiveness of the secular situation, for Stevens, is that modern people have become fully aware of the anthropomorphic operation. Stevens views secular modernity as an elucidation of the human as such. To be secular is to understand the "height" and "the depth / Of human things" (*CPP* 267). Yet to map the human, one must grasp the meaning of human history in relation to its "modern" fruition. For the empiricist anthropologists of religion, the premodern history of human consciousness was a story of immaturity and error progressively shed by the ascendance of science. For Stevens, that is only half the story. This history is not so much disavowed as reconstituted as a history of creative authorship. The later Stevens follows the thinking of Vico and Ludwig Feuerbach, for whom the religious imagination was seen as un-self-conscious anthropological imagination. Theologies were really idealizations of the human. As Stevens writes in "Two or Three Ideas," we should imagine an equivalence between the "style of men" and the "style of the gods," and further between these and the "style of a poem." The gods are "as we wished them to be . . . they have fulfilled us . . . they are us but purified, magnified, in an expansion" (*CPP* 847). The divine does not humiliate the human; it is the human objectified and ennobled.

Ultimately, the content of the religious imagination matters less to Stevens than the set of human capacities that underwrites it. Such capacities generate a way of life generalized in a "style." There is, however, a tension in this secular affirmation, one that exemplifies two modalities of secularism. On the one hand, Stevens consistently characterizes secularism as a revelation of the fundamental contours of the human, for, to reclaim our original imaginative capacities, we must understand the fundamental needs and desires that set them to work. When Stevens discusses the post-religious task of poetry in "Imagination as Value," he posits an "imagination that seeks to satisfy . . . the universal mind." This imagination must "penetrate to basic images, basic emotions" – must discover and characterize essential human feeling – and so "compose a fundamental poetry even older than the ancient world" (*CPP* 732). In "Notes," the "major abstraction is the *idea* of man" (emphasis added) because this secular anthropology emphasizes the formal or constitutive capacities of the human. By meditating on the structure of desire itself (human figures "grown furious with human wish") rather than on particular objects of desire, we "see these separate figures one by one, / And yet see only one" (*CPP* 336).

On the other hand, while Stevens emphasizes the secular human as an abstract set of faculties, capacities, and basic emotions, the imaginative content of this set is by definition fluid, provisional, and various. It is a life enveloped in a value-creating language. The secular self and the world that it "propound[s]" are abstractions that are, as in "Notes," elusive of concrete "names" (*CPP* 336). Yet the happiness of this universalized abstraction is precisely to give names, as in "The Pastor Caballero": "The flare // In the sweeping brim becomes the origin / Of a human evocation, so disclosed / That, nameless, it creates an affectionate name, // Derived from adjectives of deepest mine" (*CPP* 327–28). "Mine" sounds an ambiguity that is unresolvable in Stevens's work: it evokes both a penetration into the dense ore of inhuman reality and an articulation of deep human desire. Stevens's secular ontology is not permeated by *logos*; because it is inhuman and impersonal, it does not possess the rational intelligibility or order of a *cosmos*, nor is his world created by the Word, as in the Gospel of John. The world is not text: in "Esthétique," human speech cannot "propound" the "dark italics" (*CPP* 287). While earlier poems such as "Sea Surface Full of Clouds" ironize the gap between creative human speech and the "perplexed machine // Of ocean" (*CPP* 82–83), Stevens became increasingly uncomfortable characterizing speech as meaning projected onto a blank canvas. So we are simultaneously told that the "words of the world are the life of the world" and that poems are "Part of the res itself and not about it" (*CPP* 404). Yet even these affirmations are tenaciously ambiguous: "not about" rejects a model in which human speech layers the world with meaning from a position outside of it, but the Latin "res" ("things") calls attention to the contingent artificiality of language. The copulative "are" seems to assert an identification of word and life, poem and thing, but "res" reminds us that the things in which words participate are only experienced historically, inside a language. And so, as in "Description Without Place," human speech as description is somehow both "revelation" (rather than mere projection) and "an artificial thing that exists. . . ." This is the "thesis of the plentifullest John" (*CPP* 301) – that is, the secular reconstitution of the Gospel writer's faith that the world was made by the Word.

Ambiguities of this kind are familiar features of Stevens's playfulness. Eleanor Cook argues in *Poetry, Word-Play, and Word-War in Wallace Stevens* that, far from indicating triviality, play is "the best way of approximating *in words* some of the most vital and mysterious parts of our lives" (5). I would like to redouble Cook's observations and suggest that play for Stevens is a defining component of his secular imagination. In *Homo Ludens* (1938), Johan Huizinga – the Dutch historian and contemporary of Stevens – argued provocatively that all cultural activity was religious activity, and all religious activity was a manifestation of the phenomenon of play. Huizinga develops theses that sound remarkably like Stevens's concepts of a "supreme fiction" and a "paradise" found in imperfection: play "creates order, *is* order. Into an imperfect world and into the confusion of life it brings a temporary, a limited perfection. Play demands order absolute and supreme" (10). Even Plato, who subordinated poetry to justice, was an evangelist of play: "God alone is worthy of supreme seriousness, but man is made God's plaything, and that is the best part of him. Therefore every man and woman should live life accordingly, and play the noblest games and be of another mind from what they are at present" (qtd. in Huizinga 18–19).

Huizinga believed that the instrumentality of modern society had impoverished the play drive. For Stevens, modernity can liberate the play drive by extracting it from the religious imagination. Huizinga argues that all metaphor, or communicative play, is inevitably anthropomorphic, and that it is nonsensical to conceptualize this process as a spiritualizing error that distorts "real" perception: "There is no question of first conceiving something as lifeless and bodiless and then expressing it as something that has body, parts and passions" (136). This dimension of play allows Stevens to reclaim the anthropomorphic imagination from religion. It is striking that one of Stevens's most programmatically secular early poems, "A High-Toned Old Christian Woman," juxtaposes the ascetic, solemn religious imagination with an equally metaphysical but winking cosmic imagination that emerges out of the joyful agonism and promiscuous transmutations of play itself. Instead of taking the "moral law" and building a cosmos, the speaker takes the "opposing law" and builds "a masque / Beyond the planets." The poem suggests that the Christian imagination was "buil[t]" through the play of associations that finally yielded an enchanted cosmos ("haunted heaven") and ritual practices ("disaffected flagellants"). In the playful spirit of competition ("palm for palm"), Stevens's speaker recovers the energy of that creative action and employs its associative method to generate a rival secular cosmos: it cunningly revises religious practice such that the ascetics will "whip from themselves / A jovial hullabaloo among the spheres" (*CPP* 47).

Stevens, like Friedrich Schiller, saw play as the highest state of freedom. Secular freedom for Stevens meant autonomy, in the strong sense of self-creation. To be secular is to be "unsponsored, free," and to stand "alone," rather than "by God's help and the police" (*CPP* 56, 120). At the same time, secularism meant immanence, or "the unalterable necessity / Of being this unalterable animal" (*CPP* 285). These two values are in permanent tension. To affirm immanence is to understand human life as swept up in the "necessity" of cyclical, natural rhythms; autonomy, by contrast, requires self-direction.

For Stevens, play has the capacity to dissolve that tension. We see this in "Notes":

> Whistle aloud, too weedy wren. I can
> Do all that angels can. I enjoy like them,
> Like men besides, like men in light secluded,
>
> Enjoying angels. Whistle, forced bugler,
> That bugles for the mate, nearby the nest,
> Cock bugler, whistle and bugle and stop just short,
>
> Red robin, stop in your preludes, practicing
> Mere repetitions. (*CPP* 350)

The self at play cultivates transcendence ("all that angels can") in a world of animal necessity. Mechanical repetition is a state of unfreedom: the wren and the robin are "forced bugler[s]" driven by sexual instinct ("for the mate") into "practicing / Mere repetitions." How is mere repetition compatible with the freedom Stevens seeks? The poet must appropriate God's prerogative by calling the repetition "good": "A thing final in itself and, therefore, good." From this perspective, repetition is not compulsion, but an "occupation, an exercise, a work." "[G]oing round // And round and round" seems to mean going nowhere; there can be no finality without a *telos*, no autonomous action when future purposes are not posited and pursued. Yet if there are no ends in this world, there are also no means, which allows Stevens to affirm the "merely going round" as "final." The repetitions are transfigured as play. The player's game, too, involves a set of constraining repetitions. Play is autonomous because its repetitions are plucked out of the realm of means and performed for their own sake. In the eye of science, the birds' sounds are instrumental strategies for perpetuating the species, whereas the poet can stand back and see "vast repetitions final in / Themselves and, therefore, good...." In this mood, "mere repetition" is converted into the conviviality of ritual: "The way wine comes at a table in a wood." As in religious ritual, Stevens aspires to become "master" of "repetition" (*CPP* 350), but for the secular poet the broader ritual, the "celestial pantomime" of cosmic rhythm, is its own end (*CPP* 221). The value discovered in the repetition is aesthetic, like Kant's "purposiveness without a purpose" (65). And like the child at play, the poet is free to oscillate among multiple roles and so enjoy like angels, men, and the birds themselves.

But how stable, how satisfactory is Stevens's vision of secular play? The mode of play, I have argued, allows Stevens to cultivate a state of transcendence and freedom that remains fully immersed in the constraining cadences of the material world. In "Notes," play renders the immanent world an adequate object of desire. The earth becomes the lover: "Fat girl, terrestrial, my summer, . . . I call you by name, my green, my fluent mundo" (*CPP* 351). But immediately after these words, the poet reminds us that "there is a war between the mind / And sky." The amorous mood of play – "The fiction that results from feeling" – is shadowed by a deeper state of conflict, for the object of desire is "not our own" and "not ourselves" (*CPP* 351, 332). An essential task of secular poetry for Stevens is to generate a "music" that will be "a mode of desire, a mode / Of revealing desire" (*CPP* 100). The biblical and Platonic traditions understood desire as a spiritual energy fundamentally oriented toward God or the Good; the spiritual life was understood as the struggle of desire to extricate itself from deficient, partial objects and ascend to the transcendent reality in which it would be actualized. Stevens's secularism inverts this effort. In "Esthétique du Mal," "The greatest poverty is not to live / In a physical world, to feel that one's desire / Is too difficult to tell from despair" (*CPP* 286). For Stevens, religious desire is despairing in the sense that it cannot find immanent objects adequate to its vehemence and solves this despair by positing a transcendent object. The religious, these lines imply, see the given world as "poverty," but Stevens insists that to despair of the world is a greater poverty.

To be secular for Stevens is to "live / In a physical world," which means that the poet must find immanent satisfactions and articulate their affective validity. This task is often accomplished in play, yet it is harried by a series of predicaments. The religious education of desire is an ascetic project. Though secularism is often construed as dismissing asceticism in favor of immanent pleasure, Stevens's project for desire is equally ascetic. Because, as one poem reads, "It can never be satisfied, the mind, never," the desiring self is perpetually tempted to seek objects beyond the immediate world (*CPP* 224). Therefore, one must, as in "Credences of Summer," "Exile desire / For what is not" (*CPP* 323). The second predicament is that Stevens increasingly saw language as a mode of transcendence. Kenneth Burke maintained that language is analogous to theology insofar as it is "*not* just 'natural,' but really *does* add a 'new dimension' to the things of nature" (8). Stevens concurred, especially later in his career: "words have made a world that transcends the world and a life livable in that transcendence." Though secular life is not transcendent, Stevens's recognition that human value is inexorably linguistic and imaginative drove him to insist that even secular life must be lived in the "transcendence" of "analogy" (*CPP* 722).

In "The Sense of the Sleight-of-Hand Man," Stevens writes, "It may be that the ignorant man, alone, / Has any chance to mate his life with life / That is the sensual, pearly spouse" (*CPP* 205). We catch the secular imperative here: "to mate" one's "life with life" is to say yes to the imperfect givenness of life instead of seeking illusory transcendence. Yet the imperative is articulated as tautology, not analogy. And the erotic state imagined here has eliminated the gap between desire and object altogether. It is a state in which, as in "Chocorua to Its Neighbor," "to breathe is a fulfilling of desire, / A clearing, a detecting, a completing, / A largeness lived and not conceived" (*CPP* 267). This structural tension between immanent tautology and transcendent analogy persists in Stevens's poetry. As "sleight-of-hand" suggests, moreover, the fictions that would render secular life erotic involve a certain gamesmanship. Ignorance in this poem and others is a fresh, absolute encounter with the world on the other side of secular knowledge. The state of ignorance is paradoxically meant to rehabilitate the condition of Vico's poetic "first men," who were like children playing in the cosmos: their "metaphysics was their poetry, a faculty . . . born of their ignorance of causes, for ignorance, the mother of wonder, made everything wonderful to men . . . they gave the things they wondered at substantial being after their own ideas, just as children do" (116–17). Stevens's playfulness abides: the secular rejection of myth and metaphysics ushers in a new era of poetic metaphysics and myth. The secular rhetoric of maturity – renunciation of the childish need to see the human face reflected in the world – yields to the child's enchantments. The final questions Stevens's secular poetry puts to its readers are these: Are we willing to play the magician's elusive game? Can we inhabit "supreme fictions" while being fully aware of their fictionality? Can we "believe without belief" (*CPP* 295)? How desperate are we, really, "in the moments when / The will demands that what [we think] be true?" (*CPP* 284).

Notes

1 On "subtraction story," see Taylor. For an account of how secular epistemology does not so much discover as presuppose a particular ontology and epistemology, see both Taylor and Asad.

2 Many of these assumptions are still visible in Stevens's most compelling recent critics. While Charles Altieri persuasively argues that the later Stevens is occupied with value, and so rejected the naïve Enlightenment empiricism that shaped modern, secular reason, his "demands of modernity" take secular, metaphysical naturalism as a given: "Naturalism entailed fully grappling with everything that had been concealed by religious faith" (48). Joan Richardson, by contrast, assumes that Stevens's "pragmatism" exempts him from the challenges of secularism altogether and so sees a continuous spiritual lineage from Jonathan Edwards and Emerson to Stevens. "While [these] figures . . . understood the role of the American writer to be a religious one, it was with a sense of religion naturalized" (11). I discuss the ambiguities of "substitution" and "naturalization" in *Restless Secularism*.

3 In preparation for the lecture, Stevens read I. A. Richards's *Coleridge on Imagination*, a text that marked Richards's turn away from positivism toward a recognition that even empirical science is a symbolic mode – or what Richards calls in the essay a form of "myth."

WORKS CITED

Altieri, Charles. *Wallace Stevens and the Demands of Modernity: Toward a Phenomenology of Value*. Cornell UP, 2013.

Asad, Talal. *Formations of the Secular: Christianity, Islam, Modernity*. Stanford UP, 2003.

Burke, Kenneth. *The Rhetoric of Religion: Studies in Logology*. U of California P, 1970.

Cook, Eleanor. *Poetry, Word-Play, and Word-War in Wallace Stevens*. Princeton UP, 1988.

Huizinga, Johan. *Homo Ludens: A Study of the Play Element in Culture*. Routledge, 2002.

James, William. *Pragmatism and Other Writings*. Penguin, 2000.

Kant, Immanuel. *Critique of Judgment*. Translated by Werner S. Pluhar, Hackett, 1987.

Mutter, Matthew. *Restless Secularism: Modernism and the Religious Inheritance*. Yale UP, 2017.

Richards, I. A. *Coleridge on Imagination*. Edited by John Constable, Routledge, 2001.

Richardson, Joan. *A Natural History of Pragmatism*. Cambridge UP, 2006.

Ricoeur, Paul. *Freud and Philosophy: An Essay on Interpretation*. Yale UP, 1970.

Stevens, Wallace. *Letters of Wallace Stevens*. Edited by Holly Stevens, U of California P, 1996.

  Wallace Stevens: Collected Poetry and Prose. Edited by Frank Kermode and Joan Richardson, Library of America, 1997.

Taylor, Charles. *A Secular Age*. Belknap P of Harvard UP, 2007.

Vico, Giambattista. *The New Science of Giambattista Vico*. Translated by Thomas Goddard Gergin and Max Harold Fisch, Cornell UP, 1961.

CHAPTER 5

Transnationalism

Gül Bilge Han

Wallace Stevens, as most readers will know, did not travel extensively outside the United States, unlike so many of his modernist contemporaries. Yet his poetry may be said to be deeply concerned with expanding the boundaries of the poetic imagination to reach beyond its domestic and local settings.[1] The desire to develop a poetics that is capable of establishing new nodes of interconnection between near and far places and cultures is palpable throughout Stevens's oeuvre. From his first collection, *Harmonium*, to his last, *The Rock*, Stevens's writing is rooted in a homegrown aesthetic that is at the same time indissociable from a globally oriented poetic outlook – a paradoxical combination the poet himself insisted upon when he proclaimed that "One Must Sit Still to Discover the World" (qtd. in Lensing 188). Indeed, if the problem of the modern poem, for Ezra Pound, is to "contain history," it is in many ways, for Stevens, to "contain the world," or to bring "The Planet on the Table," as he famously put it in his late poem of the same title (qtd. in Moody 82; *L* 501; *CPP* 450). Despite his oft-pronounced provincialism, a modernist pursuit of the foreign undergirds Stevens's writings at different stages of his poetic career.

This chapter outlines and explores this aspect of Stevens's work in view of recent theoretical interventions in literary transnationalism and global modernism. It examines the significance of artistic mobility and travel for the poet's exploration of diverse cultural materials and settings, extending from the Caribbean to European and Asian contexts. The chapter maps Stevens's attitude toward the transnational affiliations and overall "worldliness" of his poetry. To do so, it will follow a trajectory that leads from teasing out the limits and possibilities of imaginative mobility and travel in his early work, through his notion of a "small relation" between diverse places and cultures in his middle poetry (*CPP* 195), to the idea of a transregionally shared lingua franca in his late poems. Stevens's impulse toward national and cultural border crossings, I argue, is composed of complex responses to the literary-political currents of his epoch, which range from the specific context of American nativism – and its pronounced focus on national identity – to more general developments of globalization and the Cold War. Situating Stevens's poetry within the contours of the transnational turn in literary studies not only reveals new cultural and historical frameworks for the critical exploration of a writer who continues to be regarded as "the quintessential American poet of the twentieth century" (Schjeldahl), but it may also help expand the scope of scholarly approaches to his poetic exploration of foreign worlds beyond the blanket condemnations of exoticism and Orientalism.

The Transnational Turn

The critical landscape of the past decade has witnessed a veritable sea change in the field of modernist literary studies. An increasing number of scholars have come to challenge the spatial and temporal boundaries that previously confined modernism to the early twentieth-century Euro-American realm of cultural production. By drawing attention to wider global networks in which various modernist practices historically unfolded, critics such as Douglas Mao, Rebecca Walkowitz, and Susan Stanford Friedman have proposed a "polycentric" understanding of multiple modernisms operating across diverse geographies and times (Mao and Walkowitz 737–42). To show how many versions of modernism take shape by way of transnational encounters, they typically focus on patterns of correspondence between local and global frames of modernist literature. Rather than reading modernist texts solely within their local contexts, they offer "a transnational optic" by which to approach works of literature, whether these be canonical, as in the case of Stevens, or peripheral (Berman, "Transnational" 116).

One of the frequently proclaimed aims of these critical approaches is to trace literature's border-traversing capacities, and the cross-cultural affiliations that may be found not only *between* but also *within* literary works. Jahan Ramazani's influential *A Transnational Poetics* has provided key points of departure for much current poetry scholarship in this vein. Ramazani reminds us of the ways in which "modern and contemporary poets" perceive the imagination as a "force that exceeds the limits of the territorial and juridical norm" (2). He shows how several writers push beyond national, socioeconomic, and historical restraints in their poetic exploration of themes such as migration, travel, decolonization, and globalization, and that they frequently do so by inventing hybrid literary forms. His discussion of "Modernist bricolage" renews our attention to "the synthetic use in early twentieth-century poetry of diverse cultural materials" (99), particularly in the case of Ezra Pound's adaptation of Japanese haiku and T. S. Eliot's incorporation of Buddhist elements into *The Waste Land*. As Ramazani argues, pursuing canonical modernism's transnational circuits provides an alternative framework to the kind of criticism that reduces modernist configurations of non-Western materials all too quickly to "orientalist theft or primitivist exoticism" (11).

Modernism's movement beyond local and national paradigms has also been the inspiration for Jessica Berman's *Modernist Commitments*, which highlights "the many nodes and circles of interconnected social and political activity among global modernisms" (31). Laura Doyle and Laura Winkiel's edited volume on *Geomodernisms* emphasizes in a similar fashion how cultural forms develop out of interactions embedded historically within inter-imperial and colonial networks of modernity and globalization. The recent work of contributors to *The Oxford Handbook of Global Modernisms* (Wollaeger and Eatough), *A New Vocabulary for Global Modernism* (Hayot and Walkowitz), and Peter Kalliney's *Modernism in a Global Context* carry on these efforts by participating in the critical reconstruction of modernism from a geographically expanded angle. For all their multiplicity of sources and claims, they participate in a collective effort to rewrite the familiar story of modernism as a mobile, circulating, and multidirectional phenomenon constitutive of textual as well as actual encounters between and among cultures, commodities, and peoples on the move.

The scholarly impact of such revisionary accounts is well attested by the breadth of recent criticism devoted to the "transnational turn" in connection to iconic modernist writers such as Pound, Eliot, Joyce, and Woolf – figures whose international ties and cosmopolitan tendencies have long been documented. But what are the implications of these methodological recalibrations when it comes to seemingly provincial writers who were neither widely traveled nor directly involved in global affairs? How do the recent framings of transnational modernism work in relation to an author like Stevens, who is most often seen as a US-American poet? And how have critics dealt with Stevens's imaginative if rather distant engagement with foreign cultural and aesthetic forms and influences? The question of Stevens's commitment to a world beyond his immediate cultural and national environment has sparked conflicting responses among his most renowned critics: Helen Vendler, for instance, has come to read Stevens as a poet deeply engrained in his national surroundings. She identifies a "resolutely American" aesthetic as the dominant mode of Stevens's writing despite his sustained passion for European literature and culture (125–26). Her remarks echo Hugh Kenner's earlier positioning of Stevens within an essentially homemade American modernism (xvii–xviii).

The counterargument against such nationalist recuperations started especially with Alan Filreis's *Wallace Stevens and the Actual World* in the early 1990s, when Filreis underlined the extent to which Stevens's poetry is founded upon a "postcard imagination," developed out of his contacts with foreign correspondents and globally perceived events of his historical moment (207). But it is only in the twenty-first century that Stevens criticism has begun to reflect more fully on the poet's use of intercultural tropes, foreign references, and translingual vocabularies: scholars have tackled his hemispheric imagination (Feinsod; Keenaghan); his poetic responses to the global news and war (Galvin); his interest in the Far East (Qian; Ragg); his various transatlantic connections with Europe (Eeckhout and Ragg); and, more generally, his sustained preoccupation with the exotic (Burt). Drawing on poems as well as contextual and biographical evidence, these works offer refreshing ways of reading Stevens that have done much to open up his poems to the world beyond his national borders.

While not devoid of exotic othering and questionable forms of appropriation, Stevens's configuration of far geographies and cultural materials, as these recent critical interventions suggest, constitutes a potential site of encounter where new cultural flows and interconnections become possible. Yet, as I will seek to demonstrate in the following pages, Stevens's imaginative vision of artistic mobility and travel characteristically interrogates, rather than simply asserts, the border-crossing capacities of the poetic imagination. His use of foreign cultural elements and references takes the form not of a simple celebration but of a thorough examination of the imagination's worldly affiliations and global circuits. Stevens's work, in other words, both displays a transnational aesthetic sensibility and reveals its moments of implosion; it explores at once the capacities and pitfalls of the imagination's movement beyond those local and national conditions by which it is necessarily shaped.[2]

The Poet as Migrant

Stevens interrogates the possibility of a transnational poetics perhaps nowhere more elaborately than in his long mock epic "The Comedian as the Letter C" (1922). The poem begins with a depiction of Crispin, the wandering hero, as an "affectionate emigrant" whose journey stretches from East to West and from South to North: from "Bordeaux to Yucatan, Havana next, / And then to Carolina" (*CPP* 26, 23). Imagined as an allegorical figure for the poet himself, Crispin is a recorder of styles, sounds, and architectures of the cities and landscapes he travels through. Dressed in foreign garments – originating eclectically from "China" and "Spain" – he roams "the harbor streets," somewhere "west of Mexico," "Inspecting the cabildo, the façade / Of the cathedral, making notes" (*CPP* 22, 26). The essentially aesthetic drive behind Crispin's wanderings is revealed by his desire to compile the musical affluence and poetic heritage of the Latin Americas and the Caribbean: he seeks to merge "the Maya sonneteers / Of the Caribbean amphitheatre," the native "music" of "rainy men," the "pampean dits" of "dark Brazilians in their cafés," and the "incantation" of "black branches" into his unwritten "anthology," that is, Crispin's work-in-progress book of verse (*CPP* 24, 30, 31).

The real and imagined "anthology" of "The Comedian" indicates the potential construction of a textual space of encounter where seemingly isolated cultural environments and diverse traditions of America converge. The poem asserts the aesthetic possibility of a hemispheric view of America in which boundaries between the United States, Mexico, Brazil, and the Caribbean are suspended. In doing so, it resists the equation of the United States with the entire continent through the formation of an aesthetic that seeks to incorporate a diverse layering of cultural forms and expressions.[3] Yet such diversity and plurality, as the poem goes on to show, cannot really be contained within a single book. The possibility of an inclusionary poetics that seeks to combine imagery, sound, and symbolism of different localities in Central and South America is shadowed by Crispin's expansionist logic, which risks producing a mode of undifferentiated globalization. As the "Progenitor of such extensive scope," Crispin, though "not indifferent to smart detail," is defined at the close of the poem as "Effective colonizer" (*CPP* 31, 35): "Was he to company vastest things defunct / With a blubber of tom-toms harrowing the sky?" (*CPP* 33). Crispin's enlarged poetic vision falls short. While projecting a far-reaching poetic map of cultural material onto his book, Crispin's voyage reveals the difficulties involved in constructing a transnational poetics: it signals the failure of assembling the foreign cultural and natural sources of poetic inspiration into "a singular collation" (*CPP* 30).

The interrogative mode in which Stevens deals with the idea of artistic mobility and transnational travel in "The Comedian" anticipates in many ways the problem he teases out later in "The Greenest Continent," the third section of "Owl's Clover" (1935), where he investigates whether "imagination, extended beyond local consciousness, may be an idea to be held in common by South, West, North and East" (*L* 370). The poetic ideal of a globally shared "consciousness" meets in both poems with obstacles as a result of the imagination's entanglement with the historical legacies of colonialism and empire, and, in the latter poem, due to the rise of fascism. In "The Comedian," however, both Stevens's projection of a hemispheric America and the figure of the poet as migrant are still anchored in the specific literary-political context of the 1920s. The artistic mobility explored in the poem offers an intricate response to the cultural model offered by proponents of a nativist aesthetic, according to which a new US-American identity could be forged with a focus on locality and native soil.

Perhaps the most critically acclaimed modernist expression of such a retrenchment into literary nation building – increasingly popular among Stevens's contemporaries – is to be found in the poetry and prose of William Carlos Williams. Both Williams and Stevens show a fascination with "narratives of how identity is necessarily and ideally actualized or transformed by the American environment" (Matterson 115). Indeed, several of Stevens's aphoristic declarations in "The Comedian," such as "his soil is man's intelligence" and "The natives of the rain are rainy men" (*CPP* 29, 30), seem at first to correspond to the nativist quest, by Williams and others, for a truly American poetic idiom immersed in locality. Read closely, however, the poem appears to negate such nativist aesthetic impulses by rendering the notion of a purely regional self-actualization and (national) identity as myth – or calling it, simply, "false" (*CPP* 37).

Stevens brings the poem to a close by staging the failure of radically insular forms of poetic regionalism or nationalism exemplified by Crispin's final withdrawal to his "Nice Shady Home" (*CPP* 32). In the end, the poet-figure settles down in his domestic surroundings (his home in Carolina) while the speaker asks, "what can all this matter since / The relation comes, benignly, to its end?" (*CPP* 37). The ending renounces "relation" altogether, and by declaring in a performative speech act, "So may the relation of each man be clipped," Stevens also clips his own attachment to Crispin as an allegorical stand-in for the poet. The literary quest for the construction of a sovereign self, embedded in native soil (Crispin's "turn" to "salad-beds"), thus equally fails: neither total attachment to locality nor the construction of a transnationally expanded vision – the "relentless contact" Crispin seeks throughout his journey – seems to suffice within the self-conscious rhetoric of the poem (*CPP* 33, 27). The mock epic reveals instead the complexities involved in constructing an all-encompassing poetics that privileges nodes of interconnectedness over dissonance, while rejecting a provincializing poetics of national and mental borders.

"A Small Relation"

Stevens's poetry from the 1930s and early 1940s continues to interrogate whether aesthetic experience can be a basis for imagining new modes of relationality and contact between different localities and cultures. This is especially the case in *Parts of a World*. While exploring new ways of figuring a common fiction in which local and foreign elements may coexist, his poems continue to acknowledge the danger of an all-inclusive global imaginary that overlooks contingencies and ruptures in favor of artistic fulfillment and connectivity. The poetic desire to incorporate "The world in a verse" in "Arrival at the Waldorf," for instance, is undercut by the speaker's recognition of the economic discrepancy and the aesthetic remoteness between the artificial extravagance of the Waldorf hotel in New York and "that alien, point-blank, green and actual Guatemala" (*CPP* 219). In "A Weak Mind in the Mountains," the meeting of the northern "wind of Iceland" with the southern "wind of Ceylon" "Grip[s]" and "grapple[s]" the poet's mind (*CPP* 192). Bringing them together is depicted as a difficult and improbable task: "The black wind of the sea / And the green wind / Whirled upon me. / The blood of the mind fell / To the floor" (*CPP* 192). The wished-for meeting of Iceland and Ceylon proves impossible except by a world-shaping mind, and only if it is raised to a higher, idealistic plane. The speaker reflects on an inner self ("a man within me") who "Could have touched these winds" (*CPP* 192–93). But in the end, even that self cannot but do violence to both winds in the course of his endeavor to arrange and design: he "Could have . . . / Bent and broken them down, / Could have stood up sharply in the sky" (*CPP* 193).

These instances engage with the problem of imaginative manipulation, that is, the imposition of an aesthetic order that may trouble the production of a transnational and globally inclusive poetics. Still, *Parts of a World* also includes poems, such as "Connoisseur of Chaos," that affirm the possibility, no matter how tentative, of a "small relation" between foreign and local places and things. In this poem, the opening propositions about "order" and "disorder" are followed by the speaker pondering on "the flowers of South Africa [that] were bright / On the tables of Connecticut" (*CPP* 194–95). The voice follows through by postulating the presence of "Englishmen" in "Ceylon" (today's Sri Lanka, still a British colony at the time) living without "tea," an image that figures a sense of British national identity inextricably tied up with imperial and colonial history.[4] Building on such images, the speaker then asserts, "a law of inherent opposites, / Of essential unity, is as pleasant as port, / As pleasant as the brush-strokes of a bough, / An upper, particular bough in, say, Marchand" (*CPP* 195) – a place-name found both in South Africa and in the United States, though Stevens is likely also referring to the French cubist painter Jean Marchand, and his painting *Les Oliviers*, which, as Eleanor Cook notes, he had then recently acquired (144). The ekphrastic reference to "brush-strokes" and "Marchand" thus reveals another transnational allusion that, furthermore, implies the artistic transformation of reality by focusing on minor details that are off-center.

As Filreis has discussed in detail, the imagined Ceylon in Stevens's middle and late poetry has specific origins in his correspondence with the young Englishman Leonard van Geyzel, who lived there as a poetry-writing coconut planter and provided him with an "unusual ethnographic encounter" (161). While the incorporation of Far Eastern places and cultural materials in Stevens's early poetry and drama leans heavily toward abstraction, later poems, as in this case, indicate a desire to seek a "much closer contact" (*L* 303). Such poems register an attempt to resist what Stevens in a late letter to Barbara Church calls an "orientalist" form of "syncretism" – the artistic intermingling of distinct cultural entities from a vantage point that claims to be "neither eastern nor western" but "universal" (*L* 797). To return to "Connoisseur of Chaos," it is precisely the logic of such would-be universalism that the poem seems to resist: the contours of a transnational meeting zone – which brings together places as diverse as Ceylon, South Africa, Connecticut, and France within a single stanza – cannot be drawn, so the speaker concedes, by means of a world-absorbing, large-scale theory: "opposite things partake of one, / At least that was the theory, when bishops' books / Resolved the world. We cannot go back to that. / The squirming facts exceed the squamous mind" (*CPP* 195). This self-critical position, however, does not appear to leave the poem at an impasse but points to the necessity of imagining relationality and connectivity in ways that are different from preordained conceptions of the world. Thus, in lieu of a "law" of "essential unity" imposed in an authoritarian, top-down manner by a monolithic – explicitly Western and Christian – view of the world to be found in the "bishops' books," an alternative measure of connectivity takes the guise of "A small relation expanding like the shade / Of a cloud on sand" (*CPP* 195). Rather than staging a mutual interplay between national and transnational frameworks, across all these instances, Stevens is more inclined to interrogate the cross-cultural reach of poetry by emphasizing distances, ruptures, and slippages that self-reflexively underline the hierarchical power dynamics and intricacies of the poetic imagination's itineraries.

In still other poems from the same period, Stevens's transnational imaginary takes on a more historically specific character responsive to the pressing geopolitical events of his time. In "A Dish of Peaches in Russia" (1938), for instance, the speaker's tasting, smelling, and touching of peaches bespeaks the experience of displacement and exile, which might be linked, as Bonnie Costello has so persuasively argued, to the experiences of those who managed to escape the Soviet Union after the Great Purge (1936–38).[5] The poem juxtaposes distinct figures and locales to capture the exiled speaker's nostalgic longing for and memory of his home (his "village"): the "Angevine" in "Anjou" (in France), the "black Spaniard," and "Russia" all populate the speaker's enclosed room. But rather than fantasizing about a pleasant integration and unification of these figures and locales, the speaker draws attention to the sense of being torn against a background of exile and war. The sensual experience of the Russian peaches results in the "ferocities" of internal division; it is incapable of acting as a basis for a renewal of the self to be effected through a rhetorical bridging of far-off places and experiences (*CPP* 206). Ideas of discontinuity and disconnection similarly underlie Stevens's wartime poem "Martial Cadenza": there, the "blank skies" over England, France, and Germany, which could seem to be linked on a planetary level by the "evening star," strike the speaker as severely "apart" from one another – both spatially and temporally – in a "world" filled with the horror of "armies" and "camps" (*CPP* 217). As in "A Dish of Peaches," the juxtaposition of foreign places and experiences in "Martial Cadenza" conveys a sense of rupture and displacement, marked by the Second World War, the news of which Stevens followed closely throughout.

Words of the "Far-foreign"

If, in Stevens's early and middle poetry, forms of artistic mobility and travel are expressed largely through place-names and cultural allusions, in subsequent works, it is more the poetic language itself that makes such movements and flows possible. Stevens's later poetry enacts imaginative forms of mobility and travel predominantly through the use of foreign words and linguistic references.[6] Stevens, as is well known, experimented with words and word stems derived etymologically from multiple sources (Arabic,

French, German, Latin, and so forth) from the very beginning of his poetic
career. Whether it is "the route taken by 'alguazil' through Spanish from
Arabic or of 'toucan' through French from Brazilian," the poetic interplay
of sonic and semantic elements in his use of foreign words often functions
as a vehicle for imaginative forms of travel in which words themselves
become "committed wanderers" (Rieke 102). Take, for instance, his early
"Bantams in Pine-Woods." In that poem, as Ramazani claims, the thematic staging of opposites (exotic/native, masculine/feminine) is foregrounded by the careful juxtaposition of words with diverse origins, from
"caftan" (derived from Persian) to "henna" (with Arabic origins) to
"Azcan" (echoing "Aztec" and "Mayan") (*CPP* 60; Ramazani 55).
Significantly, Stevens sonically connects these heteroglossic words through
the use of internal rhyme and alliteration: "caftan" with "Iffucan,"
"Azcan," and "tan" and "henna" with the Anglo-Saxon "hackles" and
"halt" (*CPP* 60). The poem thus familiarizes the unfamiliar words, or at
least establishes new relations among them within its lexical texture.

   In Stevens's poetry of the 1940s and 1950s, arguably, the imaginative act
of traveling through words increasingly adheres to the idea of a globally
shared common language envisioned through poetry. This comes to the
fore, for example, in "Prologues to What Is Possible," a poem that sets out
a parallel between the "voyaging" of a Ulysses-like figure – his "far-foreign
departure" – and the movement of "a syllable" (*CPP* 438). In the end, the
"vocabulary" of "Northern trees" is unexpectedly married to "the whole
vocabulary of the South." The hypothetical or fictional blending of
Northern and Southern vocabularies creates "a fresh universe" made out
of words that travel across borders, forming a part of Stevens's projection of
new beginnings and futurity as envisioned in the poem (*CPP* 439).
"Holiday in Reality" and "Sketch of the Ultimate Politician" showcase
slightly earlier versions of Stevens's idea of a common linguistic fiction,
although as wartime poems they do so from a less optimistic viewpoint:
whereas the speaker in the former poem reflects on the lack of a "common
speech," which he dismisses as "Palabra of a common man who did not
exist" (*CPP* 276), the latter presents the figure of the ultimate politician as
someone who does manage to hear a form of "common speech" – "Words
that come out of us" – only to conclude that the "speech falls as if to fail"
(*CPP* 294).

   But it is in "Notes Toward a Supreme Fiction" that Stevens explores
most explicitly the idea of poetry as a medium for generating a meta-
language that is capable of encapsulating a cross-cultural linguistic identity.
Recalling the figure of the poet-guitarist in "The Man with the Blue

Guitar," here Stevens imagines a poet-orator whose "string speaks for a crowd of voices" to express the "peculiar potency of the general" (*CPP* 339, 343). The notion of poetry giving expression to the "commonal" or "general" undergirds the larger quest for a "lingua franca et jocundissima" in which the ordinary ("the vulgate") converges with "the imagination's Latin" (*CPP* 336, 343). Significantly, the embodiment of a common linguistic universe here, as in "Prologues," is dependent on the poetic imagination's capacity to form new transnational linkages and nodes. This aspect of Stevens's "lingua franca" manifests itself particularly through the figure of what he calls, later in the poem, his "fluent mundo": "Fat girl, terrestrial, my summer, my night, / . . . / I call you by name, my green, my fluent mundo" (*CPP* 351). The poem's earlier merging of "North and South" as "an intrinsic couple . . . in the greenest body" (*CPP* 339) paves the way for the aesthetic construction of this "green . . . mundo" that encapsulates the expressive powers – the "fluen[cy]" – of poetic language. This poetic ideal, presented as a supreme fiction, is associated not only with the "terrestrial" or earthly but also, as Stevens explained his image of the "Fat girl" in a letter to Henry Church, with the global in its political and ideological senses: "what the politicians now-a-days are calling the globe" (*L* 426).

Indeed, as Harris Feinsod has suggested, Stevens's idea of a transnational lingua franca and a "fluent mundo" in "Notes" can be read productively within the historical juncture of a newly emerging inter-American consciousness that characterized the geopolitical and cultural climate of the war years and early Cold War era. His imaginative merging of the North and South and his "Latinization of American English" in the 1940s and 1950s arguably reflect a more general concern with inventing a common (linguistic) identity for the Americas (98). As Christopher Winks and Eric Keenaghan have also argued, Stevens shared with a host of Latin American writers, including José Lezama Lima, Jorge Luis Borges, and José Rodríguez Feo, a tendency to resist the currency of nationalistic literary formations of post-World War II America. The Cold War pushes him toward exploring new possibilities of cross-cultural referencing and contact that charge his poetic commitment to worldliness with new literary and political significance. But as I hope to have demonstrated, Stevens often approaches such border-crossing impulses of his own aesthetic with a self-conscious rhetoric that raises more questions than answers about the possibilities for poetic inclusion and expansion. This is also the case in "Notes." If in "The Comedian" his aesthetic effort to assemble the diverse materials of a hemispheric America into "a singular collation" (Crispin's book of verse) is ultimately disrupted (*CPP* 30), in "Notes" the supreme fiction of a transnational lingua franca expressed within "A single text" remains equally incomplete (*CPP* 340). To fix such a formation is to create what the speaker calls "granite monotony" – a "sound" that is bound to "end" "like any other [sound]" unless it constantly changes (*CPP* 340–41). Although in markedly different ways, both poems characterize the hemispheric ideal of a cross-cultural and transnational aesthetic by its processual and fragmentary nature rather than by its finality and/or completion.

Whether it takes the form of a poetic envisioning of a hemispheric America, an intermingling of foreign places and objects, or a tapping into the context of globally experienced events of war and exile, Stevens's aesthetic impulse to move beyond and across borders – national, geographic, linguistic – is clearly a significant and recurrent feature of his poetics. Both the spatial and cultural reach of his poems draws out linkages that bring together distant contexts and places. Yet it does so without an easy flattening of divergences or obscuring of boundaries between the entities that are engaged. The transnational registers of Stevens's work are in this sense distinct both from the cosmopolitan modernism of Pound and from the recognizably local aesthetics of Williams. His interrogative modes of artistic mobility and travel pose a limit case for those theories of transnational modernist literary studies that primarily focus on cross-cultural flows and interconnectedness. Reading Stevens from the perspective of the transnational turn nevertheless provides new directions for interpreting his exploration of distant geographies and cultures in ways that challenge the persisting critical receptions of his poetry as essentially provincial.

Notes

1 The main points made in this chapter, whether on transnational modernist studies, "The Comedian as the Letter C," or *Parts of a World*, are further elaborated in my *Wallace Stevens and the Poetics of Modernist Autonomy*.
2 I use the "transnational" throughout this chapter by drawing on Jahan Ramazani's use of the term to indicate the cross-cultural allegiances that literary texts invoke "not among" but "across the borders of nation-states" and "regions" in ways that respond to the aesthetic, socioeconomic, and political conditions of modernity and globalization (181).
3 For a detailed discussion of the poem's crossing of national boundaries in the context of American imperialism, see Rowe 293.
4 For further discussion of Stevens's preoccupation with the Orient and, more specifically, with Far Eastern literary-philosophical and artistic traditions, see Qian and Ragg.

5 As Costello argues, the figure of the exile here might as well be "the real Russian exile who kept a shack near the Hartford dump within view of the Stevens's house" (34).
6 On this point, see also Burt 321 and Haglund 122.

WORKS CITED

Berman, Jessica. *Modernist Commitments: Ethics, Politics, and Transnational Modernism.* Columbia UP, 2011.

"Transnational Modernisms." *The Cambridge Companion to Transnational American Literature*, edited by Yogita Goyal, Cambridge UP, 2017, pp. 107–21.

Burt, Stephanie. "The Exotic." *Wallace Stevens in Context*, edited by Glen MacLeod, Cambridge UP, 2017, pp. 316–25.

Costello, Bonnie. *Planets on Tables: Poetry, Still Life, and the Turning World.* Cornell UP, 2008.

Doyle, Laura, and Laura Winkiel, editors. *Geomodernisms: Race, Modernism, Modernity.* Indiana UP, 2005.

Eeckhout, Bart, and Edward Ragg, editors. *Wallace Stevens across the Atlantic.* Palgrave Macmillan, 2008.

Feinsod, Harris. *The Poetry of the Americas: From Good Neighbors to Countercultures.* Oxford UP, 2017.

Filreis, Alan. *Wallace Stevens and the Actual World.* Princeton UP, 1991.

Friedman, Susan Stanford. *Planetary Modernisms: Provocations on Modernity across Time.* Columbia UP, 2015.

Galvin, Rachel. *News of War: Civilian Poetry, 1936–1945.* Oxford UP, 2017.

Haglund, David. "Stevens, Duchamp and the American 'ism,' 1915–1919." *Wallace Stevens across the Atlantic*, edited by Eeckhout and Ragg, pp. 121–32.

Han, Gül Bilge. *Wallace Stevens and the Poetics of Modernist Autonomy.* Cambridge UP, 2019.

Hayot, Eric, and Rebecca L. Walkowitz, editors. *A New Vocabulary for Global Modernism.* Columbia UP, 2016.

Kalliney, Peter. *Modernism in a Global Context.* Bloomsbury, 2016.

Keenaghan, Eric. *Queering Cold War Poetry: Ethics of Vulnerability in Cuba and the United States.* Ohio State UP, 2009.

Kenner, Hugh. *A Homemade World: The American Modernist Writers.* Alfred A. Knopf, 1975.

Lensing, George S. *Wallace Stevens: A Poet's Growth.* Louisiana State UP, 1986.

Mao, Douglas, and Rebecca L. Walkowitz. "The New Modernist Studies." *PMLA*, vol. 123, no. 3, May 2008, pp. 737–48.

Matterson, Stephen. "'The Whole Habit of the Mind': Stevens, Americanness, and the Use of Elsewhere." *The Wallace Stevens Journal*, vol. 25, no. 2, Fall 2001, pp. 111–21.

Moody, David. A. *Ezra Pound: Poet. A Portrait of the Man and His Work.* Vol. III: *The Tragic Years, 1939–1972.* Oxford UP, 2015.

Qian, Zhaoming. *The Modernist Response to Chinese Art: Pound, Moore, Stevens.* U of Virginia P, 2003.

Ragg, Edward. "The Orient." *Wallace Stevens in Context*, edited by Glen MacLeod, Cambridge UP, 2017, pp. 55–64.

Ramazani, Jahan. *A Transnational Poetics.* U of Chicago P, 2009.

Riddel, Joseph. "Walt Whitman and Wallace Stevens: Functions of a Literatus." *Wallace Stevens: A Collection of Critical Essays*, edited by Marie Borroff, Prentice-Hall, 1963, pp. 30–42.

Rieke, Alison. *The Senses of Nonsense.* U of Iowa P, 1992.

Rowe, John Carlos. *Literary Culture and U.S. Imperialism: From the Revolution to World War II.* Oxford UP, 2000.

Schjeldahl, Peter. "Insurance Man: The Life and Art of Wallace Stevens." *The New Yorker*, 2 May 2016, www.newyorker.com/magazine/2016/05/02/the-thrilling-mind-of-wallace-stevens.

Stevens, Wallace. *Letters of Wallace Stevens.* Edited by Holly Stevens, U of California P, 1996.

    Wallace Stevens: Collected Poetry and Prose. Edited by Frank Kermode and Joan Richardson, Library of America, 1997.

Vendler, Helen. "Wallace Stevens." *Voices & Visions: The Poet in America*, edited by Helen Vendler, Random House, 1987, pp. 123–55.

Winks, Christopher. "Seeking a Cuba of the Self: Baroque Dialogues between José Lezama Lima and Wallace Stevens." *Baroque New Worlds: Representation, Transculturation, Counterconquest*, edited by Lois Parkinson Zamora and Monika Kaup, Duke UP, 2010, pp. 597–621.

Wollaeger, Mark, and Matt Eatough, editors. *The Oxford Handbook of Global Modernisms.* Oxford UP, 2014.

PART II

Recent Critical Methods Applied to Stevens

CHAPTER 6

World Literature

Lee M. Jenkins

Wallace Stevens is a poet of the earth, so much so that, according to Eleanor Cook, "If we had to name the subject of Stevens' poetry in one phrase, that phrase would be his own: a poetry 'of the earth'" (6). Stevens's first volume, *Harmonium* – and his *Collected Poems* – opens with an appropriately titled "Earthy Anecdote," and yet the title of his late poem "The Planet on the Table" presents Stevens's completed oeuvre as a proxy Earth, a world in and of itself. How do we reconcile Stevens's earthiness with his totalizing tendency to put "the world in a verse" (*CPP* 465), and to what extent, and in what sense, or senses, should Stevens be regarded as a writer of "world" literature? These queries generate more questions than answers – as Stevens says, "One goes on asking questions" (*CPP* 369) – among them the vexed question posed by David Damrosch in his 2003 study of that title: *What Is World Literature?*

As a disciplinary field, world literature is a twenty-first-century phenomenon, but the concept has a prehistory. The term "world literature" (*Weltliteratur*) was popularized by J. W. von Goethe in the 1820s to describe the circulation of literary works beyond their nations of origin: as Damrosch explains, in his conversations with Johann Peter Eckermann, "Goethe discusses Chinese, French, Greek, Serbian and Persian literature in world circulation through translation, emphasizing the authors' similarities and affinities rather than their disjunctions and asymmetries" (*World Literature in Theory* 15–16). Goethe's prediction that "National literature is now a rather unmeaning term; the epoch of world literature is at hand," however, would be gainsaid by the coterminous rise of Romantic nationalism (qtd. in Damrosch, *World Literature in Theory* 19). Repurposed to ideological ends by Karl Marx and Friedrich Engels in the *Communist Manifesto* of 1848, world literature reemerges as a signifier for the "'cosmopolitan consumption' of cultural

I am grateful to the following scholars, poets, and translators for their insights and advice: Massimo Bacigalupo, Bart Eeckhout, Rajiv Krishnan, Jamie McKendrick, Rajeev S. Patke, Jahan Ramazani, Roger T. Sedarat, and William Wall.

goods, facilitated by the bourgeois world market" (Mani 287). In the early twentieth century, world literature would be reformulated as "the supranational movement called International Modernism," an exemplar of which is Ezra Pound's idea of "world poetry" (Kenner, "Making" 367; Pound, "Tagore's Poems" 92). Recommending "the importation of models for painting, sculpture or writing," Pound opined in 1915 that "this century may find a new Greece in China" ("Renaissance" 228).

As a field-imaginary, world literature today is predicated on a more inclusive paradigm, its scholarship alert to persisting "asymmetries" in the processes of literary circulation and reception that it traces. As a pedagogy, world literature synthesizes elements of (now largely obsolescent) Great Books programs and Comparative Literature (or the "new Comparative Literature" that Gayatri Chakravorty Spivak defines as "Planetarity") with the study of (Third) World Literature, or what we now term literatures of the Global South, in an expansive geographical and temporal reach that extends from Aeschylus to Adichie (Spivak 208). But if world literature has gained institutional traction, it has yet to find theoretical or methodological terra firma, with leading scholars such as Franco Moretti and Pascale Casanova taking up opposing positions in the world literature debate. Drawing on Immanuel Wallerstein's world-systems analysis, Moretti advocates "distant" as opposed to "close" reading as a methodology for surveying global patterns in literature (57). Casanova's divergent model differentiates between the political and aesthetic economies of what she calls the "world literary space" ("Literature" 200). Acknowledging that the "skewed distribution of goods and values has been one of its constituting principles," Casanova also affirms that the "second constitutive factor of the literary world is its relative autonomy," insisting that these "two orders" – political and aesthetic – "cannot be confounded" (201–02). Since poetry demands close rather than distant reading, the subject of Stevens and world literature is better understood in Casanova's terms than in Moretti's. Casanova's two worlds or "orders" show us that Stevens's aesthetic of poetic autonomy – his planet on the table – and his relationship to the world literary space are constitutive, in equal measure, of his relationship to world literature.

Stevens, as Astradur Eysteinsson points out, was "not a part" of the supranational movement that Hugh Kenner in *The Pound Era* defines as "International Modernism" but belonged instead to what Kenner elsewhere calls the "Homemade World" of American modernism (Eysteinsson 88). Unlike the American expatriates who were his contemporaries – Pound, T. S. Eliot, H. D. – Stevens stayed at home, traveling in his capacity as an insurance lawyer within rather than outside the United States, with the rare exceptions of a vacation, as a young man, in Canada, and two trips to Cuba. Stevens was an armchair traveler, but, as Jahan Ramazani has argued, armchair as well as actual travelers write "traveling poetry," since "a poem is itself a kind of 'contact zone,'" "a site of migratory and mingling tropes, geographies, and cultural signifiers" (*Transnational* 54). Collapsing the distance between the stay-at-home Stevens and the peripatetic Pound, the poetry of both is fascinated by the visual and verbal cultures of the Far East. Edward Ragg has traced Stevens's relationship with "the Orient" to his access, in his undergraduate years at Harvard, to "the new Oriental Wing of Boston's Museum of Fine Arts (MFA), established by Ernest Fenollosa" (55). Ruth Harrison has suggested that Stevens's Orientalism – specifically his interest in Japanese Noh drama – was subsequently mediated through Pound, who was appointed literary executor of Fenollosa's Noh manuscripts in 1913, and whose translations of and writings about the Noh appeared in *Poetry* magazine in 1914 and 1915: "The Asian influence is the clearest in Stevens' two plays *Three Travelers Watch a Sunrise* (1916) and *Carlos among the Candles* (1917), which resemble Pound's translation of the play *Nishikigi* by Zeami Motokiyo (1364–1443)" (Harrison 189).

Like Pound's Imagist verse of the 1910s, Stevens's early poetry – "The Snow Man," "Thirteen Ways of Looking at a Blackbird" – is influenced by the Japanese haiku or *hokku*, albeit that Stevens eschewed the Poundian doctrine of the Image on the grounds that "Not all objects are equal" (*CPP* 903). In a 1935 letter to Ronald Lane Latimer, Stevens tells him, "I think that I have been influenced by Chinese and Japanese lyrics. But you ask whether I have ever 'tried deliberately to attain certain qualities.' That is quite possible" (*L* 291). The greater influence, however, came from the visual arts of China and Japan. The relations between Stevens's poetry and Asian painting are plain to see in the multiple perspectives of *Harmonium* poems like "Six Significant Landscapes" and, again, in his serial *hokku* "Thirteen Ways of Looking at a Blackbird." Late in his life, Stevens would write to Peter H. Lee, a Korean student and translator he had befriended; thanking Lee for the gift of a painted scroll, Stevens conflates the pictorial and poetic arts of Asia: "The scroll made the same impression on me when I first looked at it that a collection of Chinese poems makes: an impression of something venerable, true and quiet" (*L* 742).

William W. Bevis has pointed to the profound and persistent impression of Eastern thought on Stevens: conceding that "Much of Stevens' conventional understanding about the Far East was part of the Orientalism of his day and superficial," Bevis nonetheless suggests that Stevens's "meditative habits of mind" may be understood "by reference to Mahayana Buddhist models"

("Stevens" 148), a point also made with reference to Chan Buddhism by Zhaoming Qian, both scholars noting that Stevens's *Collected Poems* is bookended – in "The Snow Man" and "Not Ideas About the Thing but the Thing Itself" – by "meditations upon the thing itself and nothing" (Qian 164). These poems embody the (oriental) mode of "meditative perception" that Bevis opposes to Stevens's (occidental) mode of "imaginative perception" (*Mind* 144). Lloyd Haft notes in his survey of Stevens in Chinese translation that "in the Chinese literary tradition there is very little basis for any positive valuation of the imagination" (147), whereas, as Milton J. Bates says of Chinese readers of Stevens, "Their own poetic tradition has … prepared them well for Stevens' metonymic method, whereby he uses carefully selected details to suggest larger patterns" (179). Accordingly, it is poems in Stevens's meditative and metonymic modes – "The Snow Man," "Thirteen Ways of Looking at a Blackbird" – that have been translated into Chinese (in anthologies edited by Zhao Yiheng [1985], Fei Bai [1989], and Zhuang Yan [1990]). Ramazani warns against reducing modernist "'appropriations' to orientalist theft" (*Transnational* 11), noting that "poetry's transnational flows" may move in what the Caribbean theorist Édouard Glissant terms "detours and returns" ("Poetry" 295). Notwithstanding Ramazani's resistance to poetry in translation, translational "flows," like transnational flows, move in detours and returns (Sapiro 211). The interchange between Stevens's reception of Chinese poetry in translation and the translation of his own poetry into Chinese involves an interchange of texts, and of their source and target languages. As Susan Bassnett remarks, in translation "texts travel across borders and are received in new cultural contexts" (237).

Translation, for Bassnett, entails "processes of import and export that are not only commercial but also aesthetic and intellectual" (235). Frank Lentricchia conflates these processes in his discussion of Stevens as a consumer in the global marketplace. It is in his lifelong passion for collecting, Lentricchia says, that we witness "the fusion of the aesthetic and the economic Stevens" (*Modernist* 167): for Stevens, whose "beginning as a collector coincided with his beginning as a writer," writing constitutes "a form of collecting, the recording of impressions and reflections a kind of hunting, the quarrying and capturing of trophies by an aesthetic imperialist" (168). Stevens's booty, in his raid on what Claire Culleton and Maria McGarrity call the "global primitive" (2), included "a small jade screen, two black crystal lions and a small jade figure" (*L* 230), items obtained through the offices of Lucy Monroe Calhoun, sister of *Poetry* magazine's editor Harriet Monroe and widow of William Calhoun, who had been US ambassador to China; Stevens sent her his poems, as well as payment, in return ("it appears that *Harmonium* reached Peking" [*L* 243]). In the *Harmonium* period and beyond, "objets d'art supply . . . the poetry" (Lentricchia, *Modernist* 171). In the 1930s, in addition to asking Harriet Monroe if her sister might procure for him "say, a pound of Mandarin Tea, a wooden carving, a piece of porcelain or one piece of turquoise, one small landscape painting, and so on and so on," Stevens also sought from his correspondent in Sri Lanka, Leonard C. van Geyzel, objects from "say, Java or Hong Kong or Siam" (*L* 278, 328). "Poetry and materia poetica are interchangeable terms" for Stevens (*CPP* 901), but for Lentricchia, "third-world objects" have a "complex political signification . . . at the point of their entry, or possibility of their entry, into first-world aesthetic reflection and writing" (*Modernist* 169). Of "the things that you have sent," Stevens would tell van Geyzel, "I selected as my own the Buddha, which is so simple and explicit that I like to have it in my room," albeit that "this particular Buddha," relocated to Connecticut in December when "the air is like ice," "must wish that I put a postage stamp on him and send him back to Colombo" (*L* 327–28).

The airmail post is a marker of Stevens's orientation toward the world, as well as his means of importing its ethnic commodities. Letters – and postcards – from his network of foreign correspondents gave Stevens a vicarious sense of citizenship in what Casanova, in her book of that title, calls *The World Republic of Letters*: as Stevens put it, "One picks up a kind of freedom of the universe, or at least of the world, from the movements of other people" (*L* 727). The interpersonal dynamics of Stevens's relationships with chosen correspondents – like Thomas McGreevy in Ireland and José Rodríguez Feo in Cuba – are replicated in the intertextual filiations that individual world poets have formed with the Stevens who is the quintessential poet's poet. For instance, Derek Walcott's mode of meditative blank verse qualifies Laurence Breiner's judgment that Stevens "seems to have inspired no one" in the Caribbean (202; see also Baer 31). The global correspondence that Stevens conducted in his lifetime continues in his afterlife in world poetry, in, for example, Kashmiri American poet Agha Shahid Ali's "Postcard from Kashmir," from his 1987 collection *The Half-Inch Himalayas*. Addressed to (and from) the poet's homeland – "Kashmir shrinks into my mailbox, / my home a neat four by six inches" (1) – Ali's postcard poem is, in its "literate despair," also addressed to Stevens (*CPP* 129). "Postcard from Kashmir" is both a poem of exile and an envoi to – or, in Kazim Ali's reading, finds a "predecessor" in (36) – Stevens's "A Postcard from the Volcano," a poem to which Ali returns in *A Nostalgist's Map of America*. Here, in the sequence "In Search of Evanescence," the first sections of which are located "in Pennsylvania," Stevens's home state, the "Students of mist / climbing the stairs like dust / washing history off the shelves / [who] will never know this house" (38–39) have predecessors in the "Children" who encounter a "shuttered mansion-house" and who "Will speak our speech and never know" in "A Postcard from the Volcano" (*CPP* 128–29).

Ali's "Snowmen" is likewise a meditation on ancestry, ethnic, and poetic: an "ancestor" who has migrated "to Kashmir from Samarkand" is the first of "generations of snowmen" that, Ali tells us, he carries "on my back" in his own migration to America and in his poem's migration to the winterscape of Stevens's "The Snow Man" (*Half-Inch Himalayas* 8). In "Land," from his 2003 book of ghazals *Call Me Ishmael Tonight*, Ali remarks, "home is found on both sides of the globe" (50). As Casanova suggests, writers occupy a "dual position, inextricably national and international," in a world literary space that "is formed by all the inhabitants of the Republic of Letters, each of them differently situated within their own national literary space" ("Literature" 200). What Casanova calls "modes of domination" nonetheless operate in the world literary space (203), both in the global marketplace, where English remains the strongest linguistic currency, and, for Frank Lentricchia, in the aesthetic sphere itself.

According to Lentricchia, Stevens's "Anecdote of the Jar" reveals "the inadequacy of the modernist literary theory of aesthetic autonomy" that the poem appears to validate if it is read as a parable about poetry as "a world unto itself" (*Ariel* 6, 15). The placing of the jar "in Tennessee," Lentricchia argues, is "an echo and repetition of a politically original act of state placing," an act of imperial "dominion" (in the language of the poem) in which the jar covers the ground in the same way that "Tennessee covers up [the original Cherokee place-name of] Tanasi" (*CPP* 60–61; *Ariel* 9, 17). In Lentricchia's interpretation, the fundamental question posed by the poem, "is Stevens *for* art or *for* nature," is resolved when Stevens "lets nature get the last word in by characterizing the autonomous jar of art, at the end of the poem, as an absence of nature": "It did not give of bird or bush, / Like nothing else in Tennessee" (*Ariel* 10; *CPP* 61). "Anecdote of the Jar," then, is another earthy anecdote, a "cautionary tale" that sounds a warning to "all us actual and would-be jar placers" (*Ariel* 12).

Iranian American poet Roger Sedarat is such a jar placer:

> Stevens never placed a jar in Shiraz.
> *Voilà!* I'm placing a jar in Shiraz. (69)

In these opening lines of "Jar in Shiraz," from his 2011 collection *Ghazal Games*, Sedarat playfully contests Stevens's poetic "dominion" with a typically

Stevensian French flourish – "*Voilà!*" A rhetorical expression of satisfaction ("there you are"), *voilà* is, also, a French deictic locative ("there"). As Rachel Blau DuPlessis notes, deixis demands "situated knowledge" (27), and Sedarat's deictic "*Voilà!*" duly prepares the ground for the placing of his jar, not in the American South of Tennessee but in the southern Iranian provincial capital of Shiraz. Sedarat also transposes Stevens's "Anecdote of the Jar" into the ancient Persian (and Urdu) form of the ghazal, creating a hybrid ghazal that embodies Sedarat's own hybrid, Iranian American identity. In "Jar in Shiraz," Sedarat rescores "the reiterated sounds of jar music" that Lentricchia hears in Stevens's poem (*Ariel* 11) – "surround," "around," "round," "ground"; "everywhere," "air," "bare" (*CPP* 60–61) – to accord with the monorhyming prosody of the ghazal, a form defined by the repetition of a word or phrase in both lines of the first couplet or *matla* (Lewis 570). Where Stevens's poem enacts the ordering power of poetry, Sedarat applies the controls – the formal and stylistic protocols – of ghazal writing, albeit that these are also the controls of the handheld gaming console featured in the cover art of *Ghazal Games.*

Stevens has been "ghazaled" before, by Adrienne Rich. A participant in the American appropriation of the ghazal initiated in New York in a group experiment from the late 1960s in which Ghalib's poetry was adapted by W. S. Merwin, William Stafford, Mark Strand, and Rich, her "ghazal of 9/28/68: ii," which is "inscribed 'For Wallace Stevens' . . . begins with an allusive tribute: 'Ideas of order . . .'" (Werner 142; see Lewis 571). Like Rich, and like Agha Shahid Ali (himself a writer of hybrid ghazals) in "Snowmen," Sedarat acknowledges Stevens as a poetic predecessor in a poem that also invokes the poet's own ancestral lineage, in Sedarat's case in Shiraz in the era of the Qajar royal dynasty (1789–1925):

> I have an uncle descended from kings.
> Here's his memoir: *A Qajar in Shiraz.* (69)

Stevens's jar, spliced into Sedarat's "*Qajar,*" is not now the modernist grail or well-wrought urn of aesthetic autonomy but a leaky vessel, pervious to world history.

In keeping with the conventions of the ghazal, and with the more flexible rules of the "ghazal games" he is playing, Sedarat puts his pen name or *takhallus* in the final couplet or *maqtai* of his poem (Lewis 570): "Jar in Shiraz," which starts with Wallace Stevens's last name, ends with Roger Sedarat's first name – "'Rah-jar in Shiraz'" (69). "Rah-jar" is a play both on Stevens's jar and on *hraja*, meaning "ruler" in proto-Indo

Iranian, the ancestor language of Persian. Roger Sedarat, then, names himself as the offspring of two progenitors: the uncle who is himself descended from the *hrajas* of Qajar Iran and Wallace Stevens, his American poetic predecessor.

Shiraz, where Sedarat places his jar, is the site of the tomb of Persian ghazal writer Hafez, who, centuries before the proscription of alcohol by the Islamic Republic of Iran in 1979, had celebrated the local wine that was stored in clay jars. The original of Stevens's jar may likewise be a receptacle for alcohol, a Canadian Dominion Wide Mouth Special canning jar, used in Tennessee for moonshine liquor in the Prohibition era (see Pearce 65). The oldest surviving Shiraz wine jar is now in the University of Pennsylvania Museum in Philadelphia, in Stevens's native state (see Shams). In "Jar in Shiraz," Sedarat repatriates the Shiraz jar, sending it back to Iran in what Brenda Le calls the "bottle form, fluid" of the ghazal ("Compulsive"). Stevens's and Sedarat's jar poems are conjoined in their meditations on the limits of aesthetic and political "dominion," but their different placings of the jar – in Tennessee and in Shiraz – mark the poets' different positionalities. As DuPlessis points out, "words take on specified meaning spoken from and to a located situation" (27).

Stevens's poems, however, are spoken from and to a variety of local and global situations; sprinkled with place-names from around the world as well as within the United States, his poetry is far more widely traveled than Stevens himself. In Stevens's *Collected Poems*, as in Casanova's Republic of Letters, "the national and international are not separate spheres" ("Literature" 200). Stevens sometimes wanted people and things from different ethnicities and nationalities to be representative of the supposedly essential characteristics of their respective groups – "Cuba should be full of Cuban things," he told the Cuban poet José Rodríguez Feo (*L* 495), reiterating the dictum in his poem "Academic Discourse at Havana" that "The world is not / . . . a word / That should import a universal pith / To Cuba" (*CPP* 116). "Academic Discourse" was nonetheless published in Spanish translation in the Cuban journal *Revista de Avance* in 1929; Stevens would subsequently contribute poems, in Rodríguez Feo's translation, to the Cuban literary review *Orígenes*, and, in a transverse trajectory, Stevens would import "Cuban things" – and verbatim excerpts from Rodríguez Feo's letters – into his own writing. Examples include Stevens's poems "A Word with José Rodríguez-Feo" and "The Novel," and the academic discourse that he delivered at Harvard in 1947, "Three Academic Pieces." In the second of these "Pieces," the poem "Someone Puts a Pineapple

Together," the pineapple – in the form of a Cuban cubist painting of a pineapple by Mariano Rodríguez, which Rodríguez Feo had sent to Stevens – is a "husk of Cuba" (*CPP* 693).

Stevens may have "lived in and out of 'his own matrix'" (Coyle and Filreis 54), but his matrix sat within a global nexus. Among the audience at Stevens's 1947 lecture was the Italian critic and translator Renato Poggioli, who would be appointed Harvard Professor of Slavic and Comparative Literature – later the Department of Comparative Literature – in 1950. In the same year, Poggioli published Stevens's poem "The Rock" in a special American edition of the Italian literary journal *Inventario*, initiating a correspondence with Stevens that marks what Massimo Bacigalupo identifies as a "unique moment in the history of Stevens' international reception" ("New Girl" 254). Poggioli's "*Mattino domenicale ed altre poesie* (1954) was the only volume of Wallace Stevens' poetry to appear in another language during the poet's lifetime" ("New Girl" 254). In a 1952 letter to Poggioli, who was working on his translation of "The Man with the Blue Guitar," Stevens parses a phrase from canto XXIV, "A poem like a missal" (*CPP* 145), explaining, "I desire my poem to mean as much, and as deeply, as a missal . . . for an understanding of the world," a secular *missale plenum* (*L* 790). In a letter to Stevens, Poggioli informs him, "the original poems you gave *Inventario* and *Botteghe Oscure* . . . revealed your name to an *elite* of Italian readers" (qtd. in Bacigalupo, "New Girl" 259). Poggioli's annotated *Mattino Domenicale* would be important to the Florentine poetic movement called *Ermetismo*, which, Bacigalupo explains, "sought a symbolic poetry of implication and syntactic complexity and ambiguity. Poggioli's 'Mattino domenicale' is written in this style" ("New Girl" 258). Bacigalupo's own, comprehensive translation of Stevens, *Tutte le Poesie* (2015), makes it "safe to say that no poet writing today in Italy is unaware of Stevens" ("Re: Stevens"). Examples include Elena Salibra, Roberto Giannoni, Carlo Vita, Guido Mazzoni, Antonella Anedda, and Valerio Magrelli. A scholar of Baudelaire and of Valéry, and a translator of Valéry, Magrelli is described by his English translator, Jamie McKendrick, as "a scholarly, philosophical, cerebral poet" whose "poems describe the process of their composition and their language keeps measuring its own capacity to observe the world" (Magrelli xi). An untitled poem in Magrelli's 1987 sequence *Nature e Venature* ("Natures and Veinings") may be modeled on Stevens's "The Snow Man" and, perhaps, the desire "to know how it would feel . . . / To be a bronze man breathing under archaic lapis" expressed by the speaker of "This Solitude of Cataracts" (*CPP* 366):

I should like, one day,
to be turned to marble,
to be stripped of nerves,
glistening tendons, veins.
Just to be airy enamel,
slaked lime, the striped
tunic of a wind
ground to a halt. (Magrelli 35)

In a poem from his 1980 volume *Ora Serrata Retinae*, Magrelli reflects on his tendency to "write as if this / were a work of translation, / something already penned in another language" (23). Poggioli would tell Stevens, "Translating is one of the humblest and noblest ways to understand poetry, not by recreating, but by being recreated by it" (qtd. in Bacigalupo, "New Girl" 260). If Stevens's poems, by way of Bacigalupo's translations, have recreated contemporary Italian verse, Stevens's poetry has itself been recreated, in non-English language and in Anglophone poetries, as "world literature."

The passage of Stevens's poetry across the Atlantic has never been smooth, however. In Britain, T. S. Eliot and the establishment would take up Stevens only belatedly, in marked contrast to the earlier and more enthusiastic reception that Stevens had received from English Surrealist poets Nicholas Moore and David Gascoyne. Stevens would find a warmer welcome in Ireland, from McGreevy through the work of contemporary poets like Derek Mahon, Seamus Heaney, and Thomas Kinsella. An exception is Austin Clarke, who, writing in *The Irish Times* in 1960, alleged that Stevens's "far-off romance" with Europe constituted a virtual version of the US imperialism that would subsequently take the tangible form of "American military bases on our side of the Atlantic" (454).

In contrast to Clarke's Cold War warrior, there is the Stevens who not only stayed at home (see Williams 27) but who also presented his *Collected Poems*, in "The Planet on the Table," as a poetic embodiment of the Monroe Doctrine – as a separate sphere, rather than as a model of what Susan Stanford Friedman calls the "cultural traffic" of planetary modernisms (64), or what Stevens himself calls "the oscillations of planetary pass-pass" (*CPP* 366). Yet the *Poems* that Stevens – fashioning himself as the "Ariel" of Shakespeare's New World romance, *The Tempest* – brings to the table "bear / Some lineament or character // . . . Of the planet of which they were part" (*CPP* 450). In their own right, and in their reception in global poetries, Stevens's poems "of the earth" (*CPP* 53) also bear the lineaments of the "sea-change" effected by transnational and translational flows (*Tmp.* 1.2.399). In alignment with Casanova's "two orders" of the world literary space, Stevens's poems, as a world apart and as part or parts of a world, are a part of world literature.

WORKS CITED

Ali, Agha Shahid. *Call Me Ishmael Tonight: A Book of Ghazals.* W. W. Norton, 2003.
The Half-Inch Himalayas. Wesleyan UP, 1987.
A Nostalgist's Map of America. W. W. Norton, 1991.
Ali, Kazim. *Mad Heart Be Brave: Essays on the Poetry of Agha Shahid Ali.* U of Michigan P, 2017.
Bacigalupo, Massimo. "'A New Girl in a New Season': Stevens, Poggioli, and the Making of *Mattino domenicale.*" *The Wallace Stevens Journal,* vol. 25, no. 2, Fall 2001, pp. 254–70.
"Re: Stevens." Received by Lee M. Jenkins, 8 Oct. 2019.
Baer, William, editor. *Conversations with Derek Walcott.* UP of Mississippi, 1996.
Bassnett, Susan. "From Cultural Turn to Translational Turn: A Transnational Journey." *World Literature in Theory,* edited by Damrosch, pp. 234–45.
Bates, Milton J. "Teaching Stevens in China." *The Wallace Stevens Journal,* vol. 25, no. 2, Fall 2001, pp. 173–82.
Bevis, William W. *Mind of Winter: Wallace Stevens, Meditation, and Literature.* U of Pittsburgh P, 1988.
"Stevens, Buddhism, and the Meditative Mind." *The Wallace Stevens Journal,* vol. 25, no. 2, Fall 2001, pp. 148–63.
Breiner, Laurence A. *A History of West Indian Poetry.* Cambridge UP, 1998.
Casanova, Pascale. "Literature as a World." *World Literature in Theory,* edited by Damrosch, pp. 192–208.
The World Republic of Letters. Translated by M. B. DeBevoise, Harvard UP, 2005.
Clarke, Austin. "Business as Usual." *Wallace Stevens: The Critical Heritage,* edited by Charles Doyle, Routledge, 1985, pp. 454–56.
Cook, Eleanor. *Poetry, Word-Play, and Word-War in Wallace Stevens.* Princeton UP, 1988.
Coyle, Beverly, and Alan Filreis, editors. *Secretaries of the Moon: The Letters of Wallace Stevens and José Rodríguez Feo.* Duke UP, 1986.
Culleton, Claire A., and Maria McGarrity, editors. *Irish Modernism and the Global Primitive.* Palgrave Macmillan, 2009.
Damrosch, David. *What Is World Literature?* Princeton UP, 2003.
editor. *World Literature in Theory.* Wiley Blackwell, 2014.
DuPlessis, Rachel Blau. "Deixis." *Inciting Poetics: Thinking and Writing Poetry,* edited by Jeanne Heuven and Tyrone Williams, U of New Mexico P, 2019, pp. 25–28.
Eysteinsson, Astradur. *The Concept of Modernism.* Cornell UP, 1990.

Friedman, Susan Stanford. *Planetary Modernisms: Provocations on Modernity Across Time*. Columbia UP, 2015.

Haft, Lloyd. "Snowy Men and Ice Cream Emperors: Wallace Stevens in Some Recent Chinese Translations." *Words from the West: Chinese Texts in Chinese Literary Context*, edited by Lloyd Haft, Centre of Non-Western Studies, 1993, pp. 145–61.

Harrison, Ruth M. "Wallace Stevens and the Noh Tradition." *The Wallace Stevens Journal*, vol. 27, no. 2, Fall 2003, pp. 189–204.

Kenner, Hugh. "The Making of the Modernist Canon." *Canons*, edited by Robert von Hallberg, U of Chicago P, 1984, pp. 363–75.

The Pound Era. U of California P, 1971.

Le, Brenda. "Poem: Compulsive Repetition Ghazal." *Chronogram*, Luminary Publishing, 2019, www.chronogram.com/hudsonvalley/poem-compulsive-repetition-ghazal/Content?oid=2192228.

Lentricchia, Frank. *Ariel and the Police: Michel Foucault, William James, Wallace Stevens*. U of Wisconsin P, 1988.

Modernist Quartet. Cambridge UP, 1994.

Lewis, F. D. "Ghazal." *The Princeton Encyclopedia of Poetry & Poetics*, edited by Stephen Cushman et al., 4th ed., Princeton UP, 2012, pp. 570–72.

Magrelli, Valerio. *The Embrace: Selected Poems*. Translated by Jamie McKendrick, Faber and Faber, 2009.

Mani, B. Venkat. "Bibliomigrancy: Book Series and the Making of World Literature." *The Routledge Companion to World Literature*, edited by Theo D'haen et al., Routledge, 2011, pp. 283–96.

Moretti, Franco. "Conjectures on World Literature." *New Left Review*, vol. 1, no. 1, Jan.-Feb. 2000, pp. 54–68.

Pearce, Roy Harvey. "'Anecdote of the Jar': An Iconological Note." *The Wallace Stevens Journal*, vol. 1, no. 2, Summer 1977, p. 65.

Pound, Ezra. "The Renaissance. The Palette. I." *Poetry*, vol. 5, no. 5, Feb. 1915, pp. 227–33.

"Tagore's Poems." *Poetry*, vol. 1, no. 3, Dec. 1912, pp. 92–94.

Qian, Zhaoming. "Late Stevens, Nothingness, and the Orient." *The Wallace Stevens Journal*, vol. 25, no. 2, Fall 2001, pp. 164–72.

Ragg, Edward. "The Orient." *Wallace Stevens in Context*, edited by Glen MacLeod, Cambridge UP, 2017, pp. 55–64.

Ramazani, Jahan. "Poetry, Modernity, and Globalization." *The Oxford Handbook of Global Modernisms*, edited by Mark Wollaeger with Matt Eatough, Oxford UP, 2012, pp. 288–309.

A Transnational Poetics. U of Chicago P, 2009.

Sapiro, Gisèle. "Globalization and Cultural Diversity in the Book Market: The Case of Literary Translations in the US and in France." *World Literature in Theory*, edited by Damrosch, pp. 209–33.

Sedarat, Roger. *Ghazal Games: Poems*. Ohio UP, 2011.

Shakespeare, William. *The Norton Shakespeare*. 3rd ed., edited by Stephen Greenblatt et al., W. W. Norton, 2016.

Shams, Anahita. "Does Shiraz Wine Come from Iran?" *BBC News*, 3 Feb. 2017, www.bbc.com/news/world-middle-east-38771806.

Spivak, Gayatri Chakravorty. "Planetarity." *World Literature: A Reader*, edited by Theo D'haen, Routledge, 2011, pp. 207–17.

Stevens, Wallace. *Letters of Wallace Stevens.* Edited by Holly Stevens, U of California P, 1996.

   Wallace Stevens: Collected Poetry and Prose. Edited by Frank Kermode and Joan Richardson, Library of America, 1997.

Werner, Craig Hansen. *Adrienne Rich: The Poet and Her Critics.* American Library Association, 1988.

Williams, William Carlos. *Imaginations.* New Directions, 1970.

CHAPTER 7

Ecological Poetics

Cary Wolfe

Wallace Stevens is not typically taken to be an ecological poet, but were you to make that claim, you would probably begin by drawing attention to what Stevens called his poetic "mundo" (*CPP* 351), which is structured by the seasons and their changes, motifs that, in turn, body forth the more abstract poetic commitments (often called "philosophical") for which this poet is famous.[1] As Sebastian Gardner has noted, the world of winter in Stevens's poetry is "not the everyday world, but the world stripped of all human, anthropocentric features"; we typically arrive at it through "an operation of subtraction" of the everyday, creating a kind of "contraction" of the ordinary world, one that "involves exchanging the *world*, in the sense of something that a human subject can properly 'be in,' for mere *reality*" (to use a favorite term of Stevens's, whose problematic nature I will pinpoint later) (326). Stevens's world of winter answers to his ceaseless desire – announced throughout his poetry, beginning to end – to know the world as it is, in itself, without human mediation or transfiguration, but (or perhaps we should say "and") it sets going a dialectical movement (though "dialectical" is not the word we will want, as it turns out) that makes us long for a habitable world, a world full of life and light. Hence, we have Stevens's world of summer, the world associated with his other great theme, the imagination, but as Gardner points out, the world of summer as well does not correspond "to the ordinary world, of which it is rather a *transfiguration*" and a kind of intensification. Rather, the world of summer "restores the character of worldhood to reality and intensifies its habitability." In between these two seasons, these two worlds, Gardner writes, "hovers the *ordinary* world," which Stevens associates with "a sense of reality that is provisional and uncertain," a "place of transition between the great antitheses of winter and summer" (327). Stevens's expression "The Plain Sense of Things" (*CPP* 428) captures "the uncertainty about reality that Stevens locates in the ordinary world," sometimes denoting the everyday and the mundane, and sometimes tending toward the "*hard* sense of reality which characterizes the contracted world of winter" (Gardner 328).

Among Stevens's critics, no one has written more about the seasonal motif than George Lensing, who observes that the seasons in Stevens are "more than pastoral backdrop or lyrical evocation"; they form "a larger mythos that lends a unity to what Stevens eventually came to call his cumulative 'grand poem.'" But they also embody "a highly personal psychodrama, even a mode of survival, for a poet who found himself for the most part estranged from the supporting ties of family (parents, wife, siblings, daughter), friendships, and religious faith" (118). Indeed, as Stevens once noted, "Life is an affair of people not of places. But for me life is an affair of places and that is the trouble" (*CPP* 901). While Lensing, at least in part, indexes Stevens's seasonal cycles to biographical facts, J. Hillis Miller has seen them as part of the larger cycle of "decreation" and "recreation" in what Stevens calls his "endlessly elaborating poem" (*CPP* 415), from the poetry of autumn, where the leaves fall, and, eventually, in winter, "man is left face to face with the bare rock of reality," to the "reconstruction of a new imagination of the world" in spring (Miller 149–50). But this new world of spring obsolesces in its turn, and so, "In this rhythmic alternation lies our only hope to possess reality" (150). It's as if Stevens realizes in his later poetry that the poem of winter, once written, rapidly ossifies and becomes "part of the dead past long before he has finished it," and so, for Miller, the poet is forced to "make sterile vibrations back and forth between one spiritual season and the other, always a little behind the perpetual flowing of reality" (150–51). Stevens's solution to this impasse, Miller writes, is to achieve in the late poetry an increasingly rapid "oscillation" between the two poles of decreation (autumn/winter) and recreation (spring/summer) that "becomes a blur in which opposites are touched simultaneously, as alternating current produces a steady beam of light" (151).

Richard Macksey, for his part, combines elements of both Lensing's and Miller's interpretations in his own version of Stevens and the seasons, when he writes that "For Stevens, man lives in the weather as he lives in the changing light of his moods and new redactions of reality" (187). As he notes, this dynamic unity "is open to change from both quarters, the turning seasons and the spinning mind," and one end of that spectrum, which is "rare in the tropics of *Harmonium* and dominant in the northern world of *The Rock*," is "represented by the nothingness of winter, the 'basic slate.'" Here we find a world increasingly privileged in Stevens's later poetry, one of "immense clarity and intense poverty, an abandonment to pure content of consciousness unrefracted by convention or individuality," a "moment of contraction" from which the poet "returns without baggage or clothing to the bare fact of the world, ... a winter world of unmediated perception"

(187–88). Precisely here, however (though many such moments could be cited in many writings on Stevens), we run aground, as I have noted elsewhere, on a conundrum that has dogged Stevens criticism from the beginning to the present day, a conundrum one might associate with the names "epistemology" and "phenomenology."[2] For here – to put it bluntly – one is forced to ask, "Well, which is it?" The "bare fact of the world" (the world of the object) or rather "unmediated perception" (the world of the subject and its perceptual powers)? Here, it seems to me, we need another theoretical vocabulary to describe what Stevens is up to, and that vocabulary is *not*, I think, the vocabulary of phenomenology on which so many fine and nuanced engagements of Stevens's work have foundered.

What I want to suggest in the remainder of this chapter is that only a *nonrepresentational* understanding of ecological poetics can enable us to grasp the most profound sense in which Wallace Stevens is an ecological poet – a sense that does not exclude but reaches well beyond the thematics and imagery of seasons and climate, palm trees and snowy scenes, that furnish his poetic "mundo." Interestingly enough, if we pay attention to the understanding of the terms "ecology" and "environment" in the contemporary sciences, this nonrepresentational emphasis should not surprise anyone – and, indeed, might be seen as long overdue in rethinking what "ecological poetics" means. As we know from contemporary theoretical biology, no organism has a representational relationship to its environment, in the sense of a neutral, transparent access whose veracity and usefulness are calibrated to the degree of this neutrality and transparency. Indeed, to make their way in the world, organisms must exclude (largely unconsciously) most of what is "out there" to make a structured and functional world possible.

In this light, the term "environment" reminds us that what counts as "nature" is always a product of the contingent and selective practices deployed in the embodied actions of a living system. In biological terms, this realization reaches back to Jakob von Uexküll's pioneering theories of human and animal *Umwelten*, or "lifeworlds" (admired by Gilles Deleuze and Félix Guattari, as well as Giorgio Agamben in contemporary philosophy), and forward to work on the philosophy of mind and consciousness by thinkers such as Alva Noë, who argues that "The locus of consciousness is the dynamic life of the whole, environmentally plugged-in person or animal" (xiii). As Noë puts it, "it is not the case that all animals have a common external environment," because "to each different form of animal life there is a distinct, corresponding, ecological domain or habitat," which means, in short, that "All animals live in structured worlds" (43).

What this means is that ecological space is, in a very important sense, *virtual* space. Why? Because any such space is populated by a myriad of wildly heterogeneous life-forms who create their worlds, their environments, through the embodied enaction, unfolding dynamically and in real time, of their own self-referential modes of knowing and being, their own "autopoiesis" (to use the term invented by biologists Humberto Maturana and Francisco Varela). Paying attention to this multidimensionality and overdetermination of ecological space means understanding that, in this context, "virtual" doesn't mean "not real" or "less real" – it means "*more* real." Indeed, Maturana calls such a perspective "super-realist," in the sense of one "who believes in the existence of innumerable equally valid realities," which cannot, however, be called "relativist" because "asserting their relativity would entail the assumption of an absolute reality as the reference point against which their relativity would be measured" (Maturana and Poersken 34).

What is accented by the term "environment," then, is this wild, crisscrossing dance of an almost unimaginable heterogeneity of living beings, at different scales and at different temporalities, doing their own thing. And a hallmark of Stevens's mode of attention is to look, listen, and follow where this dance leads him. In fact, an added bonus of this shift in theoretical frameworks from "nature" to "environment" is that it helps us account for the extraordinary power of *virtualization* that Stevens exerts in such moments (think, for example, about "The Snow Man" and Stevens's conjugation of the relationship between "Nothing that is not there" and "the nothing that is" [*CPP* 8]).

It's this power of virtualization, at least in part, that gives Stevens's poetry a quality that often borders on "clairvoyance" (to borrow Harold Bloom's wonderful characterization [23], borrowed from Stevens's late long poem "Credences of Summer" [see *CPP* 323]) – his ability to disclose how that virtual space is paradoxically more "real" than "reality," precisely because the "out there" and the "in here" become so dynamically and intimately conjoined, in real time. This fact about any living being's "world" is foregrounded, persistently and paradoxically, in Stevens's poetry, framed as it is by an extreme tension between a desire for "things as they are" (*CPP* 135), things without human mediation (on the one hand) and (on the other) constant reminders of the supreme value of the imagination and how the mind of the poet makes its world. (Think, for example, about poems such as "Metaphors of a Magnifico" or "The Idea of Order at Key West," or the many moments in the poetry when the figure of the bird, and more specifically bird's song, becomes the staging ground for this

question, such as section IX of "Credences of Summer.") But the larger
ecological point here is that this is not simply an epistemological problem,
not simply about Stevens insisting that the paradoxical relationship of
organism and environment emphasizes the inescapable co-implication
and mutual enfolding of self and world. Rather, in Stevens's poetics, the
"operating program," so to speak, *reproduces* rather than *represents* the
complex logic of physical (and, specifically, biological) systems in ongoing
acts of meaning-making that are, at the same time, processes of
individuation.[3]

The issue for Stevens, then, isn't about getting an accurate picture of the
world; it's about *getting on* in the world, and the shift in emphasis is from
"being" to "doing" (to borrow Maturana's formulation) (Maturana and
Poersken 20). Indeed, this shift from "being" to "doing" is fundamental to
how Stevens recasts in his poetry the familiar problems inherited from
epistemology and phenomenology that we touched on a moment ago. As
Simon Critchley puts it,

> Stevens's poetry allows us to recast what is arguably the fundamental
> concern of philosophy, namely the relation between thought and things
> or mind and world, the concern that becomes, in the early modern period,
> the basic problem of epistemology. It [is] my general claim that Stevens
> recasts this concern in a way that lets us cast it away. Stevens's verse shows us
> a way of overcoming epistemology. (4)

The question then becomes how to do this non-dialectically, as it were
(how not to be Walt Whitman, if you like – which Stevens had not yet
figured out in a poem such as "Sunday Morning"). This leads to the second
stage of the progression of Stevens's poetics, his contention that "the
theory / Of poetry is the theory of life, // As it is, in the intricate evasions
of as" (*CPP* 415). This is so, according to Critchley, because it is "performed
in the specific poem insofar as that poem concerns itself with some real
particular, with some object, thing or fact," which in turn means, as he
asserts, that "things as they are" (to repeat Stevens's phrase from "The Man
with the Blue Guitar") "only are in the act that says they are" (19). Thus, for
Stevens, poetry "reveals the idea of order which we imaginatively impose
on reality.... The fact of the world is a *factum*: a deed, an act, an
artifice" (58).

It is, in fact, a *poiesis* in the strict sense, a "making," and it is the same
poiesis, in its fundamental structure, that we find in the *autopoiesis* of
biological life-forms. But even though that *poiesis* reproduces the "operating program" of biological life-forms, with all of the paradoxes around the

relationship between "inside" and "outside," organism and environment, that are connoted by the term *Umwelt* or "lifeworld," in Stevens's poetry, of course, it takes place in the domain of language and culture. Hence, it can hardly be called "natural" or "ecological" in the traditional sense of those terms. And hence, the "ecological" dimension of Stevens's poetics may be found in places where we might least expect to find it.

For example, several critics have explored the peculiar, nonrepresentational (but performative) rhetoricity of Stevens's style, reaching back to Helen Vendler's early essay on Stevens's "qualified assertions" and her emphasis on "the frequency with which he closes his poems on a tentative note," resorting "repeatedly to some of the modal auxiliaries – may, might, and must, could, should, and would – to conclude his 'statement'" (163–64). One effect of this, she notes, is that "the texture of Stevens' language is such that it shifts from 'reality' to the realm of 'as if' very easily, making the two almost interchangeable at times," so that he is able to use logic "not as a logician but as a sleight-of-hand man ... delighting in paradoxical logic" (174–75). Beverly Maeder, who has written the most extensive book on Stevens's grammar and syntax, similarly draws our attention to Stevens's salient use of "'function words,' such as prepositions, modal verbs, and certain uses of the verb *to be*" – words that are "weak in semantic content but that bind other words and parts of sentences together in special ways" and so are "central to the poems' tentative, speculative edge" (151). In fact, Roger Gilbert has calculated that roughly one in every twenty-seven words in Stevens's *Collected Poems* is some form of the verb "to be," and, significantly, roughly a third of those occurrences are preceded by what linguists call "dummy subjects" – words such as "there," "this," and "here." This is significant because the designation of the ontological claim "to be" thus gets referred to the provisional and contingent performativity (the "location," if you will) of "there," "this," and "here" (193–94). And even though most studies of Stevens's diction, he notes, have focused on its "florabundant" aspects (193), much of Stevens's diction is in fact centered on what Maeder calls the "functional core" of English, words that are performative and grammatically *enactive* rather than denotative and representational (158).

The result, Maeder writes, is that in Stevens, word choice "means less the search for the right word or *le mot juste* than the experimental combination ... to draw attention to, and stimulate pleasure in, the poem's constructedness or artifice" (154). Indeed, as she notes, Stevens's later poetry takes "some distance from the exotic flourishes he included in his early poems" (153). Mac Hammond puts it even more forcefully: "after the gorgeous vocabulary of the 1923 *Harmonium* volume, the bareness of vocabulary in poems beginning with 'The Man with the Blue Guitar' (1937) seems something of a desert." And when we ask, "Of what does this desert music consist?" his answer, like Maeder's and Vendler's, is astute: it aims "to lay bare the grammatical structure of the speech and to place a heavy burden on the grammar in respect to the communication of meaning. The late poetry of Stevens is, in short, a poetry of grammar" (179).

My emphasis on this "functional" or "weak" or "rhetorical" quality of Stevens's poetics is meant to underscore again that the point here is not "accuracy" or "representation" in relation to the natural world, but rather the *performativity* of poetic making that highlights at every moment the highly structured, contingent character of the organism in its world, which then gets handled within the specific (and nonnatural) technology of the poem, foregrounding the relationship between the world of "fact" (Stevens's "reality") and the *factum* of the poem itself – literally, an act, a making, as Critchley points out. (Think, for example, about key moments in the corpus such as it "*Seemed* like a sound in his mind" and "It was *like* / A new knowledge of reality," from "Not Ideas About the Thing but the Thing Itself" – the last poem in *The Collected Poems* [*CPP* 451–52; emphases added] – or all those "It was when" and "It was at that time" and "You said" and "We said" phrases in "On the Road Home" [*CPP* 186].) This rhetoricity *both* foregrounds the specificity of the poem's performative dimension *and* reminds us that this performativity, this *poiesis*, is pervasive beyond human language, directing our attention to a very different understanding of the "ecological" dimension of the poetry. Performativity and *poiesis*, in other words, are larger domains of meaning-making than human "language" proper.

Stevens is obviously quite focused on this question in some of his most famous poems (and in many of his poems about birdsong), including "Not Ideas About the Thing but the Thing Itself" and "Of Mere Being" (to name only two famous examples), both of which are framed by the fundamental question broached in "The Planet on the Table" – that "What mattered" was that the poems should bear "Some lineament or character" of "the planet of which they were part" (*CPP* 450). Roy Harvey Pearce finds Stevens working through this question in another late poem, "The Region November." In a wonderfully suggestive engagement with this posthumously published poem, Pearce writes, in a passage worth quoting at length,

> The poem see-saws between "sway" and "say" – the movement of meter and sensibility being enforced by the outrageous adverbs, "deeplier" and

"loudlier." . . . The effort of the treetops is "So much less than feeling, so much less than speech." Yet it proves a feeling and speech of some sort; and the poet can suppose that they "say / On the level of that which is not yet knowledge." "On the level of . . ." is "philosophic" diction, and so bids us think with this lyric, not sing mournfully with it. The "not yet intended" of the seventh line is in fact a bit of technical language out of Stevens' dabbling in phenomenology, in whose logic all revelations are nothing if not "intended." Now he decides that, spontaneously, without intention, to be is to say: to say what "It is hard to hear." In short, Stevens is claiming that if the treetops do "say," it is not in the language of any "speech." . . . He will not let himself be trapped in the anthropocentrism, as often as not masked as theocentrism, of his "romantic" forebears and contemporaries. He will be a radical humanist to the end. But his humanism now forces him to acknowledge both the virtual life of the non-human and its virtual capacity to "say." (131)

Here, I think we can use the questions broached so sensitively by Pearce as an invitation to pursue a theoretical framework quite different from phenomenology, one that had been taking shape during the same period in which Pearce's essay on Stevens appeared: namely, Gregory Bateson's work in systems theory on what he called "an ecology of mind." Bateson's interest is in forms of meaning – indeed, what he calls "ideas" – for which human "speech" is not a constitutive element, and in which various non-human living systems participate quite robustly, all the time. Bateson recalls the "Liar's Paradox" familiar to us from the philosophical tradition's confrontation with the problem of paradoxical self-reference. "If Epimenides was right in saying that Cretans always lie," Bateson writes, "and he was a Cretan, was he a liar or not a liar? If he was a liar, then he was not a liar. If he was not a liar, then it was untrue that Cretans are always liars, and so on. Now," he continues, in a crucial advance on Pearce's quarry, "look at the 'then' in that paradox. If yes, then no. If no, then yes. If the 'then' is logical, there is a paradox, but if the 'then' is causal and temporal, the contradiction disappears" (181). Why? Because the temporalization of the "then" means that the same element in a system can have a different, even opposed, meaning at a different point in time, depending on the dynamic state of the system as a whole. Such systems do not operate with, and are not constituted by, *substances* that have fixed and permanent meanings. As it turns out, this is how biological and ecological systems operate (take, for example, the phenomenon of autoimmunity, where the same substance can have different, even opposite, effects on an organism, depending on that organism's dynamic state in real time). And this is one of the reasons, Bateson writes, that "*logic is a very poor model of the world of mental process*" and of the complex, even paradoxical organism/environment relationship, unfolding in real time, from which they arise (204).

Bateson's account gives us a robustly naturalistic way to understand the problem that captivates so many of Stevens's critics (and captivated Stevens himself): how poetry can take on and explore philosophical problems that philosophy *qua* logic can't handle because it isn't complex enough; and it isn't complex enough because for philosophical logic, *time* is not a constitutive element. To put it bluntly, the poetic strategies for handling the philosophical problems that Stevens is so interested in may be less "logical," but, for that very reason, they are more "effective" insofar as they are more *ecological* – that is to say, they partake of the same nonlogical integration that characterizes biological, ecological, and evolutionary systems.

It is worth emphasizing one last time that such systems *are not representational*, because they do not operate with fixed substances but rather with elements whose function and significance in the system will always vary in the context of the temporalized complexity that Bateson emphasizes. But they are also not representational in an even more important sense elucidated by Bateson – important, given the habitual recourse to phenomenology and intentionality in the critical literature on Stevens. If it is true that meaning-making systems and biological systems are nonrepresentational in the first sense discussed earlier, then it is also true, as Bateson puts it, that "Mind always operates at one remove away from matter," at "one *derivative*" from the so-called "'external' world" (188). As Bateson notes, in fact, we "have sense organs specially designed to keep the world out," but "Very few people seem to realize the enormous theoretical 'power' of this distinction between what I 'see' and what is out there" (182, 204). Most people, Bateson continues, assume that

> they see what they look at and they assume this *because* there is total unconsciousness of the processes of perception.... My mental machinery provides me not with the news of its processes, but with news of its products. Indeed, there is a certain common sense in a world so constructed that organisms shall not be bothered with news of processes and they shall be given the product only. But, in fact, the processes of *making* images are of very great complexity, and can be experimentally investigated [as in, for example, the famous false parallax experiments of Adelbert Ames that Bateson describes]. (204–05)

Interestingly enough, Bateson invokes Stevens's "The Man with the Blue Guitar" as a meditation upon this very process. "The poet sees himself as divided from 'Things as they are,'" Bateson observes. "*But this, after all,*" he continues, "*is the circumstance for all organisms....* The 'Blue Guitar,' the creative filter between us and the world, is always and inevitably there. This it is to be both creature and creator. This the poet knows much better than the biologist" (264; emphases added).

In Stevens's terms, this fact about what I have elsewhere called "openness from closure" (*What Is Posthumanism?* xxi) might be rephrased as follows: our intense concentration on what Stevens called the "august" activity of the mind's formation of its perceived reality actually makes us more attuned to the world, and to our own ongoing immersion in it, precisely because of the contingency of our own self-reference. Or as Bateson puts it, "most people are not aware that they do this, and as you become aware that you are doing it, you become in a curious way much closer to the world around you. . . . The world is no longer 'out there' in quite the same way that it used to seem to be." What we find instead, he writes, is "neither pure solipsism nor its opposite" (which is, of course, the impasse in which we land in an epistemological framing of the problem). As Bateson sketches it, "In solipsism, you are ultimately isolated and alone, isolated by the premise 'I make it all up,'" but at the other extremity (what is often called "realism"), "you would cease to exist, becoming nothing but a metaphoric feather blown by the winds of external 'reality.'" And in "between these two," he continues, "is a region where you are partly blown by the winds of reality and partly an artist creating a composite out of the inner and outer events" (222–23). Or as Stevens will put it in "Reality Is an Activity of the Most August Imagination," musing about driving home in the lights of the roadway, late on a Friday night – one of the many poems that wonderfully exemplifies this "composite" process – "It was not a night blown at a glassworks in Vienna," something "gathering time and dust." On the contrary, we found that "things emerged and moved and were dissolved," "An argentine abstraction approaching form / And suddenly denying itself away" (*CPP* 471–72).

Notes

1 The points covered in this chapter are explored in greater detail in Wolfe, *Ecological Poetics*.
2 Specifically, in Wolfe, *What Is Posthumanism?* 268–70.
3 I thank Marjorie Levinson for helping me to articulate this very important point in precisely this way.

WORKS CITED

Bateson, Gregory. *A Sacred Unity: Further Steps to an Ecology of Mind*. Edited by Rodney E. Donaldson, HarperCollins, 1991.

Bloom, Harold. *Wallace Stevens: The Poems of Our Climate.* Cornell UP, 1977.

Critchley, Simon. *Things Merely Are: Philosophy in the Poetry of Wallace Stevens.* Routledge, 2005.

Gardner, Sebastian. "Wallace Stevens and Metaphysics: The Plain Sense of Things." *European Journal of Philosophy*, vol. 2, no. 3, December 1994, pp. 322–44.

Gilbert, Roger. "Verbs of Mere Being: A Defense of Stevens' Style." *The Wallace Stevens Journal*, vol. 28, no. 2, Fall 2004, pp. 191–202.

Hammond, Mac. "On the Grammar of Wallace Stevens." *The Act of the Mind*, edited by Pearce and Miller, pp. 179–84.

Lensing, George S. "Stevens' Seasonal Cycles." *The Cambridge Companion to Wallace Stevens*, edited by John N. Serio, Cambridge UP, 2007, pp. 118–32.

Macksey, Richard A. "The Climates of Wallace Stevens." *The Act of the Mind*, edited by Pearce and Miller, pp. 185–223.

Maeder, Beverly. "Stevens and Linguistic Structure." *The Cambridge Companion to Wallace Stevens*, edited by John N. Serio, Cambridge UP, 2007, pp. 149–63.

Maturana, Humberto, and Bernhard Poersken. *From Being to Doing: The Origins of the Biology of Cognition.* Translated by Wolfram Karl Koeck and Alison Rosemary Koeck, Carl-Auer Verlag, 2004.

Maturana, Humberto, and Francisco Varela. *The Tree of Knowledge: The Biological Roots of Human Understanding.* Rev. ed., Shambhala P, 1992.

Miller, J. Hillis. "Wallace Stevens' Poetry of Being." *The Act of the Mind*, edited by Pearce and Miller, pp. 143–62.

Noë, Alva. *Out of Our Heads: Why You Are Not Your Brain, and Other Lessons from the Biology of Consciousness.* Hill and Wang, 2009.

Pearce, Roy Harvey. "Wallace Stevens: The Last Lesson of the Master." *The Act of the Mind*, edited by Pearce and Miller, pp. 121–42.

Pearce, Roy Harvey, and J. Hillis Miller, editors. *The Act of the Mind: Essays on the Poetry of Wallace Stevens.* Johns Hopkins P, 1965.

Stevens, Wallace. *Wallace Stevens: Collected Poetry and Prose.* Edited by Frank Kermode and Joan Richardson, Library of America, 1997.

Uexküll, Jakob von. *A Foray into the Worlds of Animals and Humans*, with *A Theory of Meaning.* Translated by Joseph D. O'Neil, U of Minnesota P, 2010.

Vendler, Helen Hennessy. "The Qualified Assertions of Wallace Stevens." *The Act of the Mind*, edited by Pearce and Miller, pp. 163–78.

Wolfe, Cary. *Ecological Poetics; or, Wallace Stevens's Birds.* U of Chicago P, 2020. *What Is Posthumanism?* U of Minnesota P, 2010.

CHAPTER 8

Urban Studies

Julia E. Daniel

At first blush, Wallace Stevens seems an unlikely candidate for an urban studies analysis. When other poets turned to skyscrapers and city trains, Stevens placed his readers in banana boats, gazebos, and palace dreamscapes. However, as scholars have come to note, many of his poetic landscapes have understudied or even hidden urban contexts (including that gazebo). His literary output and poetic imagination were also embedded in the artistic, social, and economic ecosystems of modern urbanism. Attending to Stevens as a poet of the city is to find him playing on felicitous ground. Stevens's urban sites are stages on which he performs his lifelong study of the imagination's relationship to reality. In some ways, this was the selfsame issue confronting urban planners and designers at the turn of the twentieth century through the 1940s and 1950s. Like Stevens, the first generation of American city planners believed that their art form could ameliorate the crushed psyche of a populace overwhelmed by the new conditions of modernity. Stevens's journals, letters, and poetry attest to the uneven successes of those ideals. His cities are most often ambiguous places, at times marred by a lack of sociability and contact with nature while, at other moments, they crackle with organic beauty and aesthetic inspiration. That Stevens's urbanism defies easy categorization, and sometimes even invites contradiction, testifies to the complexities of the modern city and the poet's own capacious engagements with these overdetermined modern spaces.

If Stevens's attitude to the city is difficult to define, the same may be said for the actual object one considers when undertaking an "urban studies" approach to literature. This multidisciplinary field has its roots back in the same period when Stevens was strolling through Elizabeth Park in Hartford. In the United States, the character of urban living altered dramatically following the massive population drift from the country to the city that began as a drip in the mid-1800s and crested to a tsunami in the 1910s and 1920s.[1] Not only did the city now present itself as a "problem" due to its cramped, unsanitary, and poorly designed work and living environments, but living in the shadow of skyscrapers instead of mountains and trees was also thought to herald a change in the very character of the citizenry. Emerging technologies also made the modern city a profoundly new kind of site, one filled with towering structures impregnated with elevators and telephone wires, rackety motorized traffic, and electrified advertisements winking into the wee hours of the night. Cities, furthermore, threw into dramatic relief the widening gulf between the wealthy elite and a growing working-class population now living elbow to elbow. At the same time, the metropolis was upheld as emblem of and ground for a modern utopianism. If only planners and politicians could get the city *right* (whatever that might mean), culture might progress into a new era when everyone had access to work, museums, parks, and the bountiful goods proffered by department stores. World's fairs presented streamlined, urban futures as the deco-inflected destiny of Western culture. A host of professional fields responded to both this utopian call and the cries of woe that urban living presented for modern citizens. By the middle of the twentieth century, professional associations and academic programs coalesced around the title "urban studies," which most often addressed technical questions of city design with an eye toward the many ways in which answers to those questions might facilitate community wellness and human flourishing. In this regard, urban studies was always preoccupied with historical, philosophical, aesthetic, psychological, and even spiritual dimensions of the urban.

Today, urban studies is a multidisciplinary field that asks how cities create, enable, or prevent different kinds of identities, communities, economies, and habitats through both their material geography and intangible powers. It considers how they might be bodied forth in imagined futures or how they haunt us from similarly imagined pasts. It also asks how certain spaces, architectures, actions, subjects, and, for our purposes, texts become understood as "urban" and what is at stake in that designation. As I have argued elsewhere, urban studies of modernist literature can be placed on a kind of spectrum "defined by two poles: the city as a literary, imaginative, and mythic construct on the one hand, and the city as a materialized, spatial, sociopolitical zone on the other" ("Urbanism" 25). In the language of Burton Pike, there is a complex weave of relationships between "the real city and the word-city" (x). The current tendency is to honor the multiple avenues of influence and even co-creation between the real cities and word-cities of modernism. In this respect, the city presents itself as a deeply Stevensian object in both urban studies and the modernist imagination, for it figures as a site held in humming tension between the flights of the imagination and the weight of lived reality.

As such, there is no one path an urban studies approach might take into the world of Wallace Stevens. What this chapter offers is a brisk walking tour of different modes of study an urbanist offers to readers of Stevens's verse. The first is a historical and biographical survey of how contact with cities formed Stevens's aesthetic sensibilities. Put differently, in what way does Stevens's work demonstrate his urbanization of mind? The second is a place-based approach that identifies or recovers city sites, both real and fictional, in Stevens's works to question how the poet frames them either pessimistically or optimistically as locations for the creation of both art and community. To limit the parameters of this jaunt, I have primarily focused here on Stevens's American urban- and suburban-isms, as they constitute the majority of named or identifiable cityscapes in his verse and arguably most influence his sense of what a city can and should be. We will conclude by glancing outward at the other geographical and fictive urban landscapes that are both trope and theater in his verse.

When considered from a literary perspective, urban studies usually first brings to mind a location's representation within a work of literature. As Arnold Weinstein argues, "One thinks initially – but perhaps wrongly – that the privileged dimension of cities is *space*" (139; italics in original). However, scholars of urban studies are equally fascinated by the intangibles of the city, such as the way its logic shapes the identities, tastes, and behaviors of inhabitants. In the words of Carlo Rotella, "Urbanization refers not only to the transformation of landscape but also to what goes on inside the minds of people who come to the city" (799). Concern about the urbanization of mind is in many ways a hallmark of the modernist period. In 1903, the influential German sociologist Georg Simmel set out to describe the effects of urbanization on individual psychology in his classic work "The Metropolis and Mental Life." For Simmel, the "metropolitan type" was coextensive with the modern mind. This new way of being in the world arose from the trauma of anonymity in crowds the likes of which individuals had not yet experienced on a daily basis. Simmel describes that mind as lonely and liberated, protectively blasé while suffering the agony of solitude. Stevens, in an attempt to prepare his fiancée Elsie for life in New York City after their marriage, voices a similar admixture of freedom and isolation in urban crowds: "It is one of the oldest observations that, in a city, one does not know the people around one. . . . You lose your individuality in a sense; in another sense you intensify it, for you are left to your own devices to satisfy your desires" (*L* 127–28). Simmel further argues that the urban mind turns away from emotion and toward reason, especially as the inconceivable scale of modern cities forced city dwellers into acts of abstraction. As the impressed twenty-one-year-old Stevens commented in the early months after his arrival, "New York is so big that a battle might go on at one end, and poets meditate sonnets at another" (L 47).

In their introduction to *Wallace Stevens, New York, and Modernism*, Lisa Goldfarb and Bart Eeckhout suggest that some of Stevens's most characteristic qualities as a poet in fact map onto Simmel's description of this metropolitan subject. Their 2012 collection heralded a reconsideration of Stevens's previously overlooked urban investments. Since then, Stevens scholarship has turned to a nuanced consideration of how the poet's contact with urban environments molded his aesthetic sensibility. Because his substantive works appeared in print after his move to Hartford in 1916, there was a tendency in earlier criticism to overlook his character as a city dweller. However, as George Lensing has argued, "New York was Stevens' first 'home' in his postcollegiate years, and his life in the city formed him, for better or for worse, during the impressionable years beginning when he was twenty" (21). And a perusal of Stevens's letters and journals during his New York sojourn reveals that it was, indeed, both for better and for worse. Stevens had an ongoing love-hate relationship with the city. At some moments, his complaints render New York nearly uninhabitable: "I am beginning to hate the stinking restaurants that line the street and gush out clouds of vegetable incense as I pass" (L 39). And yet, at others, it offers space and material for poetic composition: "A city is a splendid place for thinking. I have a sonnet in my head the last line of which is – And hear the bells of Trinity at night – bells which start ringing in my remotest fancies" (L 42). His letters from this period are like a swinging pendulum: he can bemoan the crowds in one and exalt the beauties of the city in another, sometimes even in the same missive. Such vacillation is arguably the hallmark of a fundamentally New York state of mind: those who love it also have the privilege of complaining about it.

Other scholars have linked capacious webs of influence and granular peccadilloes with Stevens's urbanization of mind in his New York milieu. Many have commented on the poet's engagement with the modern art scene as manifest in the lively tangle of New York galleries, museums, theaters, and concert halls he frequented.[2] Axel Nesme and Juliette Utard have connected philosophical and affective tendencies toward abstraction and disappointment with Stevens's interactions with the large, lonely city.

Still others have opened up parallel avenues of exploration to consider what we might call Stevens's subsequent suburbanization of mind, particularly in his engagement with Hartford. Stephanie Burt relates Stevens's ambulatory habits and his use of public transport to a suburban kinetics that "transforms the commuter's mood" in a manner that facilitates poetic perception (333), just as Peter Monacell links a mode of pastoralism in Stevens with suburban aesthetics. And in "Wallace Stevens and the American Park," I have argued that Stevens's city park rambles, both in Hartford's Elizabeth Park and across the New York public park system, inflect his presentation of nature as an organic artistic media that blurs the nature-culture divide while providing a setting for explorations of the failed civic ideals of park designers and city planners.

Given the sundry ways city environments shape Stevens's personal and poetic character, it is fitting that he turns to urban spaces in his ongoing study of how imagination and reality are to find equipoise in the modern moment. Stevens's cities often embody the weight of reality that overwhelms the imagination, which has poetic and even spiritual consequences. "Cities" in the plural is functional here. One does better to argue for different kinds of urbanism in Stevens, as, for example, his Boston is nothing like his Key West. One major, late-Romantic vein of Stevensian urbanism is city-as-anti-poetry, a dark urbanism that ultimately criticizes these built habitats for preventing meaningful contact with nature, with other people, and with an inspiring force often accessed through the prior two. In this mode, Stevens's urbanism manifests a slumbering bourgeois malaise endemic to modernity: "The feeling of piety is very dear to me," he notes in 1899, "I would sacrifice a great deal to be a Saint Augustine but modernity is so Chicagoan, so plain, so unmeditative" (*L* 32). Chicago is no Carthage, and Stevens here frets over a modernity that cannot offer an urbanism wicked enough to inspire epic conversion. With some luminous exceptions, Stevens often singles out Midwestern and New England cities as nodes of banality. He elsewhere complains of the disenchantment of American urbanism in similarly theological tones: "There are no saints at all in Hartford" (*L* 599). Boston suffers from a similar diminishment. In section VI of "New England Verses," titled "Boston without a Note-book," Stevens frames the city in its geological features and imagines its monuments as a response to a stifled mythic longing in its citizens: "Let us erect in the Basin a lofty fountain. / Suckled on ponds, the spirit craves a watery mountain" (*CPP* 87). Perhaps a reference to the large, classical Brewer Fountain in Boston Common, the "lofty fountain" hovers between harmony and dissonance with its watery, low-lying basin environs. The fountain tries to remediate a Bostonianism of the mind, in which the imagination has been nourished only by docile park ponds. The nigh-biblical command to order the waters feels gently but comically unfit when addressed to municipal water features, and the hungry spirits of the city dwellers appear more ravenous than can be appeased by a simple public fountain.

Similarly, in his ruminations on William Carlos Williams, Stevens diagnosed an urbanization of spirit that threatened the very creation of poetry: "But as a phase of a man's spirit, as a source of salvation, now, in the midst of a baffled generation, as one looks out of the window at Rutherford or Passaic, or as one walks the streets of New York, the anti-poetic acquires an extraordinary potency" (*CPP* 769). In "A Thought Revolved," the city becomes a dull hellscape for the poet who strolls among the cigar shops and restaurants. Rather than Augustine's cauldron of unholy loves, the poet is trapped in a grey urban box that defies his language. And, in keeping with Simmel's critique of urban scale, the very size of the city stifles poetic sensibility: "These are his infernal walls, / A space of stone, of inexplicable base / And peaks outsoaring possible adjectives" (*CPP* 171). The massive city becomes a vicious, incomprehensible container as its spatiality defies meaningful language, from its foundations to its heights. It is a "space," rather than a place, hard in its stony composition and notable only for the way in which it entombs both poet and language.

Urban architecture can also create a kind of shell that forecloses an aesthetic, poetic encounter with the elements, seasons, and organic life. In "Six Significant Landscapes," the lampposts, streets, and towers are cast as "knives," "chisels," and "mallets," all of which are impotent tools compared with the carving work of starlight through grape leaves (*CPP* 59). The cutting action of the urban hardware fails and threatens because it addresses itself to no clear media: what is it the lamppost must cut, the towers beat? The scale, moreover, is alarming, as the city apparatus seems capable of delivering only massive hacks and slashes. Streetlamps were early icons of the unsleeping city, facilitated by networks of modern power grids. While many celebrated them as a needed safety advancement, others lamented the imposition of artificial daylight that disrupted the rhythms of life. As in "Six Significant Landscapes," Stevens's streetlights most often fall into the latter category. For example, in "Metamorphosis," Stevens contrasts the season-defying technology of the streetlamps with the logic of nature, here realized in the seasonal shift into fall. While the "wind spells out / Sep – tem – ber," the world moves downward as the autumnal "leaves fall. / The rain falls" (*CPP* 238–39). Against this descending natural logic, the streetlamps are suspended on high: "those that have been hanged, / Dangling in an illogical / To and to and fro / Fro Niz – nil – imbo" (*CPP* 239). They are cold in an unnatural manner, as their disordered two-step rocking, to-and-to, fro-fro, slides into "Fro Niz," which scrambles the sonic form of "frozen." Similarly, while the wind sings the syllables of "September," the lights make a hash of letters that ultimately land the reader nowhere in the cityscape: the zero land of "nil," the seasonless borderland of "limbo." Unlike the nowhere of "The Snow Man," this eutopia offers not a Zen-like attentiveness to reality but a glaring distraction from it.

As with these lofted streetlights, cities allow Stevens to work along the y-axis whenever some of his urban pieces feature the tall structures associated with urbanism. As Eeckhout has compellingly demonstrated, even though Stevens comments on New York skyscrapers throughout his journals and early letters, they are remarkably absent in his verse at a time when poets like E. E. Cummings or Sara Teasdale were praising this ambitious new architecture (87–88). However, Eeckhout shows how Stevens inserts modern skylines in subtle ways – for instance, in the glowing silhouettes in "Carlos Among the Candles," where Carlos says of his six burning candles, "They are a city" (*CPP* 617). Urban skylines do make some other notable appearances as well, as in "The Common Life," where a church steeple and the stack of an electric plant create a minimalist "down-town frieze": "A black line beside a white line; / And the stack of the electric plant, / A black line drawn on flat air" (*CPP* 204). The divine and the mundane, the revelatory and the utilitarian, are indiscriminately reduced to the dashed outline of a planner's design. Provocatively, this oppressively thin frieze, all height and no depth, is chiseled on air, as the skyline makes the atmosphere a form of artistic media that participates in upholding both bare steeple and stack.

The flatness of this air is nonetheless disconcerting and is one of many instances where Stevens's cities prevent meaningful contact with the elements. As he once lamented, "I thought, on the train, how utterly we have forsaken the Earth, in the sense of excluding it from our thoughts. . . . Man is an affair of cities. His gardens + orchards + fields are mere scrapings" (*L* 73). When his human figures become only "an affair of cities," they lose vital contact with a more-than-human world. In "The Man Whose Pharynx Was Bad," an excluded wind prevents poets from their nighttime reveries: "The wind attendant on the solstices / Blows on the shutters of the metropoles, / Stirring no poet in his sleep" (*CPP* 81). "Metropoles" refers to the mother city of a colony or the largest, often most diverse urban center in a nation. These are uber cities that exist in a vague nowhere, perhaps American or perhaps European, because they are perfectly interchangeable, as global metropolitanism translates into a cultural flattening. As Stevens once reflected, "Cities, I imagine, are more or less alike the world over" (*L* 127). Here, the magically sibilant "solstices" counter the "metropoles" that are shuttered against them. Poets are sealed off from fresh air, inspiration, and the lunar shift of seasons in their city garrets, in whatever city they find themselves.

In this negative mode, Stevens's cities induce the kind of profound isolation that Simmel linked with the effect of living in massively crowded locations. As the poet ruminated in a 1909 letter to Elsie, "Such numbers of men degrade Man. The *teeming* streets make Man a nuisance – a vulgarity, and it is impossible to see his dignity" (*L* 141). The tension between the suffering individual and the teeming masses often has a distinctively urban character in Stevens, as we notice in "Loneliness in Jersey City," where the speaker is reduced to the apartment number associated with his singular window in a high-rise. From 1917 through the 1940s, Jersey City was a booming dock city swelling with an influx of immigrant laborers, connected to Manhattan via underground trains. Stevens's Jersey City is nonetheless eerily vacant: "My window is twenty-nine three / And plenty of window for me. / The steeples are empty and so are the people, / There's nothing whatever to see" (*CPP* 191). The merciless sing-song rhyme traps the speaker in an equally claustrophobic glass house that is utterly and uselessly transparent to unfolding absences. Plentitude here testifies to the bizarre placelessness of urban dwelling: any window is plenty when there's "nothing whatever to see," even in one's neighbors, and the speaker seems to have naturalized himself to this literal point of view. Once again, Stevens's dark urbanism is a desacralized one, as God and his bells have vacated the steeples, which the poem casts as a direct consequence of urban indoor seclusion. When "The people grow out of the weather; / The gods grow out of the people" (*CPP* 191): cities become secular when the people lose immediate contact with their climate.

Without a guiding myth or spiritual bearings, Stevens's urban crowds become tragically malleable in the hands of the city's shaping pressure, as when Bostonians are utterly compelled by the "Scaffolds and derricks" that impose their will upon them in "New England Verses" (*CPP* 88). And yet, at other moments, cities fail to discipline their unruly inhabitants, becoming instead the theater for revolution. In playing with these extremes, Stevens lays bare a core concern for urban planners and designers: to what degree does urban architecture shape the public's behavior? Early planners in the City Beautiful Movement believed that the passive reception of well-ordered city environments would infuse middle-class comportment and civic virtue into an increasingly heterogenous immigrant population, and many American cities were designed (or redesigned) based on this philosophy. As I have argued elsewhere, Stevens is equally alarmed by the prospect of success and failure for this spatial determinism.[3] His urban crowds either lose their vigor under the persuasive power of their surroundings or move as an aggregate automaton against it, as we see in his long poem "Owl's Clover," which offers an extended exploration of the compelling force of urban architecture on its inhabitants while also considering how art can best address this population. Stevens sets "Owl's Clover" in Brooklyn's sprawling Prospect Park, a space that made visible the crisis of homelessness during the Great Depression, as did countless American parks at the time. In his rebuttal of the Marxist critic Stanley Burnshaw, he presents the masses destroying the effete classical park sculptures that brought them no consolation in their need, as they tear down the "columns intercrossed, / White slapped on white" and behead the statuary (*CPP* 572). However, in the later section "A Duck for Dinner," the Bulgar argues that the park in fact creates a sheeplike docility in the urban public, to the point of forestalling any political uprising: "Apocalypse was not contrived for parks" when the public "keep[s] to the paths of the skeleton architect" and are lulled by the "sheep-like falling-in of distances" in the park's pastoral architecture (*CPP* 583–84). Against these alternately revolutionary or enervated masses, Stevens juxtaposes another urban figure, a solitary woman experiencing homelessness, as a reminder of the failures of urban utopianism, whether of the Marxist or City Beautiful variety. This woman becomes the intimate audience to whom the artist must address his work, since the park's equestrian statuary is too frothy to speak to her. It is her kind of city-crushed imagination that most needs the enlivening work of the artist even as it presents the greatest challenges to the art's reception. Remarkably, here Stevens casts the modern audience as a distinctively urban one. And the city environment helps artists to address a wider public craving the therapeutic intervention of their imaginative works, whether a bad sculptor or an excellent poet.

As with his hope for a "garlanded . . . way" in the city habitat of Prospect Park (*CPP* 588), Stevens occasionally imagines a positive urbanism as well. The city becomes a site where the imagination might stretch, often in its lush dusk or moonlit guises, as it does for the poet at nightfall in "Owl's Clover" or the speaker in "The Idea of Order at Key West." In Stevens's more optimistic moments, cities can facilitate poetic creation and contact with the more-than-human world – for instance, in several city park poems like "Vacancy in the Park," "Nuns Painting Water-Lilies," "Tea," and the Elizabeth Park setting embedded in "Notes Toward a Supreme Fiction." These cityscapes are often presented as works of visual art that undermine the nature-culture divide on which his pessimistic urbanism is prefaced. "Of Hartford in a Purple Light" captures this pivot between a utilitarian urbanism and a feminized, aesthetic, organic urbanism. The "light masculine" view of the daytime city nakedly delineates "the town, the river, the railroad" but ultimately gives way as the sunset "sets purple round." These "lights feminine" recast the city into a melting impressionism of "the spray / Of the ocean, ever-freshening, / On the irised hunks, the stone bouquet." Hartford is both floral still life and fancifully coastal habitat. Seen under "this purple, this parasol," the city becomes a violet botanical arrangement that blurs with the lively ocean on its distant permeable border (*CPP* 208).

A similar magic is cast in Stevens's rendering of an actual coastal city, Key West. Arguably, almost no city character is felt at all in "The Idea of Order at Key West." However, the urban tag in the title prevents the ocean setting from becoming merely mythic and unmoored in the early stanzas: we know we are in Florida on a beach in a well-known tourist resort. Indeed, whatever idea of order the poem presents, Stevens ultimately circumscribes it "at Key West," as the title insists on an abstraction with emphatically local and urban grounding. By the time Stevens was frequenting the Casa Marina hotel in Key West, the city was thriving thanks to a booming tourism industry but also maintained its character as a busy Floridian port and fishing center, as his speaker notes "the glassy lights, / The lights in the fishing boats at anchor there" (*CPP* 106). Many critics have commented on the aesthetic order that emanates from the singer, the speaker, and even Ramon Fernandez in his "rage" for political order. However, there is yet another node of order that ultimately "Mastered the night": the lights themselves. The grammar that begins the sixth stanza, when trimmed of its clauses, ultimately asks "Why ... the glassy lights ... Mastered the night" in the silence after the song (*CPP* 106). If the woman's music makes a world, so too do the glassy lights from the marinas and docks where veiled fishermen are anchored. The agency of the verb adheres to these non-human extensions of the city's electrical grid and the lights of the boats bobbing beyond them. Just as Hartford bled into the distant ocean spray, the twinkling extension of urban infrastructure, transportation, economy, and community quietly blurs into the watery field of ocean-as-night-as-cosmos. Unlike the mess of illogical streetlights in "Six Significant Landscapes," these lights enchant the darkness with the order *of*, not simply at, Key West.

Like the real cities that inspired him, Stevens's urban poetics has a nearly inexhaustible number of boulevards and alleyways left to explore. For example, this survey has intentionally neglected Stevens's British and European city centers, which often function as a chronotope for past moments in Western art and philosophy while doubling in their modern guise as the vacationer's spot of choice. The current chapter also overlooks Stevens's wholly imaginative cities, like the many capitols that spatialize the mind at its height, let alone the non-Western court cultures, with their temples and palaces, that Stevens adored, all of which were prefaced on earlier modes of urbanization. Whether in their anti-poetic or enchanting costuming, Stevens's cities invite his readers into deeper acts of contemplative dwelling. In the words of "To an Old Philosopher in Rome": "The life of the city never lets go, nor do you / Ever want it to" (*CPP* 434).

Notes

1 City plans predate the twentieth century, but this genealogy presents the roots of the contemporary disciplines we call urban studies and planning. For a long history of urban planning, see Bussell.
2 For more on Stevens and the New York art scene, see Costello; for an exploration of Stevens and music in a New York context, see Goldfarb; and for a wider study of Stevens's engagement with New York cultural institutions, see also Lensing.
3 See my "Wallace Stevens and the American Public Park" for an extended study of Stevens's portrayal of Prospect Park in "Owl's Clover."

WORKS CITED

Burt, Stephanie. "Wallace Stevens: Where He Lived." *ELH*, vol. 77, no. 2, Summer 2010, pp. 325–52.
Bussell, Mirle Rabinowitz. *History of Urban Planning and Design*. Cognella Academic Publishing, 2012.
Costello, Bonnie. "'My Head Full of Strange Pictures': Stevens in the New York Galleries." *Wallace Stevens, New York, and Modernism*, edited by Goldfarb and Eeckhout, pp. 37–53.
Daniel, Julia E. "Urbanism." *A Companion to Modernist Poetry*, edited by Gail McDonald and David E. Chinitz, Wiley Blackwell, 2014, pp. 23–33.
"Wallace Stevens and the American Park." *Building Natures: Modern American Poetry, City Planning, and Landscape Architecture*, U of Virginia P, 2017, pp. 50–86.
Eeckhout, Bart. "The Invisible Skyscraper: Stevens and Urban Architecture." *Wallace Stevens, New York, and Modernism*, edited by Goldfarb and Eeckhout, pp. 85–104.

Goldfarb, Lisa. "'The Whispering of Innumerable Responsive Spirits': Stevens' New York Music." *Wallace Stevens, New York, and Modernism*, edited by Goldfarb and Eeckhout, pp. 54–70.

Goldfarb, Lisa, and Bart Eeckhout. "Introduction: Back at the Waldorf?" *Wallace Stevens, New York, and Modernism*, edited by Goldfarb and Eeckhout, pp. 1–20.

editors. *Wallace Stevens, New York, and Modernism*. Routledge, 2012.

Lensing, George S. "Stevens and New York: The Long Gestation." *Wallace Stevens, New York, and Modernism*, edited by Goldfarb and Eeckhout, pp. 21–36.

Monacell, Peter. "In the American Grid: Modern Poetry and the Suburbs." *Journal of Modern Literature*, vol. 35, no. 1, Oct. 2011, pp. 122–42.

Nesme, Axel. "On Stevensian Transitoriness." *Wallace Stevens, New York, and Modernism*, edited by Goldfarb and Eeckhout, pp. 105–20.

Pike, Burton. *The Image of the City in Modern Literature*. Princeton UP, 1983.

Rotella, Carlo. "Urban Literature: A User's Guide." *Journal of Urban History*, vol. 44, no. 4, Sept. 2017, pp. 797–805.

Simmel, Georg. "The Metropolis and Mental Life." *The Sociology of Georg Simmel*, translated by Kurt H. Wolff, Free Press, 1950, pp. 409–24.

Stevens, Wallace. *Letters of Wallace Stevens*. Edited by Holly Stevens, U of California P, 1996.

Wallace Stevens: Collected Poetry and Prose. Edited by Frank Kermode and Joan Richardson, Library of America, 1997.

Utard, Juliette. "'Unless New York Is Cocos': Stevens, New York, and the Discourse of Disappointment." *Wallace Stevens, New York, and Modernism*, edited by Goldfarb and Eeckhout, pp. 133–43.

Weinstein, Arnold. "Fragment and Form in the City of Modernism." *The Cambridge Companion to the City in Literature*, edited by Kevin R. McNamara, Cambridge UP, 2014, pp. 138–52.

CHAPTER 9

Queer Studies

Bart Eeckhout

Part of the continuing appeal of queer studies is that it allows for historical reconsiderations of sexuality without requiring a fixation on identity categories or conclusive empirical evidence. On the face of it, the biographical facts about Wallace Stevens's sexuality are fairly straightforward. The first love of his adult life appears to have been a lively and intelligent young woman named Sybil Gage, whom he was somehow too diffident to court very actively. After spending a few years in New York as a lonely bachelor, he then fell in love with Elsie Kachel, a beautiful eighteen-year-old from his hometown, with whom he started on a long courtship and engagement. The marriage in 1909 quickly led to mutual disappointment, yet the couple stayed together and eventually a daughter, Holly, was born in 1924. During the biographical interviews Peter Brazeau conducted in the 1970s or in later research, no extramarital affairs were ever suggested. Stevens was, it would appear, a married straight man largely deprived of a satisfying love life. His name is nowhere to be found in *The Cambridge Companion to American Gay and Lesbian Literature*.[1]

And yet. There will be rumors, even about (or precisely about?) a man with as private and sexually uneventful a life as Stevens seems to have led. For a long time, such rumors had no place in responsible scholarship. But at least one pioneer of queer studies, Henry Abelove, has suggested there might be some value in attending to what he calls, borrowing a phrase with which Allen Ginsberg memorialized Frank O'Hara, "deep gossip" (xi). If gossip, as Abelove contends, involves "illicit speculation," it has historically nevertheless been "an indispensable resource for those who are in any sense or measure disempowered, . . . and it is deep whenever it circulates in subterranean ways and touches on matters hard to grasp" (xii). The gossip I've personally heard about Stevens's sexual orientation over the years would still remain unmentioned here if on one occasion a major queer writer hadn't also recorded it in print. In an essay on Hart Crane from the early 1990s, the novelist and cultural critic Samuel R. Delany notes

123

laconically, "after Eliot, Pound, and Yeats, the only poet of his era who precedes Crane in reputation is Wallace Stevens – another male homosexual poet" (199).

 While there is little point in continuing down the road of unverifiable gossip, there may be some value in attempting to redraw a number of circles around Stevens. What happens when, with the knowledge and insights gained from queer studies and other relevant scholarship, we try to resituate Stevens not only within the aesthetic circles that may be drawn around his work but also and especially within the social circles in which he moved during his lifetime, and the poetic circles of those who have been attracted to his writings? In an attempt to further diversify the types of scholarship presented in this volume, my contribution will tilt more toward the biographical than other chapters do. From the new modernist studies, my investigation derives an interest in social networks at the expense of a narrow focus on self-reliant individuals; from queer studies, it borrows a fundamentally querying spirit about sexual identities and desires.

Queer Genealogies

Stevens's biography and poetics are worth revisiting as the lives of those who mattered to him have come into sharper focus. Because of research conducted in the context of queer studies and by historians and biographers more generally, a twenty-first-century revision of Stevens in relation to questions of sexuality is almost inevitable. To undertake such a revision, we might start by distinguishing among precursors, contemporaries, and heirs. As soon as we do so, it seems that the least effective level may be that of the poet's precursors. There is nothing particularly new to tracing aesthetic genealogies from Stevens back to the fin-de-siècle Aestheticists Walter Pater and Oscar Wilde; the French Symbolists Arthur Rimbaud and Paul Verlaine; or some of the great American writers of the nineteenth century, Walt Whitman, Emily Dickinson, and Henry James. As the submerged queer dimensions of these writers' heritage have been gradually brought to light, they have barely altered the critical perception of Stevens's relation to them.

To be sure, already in the 1980s, the first attempts were made to establish significant queer genealogies. In his first book on Stevens, Glen MacLeod showed that "Le Monocle de Mon Oncle" has an insufficiently acknowledged homosexual context. During the 1910s, Stevens was close to the "Patagonians," a quartet of writers that included Carl Van Vechten and for whom the British 1890s were the chief inspiration (*Stevens and Company* 70, 106). Wilde was their literary hero, and Stevens appears to have followed suit in "Le Monocle" by including a series of allusions to Wilde (74). Although scholars have come to see the Wildean dandy of "Le Monocle" as a persona Stevens soon shied away from, Lee Edelman, writing only a few years after MacLeod, advised that we take another hard look at the poet "in terms of a fin-de-siècle aestheticism" and a "'decadence' inseparable from associations with sexual irregularity" (36). Edelman reminded us that different early reviewers associated Stevens's poetry with Aubrey Beardsley, Marcel Proust, and Ronald Firbank, and that as late as 1953, William Empson kept suggesting that "growing up in the hey-day of Oscar Wilde, [Stevens] was perhaps more influenced by him than by Whitman" (qtd. in Edelman 36).

As Empson's cautious formulation signals, however, the pursuit of such queer genealogies might not always take us very far. Even though in recent years entire issues of *The Wallace Stevens Journal* have been devoted to a juxtaposition of Stevens with, respectively, James and Whitman, contributing experts in either case have felt little inclination to revisit the relation from a queer-studies perspective.[2] If anything, critics have become more and more wary of positing any strong influence exerted by precursors on Stevens, preferring instead to remain tentative about temperamental and aesthetic affinities.

Living among Unfathomable Men: The Examples of Santayana and Rodríguez Feo

Among the Patagonians, probably only Van Vechten slept around with men (he doesn't seem to have cared for translating this into a sexual identity). In George Chauncey's groundbreaking history of male homosexuality in early twentieth-century New York, Van Vechten is described as "a gay married man" who "played a key role in the 1910s in organizing Mabel Dodge Luhan's famous salons on lower Fifth Avenue, at which socialists and anarchists, Freudians and free-lovers, artists and activists debated the issues of the day" (232). In due course, Van Vechten developed a reputation for "the gay, artistic, and theater circles around" him (175). Stevens's friendship with the man could easily be dismissed as being of marginal importance if it weren't for the fact that it seems to have been part of a pattern in his life.

Indeed, if we had better be careful about overestimating queer genealogies that link Stevens with his precursors, the information that has emerged on his circle of personal friends does prompt some serious reconsideration. In addition to Van Vechten, Stevens is well known for his friendships with the poet and philosopher George Santayana (while a student at Harvard); two lifelong friends from his Harvard days, Witter Bynner and Pitts Sanborn; the shady pseudonymous publisher Ronald Lane Latimer during the 1930s; the museum director of the Wadsworth Atheneum, A. Everett Austin Jr., who was like a second father to Holly; the young Cuban literatus José Rodríguez Feo, whose epistolary exchange with Stevens is so colorful that it was published in a separate edition; and the Irish poet and museum director Thomas McGreevy, who vied with Rodríguez Feo for the role of Stevens's all-time favorite correspondent. Yet, it has only gradually been established that all of these men were either gay or bisexual.

In and of itself, such a constellation doesn't allow us to second-guess Stevens's own sexual preferences. It barely allows us even to conclude that he was, in today's terms, more gay-friendly than we might have assumed from a man who never showed a strong commitment to emancipatory social movements. What it does remind us of, however, is the value of the central concept launched by Eve Kosofsky Sedgwick in her first book, *Between Men: English Literature and Male Homosocial Desire*. If homosexuality has a doubtful place in Stevens's libidinal fantasies (let alone sexual practices), there should be no hesitancy about affirming the powerful *homosociality* that structured his life in a still heavily patriarchal society – from his student days at an all-male university to his life as a lawyer and businessman, down to his largely male network of correspondents; his similarly gendered interest in artists; his membership in gentlemen's clubs like the St. Nicholas Society; and his habitual way of referring to humankind, in prose as in poetry, through the generic use of "man" and "men." Sedgwick's critical inquiries have interestingly complicated our understanding of such historical relations among men because, as that other founding figure of queer theory, Judith Butler, notes, she didn't argue "that the homosocial bond comes at the expense of the heterosexual, but that the homosocial (distinct from the homosexual) is articulated precisely through the heterosexual." Still according to Butler, this "has had far-reaching consequences for the thinking of both heterosexuality and homosexuality," since Sedgwick's analysis has had a "confounding" effect on "the identificatory positions" for every party involved (138).

Complications of identification have been at the heart of queer studies ever since. If we wanted to unpack Stevens's shifting attitudes to the unstable nexus of homosociality, homosexuality, and heterosexuality, we would in fact have to return to another staple text from queer theory as well, David M. Halperin's "How to Do the History of Male Homosexuality." Only a careful application of Halperin's historical framework would allow us to trace the precise cultural effects on Stevens of the entire range of "prehomosexual discourses, practices, categories, patterns, or models" of same-sex desire identified by Halperin, because all of these lingered during Stevens's lifetime and went into his thinking – from the notion of effeminacy to the Platonic idealization of male friendship and love or the idea of inversion (264). This kind of complex genealogical investigation hasn't been undertaken yet for Stevens with any real systematicity.

To demonstrate some of the opportunities for queering our perspective on Stevens's homosocial relations, I will limit myself here to a succinct consideration of two case studies from either end of his adult life: his friendships with Santayana and Rodríguez Feo. Every Stevens scholar knows that during Stevens's days as an undergraduate student at Harvard, he and Santayana were sufficiently interested in each other to seek out each other for private conversation (despite Stevens not taking any classes with the philosopher); that they wrote sonnets for each other (as a form of aesthetic debate); and that late in life Stevens cherished these memories so much that he composed a moving imaginary portrait, "To an Old Philosopher in Rome." But it is nearly impossible to pinpoint the extent to which the two writers' mutual appreciation channeled any erotic desires. The critical consensus today is that Santayana was gay, though what biographers and historians have revealed is a typically oblique, late-Victorian story. On the one hand, we now know that the philosopher's bachelordom and aestheticist literary inclinations were frowned upon by the university administration; as a result, the man Stevens engaged with wasn't a professor but a mere instructor. On the other, by his own later admission, Santayana came to realize his sexual orientation only retroactively, years after he had left Harvard; his autobiography limits itself to rhapsodic evocations of male friendship typical of one of those prehomosexual traditions identified by Halperin.[3]

Considering the particular homosocial environment in which Santayana and Stevens befriended each other – one that validated the exchange of literary enthusiasm and intellectual affection through a Socratic mentor-student dialogue – subsequent investigations have had to assume the form not of further, probably fruitless, biographical sleuthing but of speculation about which of Santayana's published ideas might have oriented Stevens's worldview in a queer direction. This is what David Jarraway has done in the most elaborate injection of queer studies into Stevens criticism so far, his 2015 book *Wallace Stevens among Others*. On and off there, Jarraway argues for Stevens as something of an identitarian skeptic, with Santayana serving as one of his main sources of inspiration. To Jarraway, "it was the 'both sides and neither' aspect of [Santayana's] identity that insistently won Stevens's attention" – the "categorical ambiguity" that he both embodied and stimulated (7). Quoting from Ross Posnock's study of William and Henry James, in which Posnock establishes a connection between Henry James's and Santayana's ideas on androgyny, Jarraway inserts Stevens into a triangle with these two writers: "Relaxing all categorical ascriptions of gender like heterosexual and homosexual, a man of feeling like Santayana perhaps taught Stevens the greater virtue of androgyny as 'more a dimension of sensibility and psychic economy than of actual behavior,' and thereby sensitized Stevens, and writers like him, 'to a variety of possibilities and options . . .'" (62). Further embroidering upon the connection, Jarraway proposes that "the point of the erotic poetics in both Santayana and Stevens is to establish a necessary *ambivalence* about gender identity" – an ambivalence undercutting both heteronormative thinking and later critical attempts at "gay-affirmative" interpretation (124–25). What Stevens seems to have taken away from his Harvard mentor, above all else, was the value of relinquishing his cognitive grasp. "To be irrational and unintelligible is the character proper to existence," proclaimed Santayana (qtd. in Jarraway 112). Stevens conspicuously paid tribute to this idea in "To an Old Philosopher" by surrounding Santayana with "Unintelligible" singing and having him ponder the world "in the presence of the extreme / Of the unknown" (*CPP* 432).

Stevens's decision to compose a tribute to his dying mentor is itself indissociable from the friendship he struck up with Rodríguez Feo during the final decade of his life. As Beverly Coyle and Al Filreis note in their introduction to *Secretaries of the Moon: The Letters of Wallace Stevens and José Rodríguez Feo*, it was, in fact, "José's affinity with George Santayana's insights into matters North and South" that "revived Stevens' interest in Santayana after four decades," so much so that the letters between the two men "have Santayana very much as their source" (17, 21). The critical attention to Rodríguez Feo as Stevens's most valued young friend nevertheless offers a somewhat different case history in that it illustrates how sensitive biographical work about the sexual lives of surviving people may be when it is conducted in a transnational context and against a background of quickly shifting cultural values and attitudes. Writing in the middle of the 1980s, at a time when gay men in the United States were in dire need of public acknowledgment and solidarity, Coyle and Filreis would have undoubtedly favored being transparent about the Cuban's homosexuality. But Rodríguez Feo was still alive (he died in 1993), living in Havana as a celebrated man of letters, one of the great patrons of Cuban culture and a supporter of Fidel Castro – not in a position, therefore, to be outed by North American critics with their own domestic political agendas. In the end, the editors chose to remain so coy that their introduction, for all its intellectual brilliance, today reads like a narrative from the age of the closet. We are told, most allegorically, that Stevens's Cuban friend was "the author of a revealing prose-poem entitled 'The Closed Door'" (Coyle and Filreis 22) – though *what* had been revealed by it remained for everyone to guess – and that the young man recognized in the withdrawn poet from Hartford someone who likewise shut doors, not only to his home (which Rodríguez Feo was never allowed into) but also within it (to retreat from wife and daughter). We are given a number of hints that, cumulatively, gay readers at the time might have picked up on – selected quotations from Rodríguez Feo in which he wistfully notes, "I write, read and frequent the company of a few and selected amigos. I am as lonely as ever" (qtd. on 5), or in which he mentions the "suffering and misery" he endures, forcing him to "remain platonic" (qtd. on 6). We hear of his attempt to open up about his fatherlessness, and his complaint, channeled through a discussion of Henry James, about the sexlessness of life at Princeton and the fate of bachelors (24, 27). In his written responses, Stevens preferred to ignore such hints of desired intimacy. Early on, he described his Cuban correspondent to Henry Church by calling him a "platonic young intellectual" who lived "like the perpetual reader, without sex or politics" (*L* 508), and on one painful later occasion, he dismissed his young friend's personal worries by telling him he should eventually get married and find a regular job (Coyle and Filreis 25).

Still, Rodríguez Feo afterward remembered his handful of meetings with Stevens – socially eased by heavy drinking on either side – with pleasure, insisting that Stevens had been "very warm" to him (qtd. in Coyle and Filreis 11). Here the case history may be extended by the interview he gave in 1978 to Peter Brazeau in Havana. Though Brazeau, too, was gay, the time and circumstances again weren't ripe to address sexual issues up front. And so Rodríguez Feo's recollections in *Parts of a World* – Brazeau's oral biography of Stevens – offer another instance of closeted indirection, with the Cuban reporting how he had built up a "romantic idea" of Stevens before meeting him (Brazeau 138); that Stevens struck him as a "hedonist" who was un-American inasmuch as he knew how to relish "anything that is joyful for itself – for instance, sex" (140); that Stevens's love of Florida and Havana was "something sensuous" that had to do with "what he felt in the skin" (141); how "very evident" it should be that Stevens "was, inside, something very different from the outside" (141); and that Stevens must have enjoyed José because he was "a fresh young man" (144). "I never talked about my amorous life," Rodríguez Feo adds, "so I think he got the impression I was more or less of an asexual sort of Platonist. Doesn't he say in one of his letters, a little bee going from flower to flower to acquire a lot of knowledge on literary matters?" (142).

In the four poems this "little bee" inspired, Stevens, unsurprisingly, wouldn't address amorous issues either. He might perhaps still be flirting with camp imagery when addressing Rodríguez Feo as "one of the secretaries of the moon, / The queen of ignorance" (*CPP* 292), yet his attention appears to have been much more clearly on revisiting Santayana's ideas. If we wish to pry into "man's interior world," Stevens tells his Cuban friend in "A Word with José Rodríguez-Feo," we shouldn't strive to find any fixed identities (sexual, ethnic, or other) but be willing "To pick up relaxations of the known" (*CPP* 293). The concluding lines of "The Novel" similarly push back against the wish for conceptual mastery: "one trembles to be so understood," Stevens writes, "as if to know became / The fatality of seeing things too well" (*CPP* 392).

Poetic indirections of this sort are precisely why Eric Keenaghan in *Queering Cold War Poetry* has been able to enlist Stevens as a major source of inspiration for "a transnational poetic line interested in elaborating ethics of vulnerability," to which Stevens's "poetic rethinking of identity and difference" contributed – not quite intentionally, we may presume – "a kind of critical queerness" (29). Keenaghan shows how in his letters to Rodríguez Feo, Stevens repeatedly "rankled at any compulsory group identification" and connects this in turn to the "unfamiliar and defamiliarizing" quality of his modernist poetics (38). (His recycling of the established critical language of "defamiliarization" reminds us that a queering of family structures may in fact be an essential component of modernist writing.) What Stevens seems to have looked for in his friendship with the young José, despite his famous protestation that "Cuba should be full of Cuban things" (*L* 495), was an opportunity for "unfixing" his own identity (Keenaghan 39). In this respect, Keenaghan hints at the possible relevance of José Esteban Muñoz's concept of *disidentification* for a reading of Stevens (43). Instead of pitting counter-identifications against normative identities, Muñoz indeed proposes a "third mode of dealing with dominant ideology, one that neither opts to assimilate within such a structure nor strictly opposes it; rather, disidentification is a strategy that works on and against dominant ideology" by trying to "transform a cultural logic from within" (11). Although Stevens during his friendship with Rodríguez Feo was very far from seeking to enact the kinds of social change dreamed up by Muñoz in his study of queer performance artists of color, Stevens's "queer assertion of humanity" has genealogical links with it for those who care to pursue them (*CPP* 445).

Queering a Fictive Stevens: The Examples of Merrill and Howard

Just as our understanding of the queer circles we may draw around the biographical Stevens has changed, we have needed the lengthening perspective of time and additional scholarship to see a queer pattern emerge among younger writers gravitating toward his poetry. This lineage may be taken to start with Hart Crane and Elizabeth Bishop, continuing with a range of younger poets who began to write by the end of Stevens's life (from James Merrill, Adrienne Rich, and José Lezama Lima to the New York School poets Frank O'Hara, John Ashbery, and James Schuyler), and on to several later writers, including Robert Duncan, Tennessee Williams, Richard Howard, Mark Doty, Rafael Campo, Michael Cunningham, and Alison Bechdel.[4]

Once more, a list of this kind doesn't build an argument; more elaborate study would be needed to characterize Stevens's individual appeal to each of these writers. For the current bird's-eye exploration, I will limit myself again to two case studies. Collectively, these suggest that the combined image of a very private citizen who in his poetry nevertheless emerged as the great champion of the resilient imagination has been particularly appealing to queer writers. To illustrate this briefly, James Merrill might serve as a transitional example – transitional because the twenty-eight-year-old Merrill met Stevens once, and not on the least of occasions: he was invited to sit at the table of honor when Alfred Knopf threw a gala luncheon for Stevens's seventy-fifth birthday and the simultaneous publication of *The Collected Poems* (Hammer 188). The meeting gave rise to one of those Stevensian elliptical comments afterward that acquire different overtones now that Merrill's sexuality is no longer a secret and we've also become aware of the sexuality of the letter's addressee, Witter Bynner. Reporting to Bynner two months after the celebration, Stevens notably singled out Merrill's presence in terms that are strikingly inclusive: "There were a lot of people there whom you would have enjoyed quite as much as I did, including young James Merrill, who is about the age which you and I were when we were in New York" (*L* 859). The coded quality and desire to bond seem hard to miss for an informed reader today, but these were still the 1950s, when speech that went in and out of the closet avoided explicitness.

Merrill, for his part, had become an admirer of Stevens several years earlier. As Langdon Hammer explains in his magnificent biography, the admiration began during Merrill's undergraduate days at Amherst. There, "The Noble Rider and the Sound of Words," the 1942 essay "in which Stevens speaks of the imagination pressing back against the brute 'pressure of reality,' became a touchstone text for Jimmy, providing a way to understand poetry's relation to history and politics" (108). Hammer's terms "history and politics" are sufficiently capacious to allow for the hypothesis that the "pressure of reality" so eloquently resisted by Stevens (*CPP* 665) must have included, for Merrill, the homophobic culture against which he needed to press back by asserting his proper aesthetic imagination. In the poetry he held up as an example, moreover, Stevens appeared ready to tutor an eagerly listening "ephebe," since he sported that Wildean, homoerotic image at the outset of "Notes Toward a Supreme Fiction" (*CPP* 329) – the main poem through which Merrill came to know Stevens's verse as an undergraduate (Hammer 108).

From a gossipy letter written by Merrill the day after Stevens's birthday party, we learn that the fêted poet showed up as a dandy in green shirt and gaudy tie, was joined at the central table by W. H. Auden as well, and gave a speech that made Carl Van Vechten blush.[5] The scene sounds almost as queer and improbable as Merrill's posthumous meetings with Stevens, for less than a year after the party and barely a month after the poet's death, Merrill and his lover David Jackson got in touch with the deceased during one of their séances. Stevens reported that he now wrote "poems on cloud" all day and compared it to a blackboard "always being erased after each word so I have the charming experience of completely private poetry" (qtd. in Hammer 204). After some compulsory shoptalk about poetry, Stevens "switched topics: 'E. tells me you are all quite homosexual. (Yes.) Interesting. So has been a good number of my oldest friends. . . . I was only able to experiment with 2 men. At 17 + 21,' Stevens confided, but he had all but forgotten these long-ago 'experiments'" (Hammer 204). Such appears to have been the deep – or should we say, in this case, high? – gossip Merrill craved, and the posthumous Stevens didn't seem to mind providing it.

Hammer proposes that, ultimately, what Merrill found in Stevens was a poet who sanctioned the artistic desire to submit "to a fiction" (612). In the speculative queer mode I'm pursuing here, one might thus draw a line from his work to that of Richard Howard. When Howard in 1987 composed "Even in Paris," his thirty-page epistolary-narrative poem recounting a surprise meeting with Stevens in Paris during the Christmas season of 1952–53, he seems to have been similarly interested in imagining the dead writer as a poetic guardian angel who affirmed the necessity of believing "in a fiction, which you know to be a fiction, there being nothing else" (*CPP* 903). And so, in the middle of the emerging AIDS crisis, when so many gay friends around him were dying (as would Merrill before long), Howard turned to the phantom ghost of Stevens to imagine him continuing the poetic conversation in ways that might offer a measure of aesthetic consolation.[6] This Stevens arose from the grave to share a collection of rather queer aphoristic proclamations in the tradition of Wildean paradox: "an attempt to escape self / is likely to be identical with / an attempt to discover it"; "I suppose I am one of those . . . / who can tell you at dusk what others deny by day"; "how hideous the happiness one wants, / how beautiful the misery one has!"; and, in an example of dizzying queer temporality, "The future of the past is never sure" (Howard 6, 11, 13, 23).

Together, the examples of Merrill and Howard suggest that at least some of Stevens's poetic heirs who have felt the need to resist the "pressure of reality" in their own lives have been drawn to the older poet as an artist who understood that the quest for an identity could be a very queer business indeed, depending fundamentally on the fictions one chose to carve out for oneself. Who, after all, was that poet mysteriously hiding behind the mask of Hoon and magisterially "descend[ing]" "in purple" through the "loneliest air"? Someone, apparently, with the mental strength to affirm "And there I found myself more truly and more strange," in a grammatical construction aptly twisted to enact the very queerness of the most truthful self-identification (*CPP* 51).

Coda

"One likes what one happens to like." It's one of those liberating Stevensian tautologies, tossed off as mere "Table Talk." "Life," after all, "is largely a thing / Of happens to like, not should" (*CPP* 566). We don't need to speculate retroactively on Stevens's forever private sexual feelings to understand how his biography and poetic legacy repay analysis also from a twenty-first-century queer-studies perspective. His distrust of established norms and fixed thinking was such that it may be extended readily into the realm of sexuality. As he proclaims in his "Adagia," "I don't think we should insist that the poet is normal or, for that matter, that anybody is" (*CPP* 906).

Notes

1 See Herring. In *The Gay and Lesbian Literary Heritage*, Stevens receives four fleeting mentions in discussions of aestheticism, transgressive writing, Santayana, and, oddly, the literary use of the figure of Sebastian (Summers 4, 582, 629, 650).
2 See, for both special issues, under MacLeod.
3 This brief sexual biography of Santayana has been assembled from two sources (Jarraway and Osvaldini) that in turn summarize several book-length studies of the man's life and writings.
4 For a discussion of Stevens's influence on the New York School poets, see Epstein's chapter in this volume and his book *Beautiful Enemies*.
5 Details derived from an as yet unpublished letter by Merrill to Claude Fredericks, dated October 3, 1954, in a transcript provided by Langdon Hammer to the author on October 24, 2018.
6 For more extended analyses of Howard's imagining of Stevens in "Even in Paris," see Longenbach 134–39 and my own "A Queer Visit to Paris."

WORKS CITED

Abelove, Henry. *Deep Gossip*. U of Minnesota P, 2003.
Brazeau, Peter. *Parts of a World: Wallace Stevens Remembered; An Oral Biography*. Random House, 1983.
Butler, Judith. *Undoing Gender*. Routledge, 2004.
Chauncey, George. *Gay New York: Gender, Urban Culture, and the Making of the Gay Male World, 1890–1940*. BasicBooks, 1994.
Coyle, Beverly, and Alan Filreis. Introduction. *Secretaries of the Moon: The Letters of Wallace Stevens and José Rodríguez Feo*, edited by Coyle and Filreis, Duke UP, 1986, pp. 1–31.
Delany, Samuel R. *Longer Views: Extended Essays*. Wesleyan UP, 1996.
Edelman, Lee. "Redeeming the Phallus: Wallace Stevens, Frank Lentricchia, and the Politics of (Hetero)Sexuality." *Engendering Men: The Question of Male Feminist Criticism*, edited by Joseph A. Boone and Michael Cadden, Routledge, 1990, pp. 36–52.
Eeckhout, Bart. "A Queer Visit to Paris: Richard Howard's Encounter with Stevens on French Soil." *Wallace Stevens, Poetry, and France: "Au pays de la métaphore,"* edited by Juliette Utard, Bart Eeckhout, and Lisa Goldfarb, Éditions Rue d'Ulm / Presses de l'École normale supérieure, 2017, pp. 97–110.
Epstein, Andrew. *Beautiful Enemies: Friendship and Postwar American Poetry*. Oxford UP, 2016.
Halperin, David M. "How to Do the History of Male Homosexuality." *The Routledge Queer Studies Reader*, edited by Donald E. Hall and Annamarie Jagose, with Andrea Bebell and Susan Potter, Routledge, 2013, pp. 262–86.

Hammer, Langdon. *James Merrill: Life and Art*. Alfred A. Knopf, 2015.

Herring, Scott, editor. *The Cambridge Companion to American Gay and Lesbian Literature*. Cambridge UP, 2015.

Howard, Richard. *No Traveller*. Alfred A. Knopf, 1989.

Jarraway, David R. *Wallace Stevens among Others: Diva-Dames, Deleuze, and American Culture*. McGill-Queen's UP, 2015.

Keenaghan, Eric. *Queering Cold War Poetry: Ethics of Vulnerability in Cuba and the United States*. Ohio State UP, 2009.

Longenbach, James. *Modern Poetry after Modernism*. Oxford UP, 1997.

MacLeod, Glen. *Wallace Stevens and Company: The Harmonium Years, 1913–1923*. UMI Research P, 1983.

⸻, editor. *Wallace Stevens and Henry James*. Spec. issue of *The Wallace Stevens Journal*, vol. 34, no. 1, Spring 2010.

⸻, editor. *Wallace Stevens and Walt Whitman*. Spec. issue of *The Wallace Stevens Journal*, vol. 40, no. 1, Spring 2016.

Muñoz, José Esteban. *Disidentifications: Queers of Color and the Performance of Politics*. U of Minnesota P, 1999.

Osvaldini. "George Santayana." *iCalShare*, 27 Feb. 2010, icalshare.com/calendars/4093/events/1200996#.

Posnock, Ross. *The Trial of Curiosity: Henry James, William James, and the Challenge of Modernity*. Oxford UP, 1991.

Sedgwick, Eve Kosofsky. *Between Men: English Literature and Male Homosocial Desire*. Columbia UP, 1985.

Stevens, Wallace. *Letters of Wallace Stevens*. Edited by Holly Stevens, U of California P, 1996.

⸻. *Wallace Stevens: Collected Poetry and Prose*. Edited by Frank Kermode and Joan Richardson, Library of America, 1997.

Summers, Claude J., editor. *The Gay and Lesbian Literary Heritage: A Reader's Companion to the Writers and Their Works, from Antiquity to the Present*. Henry Holt and Company, 1995.

CHAPTER 10

Intersectional Studies

Lisa M. Steinman

Intersectional studies is not a uniformly defined discipline. Moreover, it is in some ways difficult to discuss how critics of Wallace Stevens's work have used or might use the various critical strategies associated with the term "intersectionality" as it is currently, if variously, understood. Kimberlé Williams Crenshaw, an activist and law professor, brought the word into prominence in her 1989 article "Demarginalizing the Intersection of Race and Sex," in which she analyzed a 1976 employment lawsuit – *DeGraffenreid* v. *General Motors* – brought against General Motors St. Louis by a group of Black women. General Motors won that lawsuit by showing that they had hired Black men and white women; the Civil Rights Act of 1964 did not allow the court to examine a combined claim of race and sex discrimination. That is, race discrimination and sex discrimination were legally separate rather than interlocking categories. Attending to how race and gender combined should form a distinct category, Crenshaw used the word "intersectional."

The term thus first suggested a way of addressing a legal issue and was not concerned with literary analyses. By 2015, however, the term had taken on a life of its own, appearing in the *Oxford English Dictionary*, which noted that "intersectionality" was a term used primarily in sociology (citing three sources beginning with Crenshaw's article); the entry defines the word as follows: "The interconnected nature of social categorizations such as race, class, and gender, regarded as creating overlapping and inter-dependent systems of discrimination or disadvantage; a theoretical approach based on such a premise." Within a few years, the word was being used even more broadly in the popular press in journals like *Vox, The Denver Post,* and *The Boston Review* – the latter two cited in the *Merriam-Webster Dictionary* by 2019 – as well as in classes and papers on critical race theory and critical social theory. As used in the popular press, to cite the first sentence of Eleanor Robertson's 2017 article "Intersectional – what? Feminism's problem with jargon is that any idiot can pick it up and have a go": "Nobody knows what intersectionality means." Robertson goes on to quote Crenshaw herself saying that she has been "amazed at how [the term 'intersectionality'] gets over- and under-used," despite her own and others' recent attempts to define a more rigorous theory of intersectionality within legal and sociological thinking, and to reaffirm intersectionality's association with social justice, without denying the ways in which since the 1990s a "copious body of scholarship within the humanities and the social sciences now self-identifies as intersectional" (Collins 22).

"Intersectionality" for the most part continues to be used and theorized as related to praxis, that is, to action in the world. Yet, while it was first used as a legal term, and laws patently do affect action in the world, it is also the case that "law is done through words. It is a profession of words" (Constable 1123). The term "intersectionality" itself began life as a rhetorical device; in her 2016 TED talk, Crenshaw said that it "occurred to [her], maybe a simple analogy to an intersection [where roads come together] might allow judges to better see [the defendant's] dilemma" (Robertson). And poetry, of course, although not as obviously a form of action in the actual world, is also a profession of words. Furthermore, the poet and lawyer Lawrence Joseph has argued that not only Stevens's use of language but also his "sense of the individual in his poetry" is related to legal recognitions of how the realities of race and gender reveal "the need for a changing sense of individual rights" (300).

Stevens was both a poet and a lawyer who for most of his life worked for the Hartford Accident and Indemnity Company on surety bond claims. Dealing as he did with complicated legal decisions, he would surely have understood the issues Crenshaw and others raise. As he said in a 1954 interview, "Poetry and surety claims . . . aren't as unlikely a combination as they may seem. There's nothing perfunctory about them" (qtd. in Joseph 303). As certainly, Stevens would not have found the looser – or as he might have said, more "perfunctory" – uses of the term to his taste. By the mid-1930s through the following decades, Stevens characterized the political rhetoric of the day as devalued and commodified, not to mention ineffective; through at least 1951, he dismissed sloganeering and advertising, along with widely disseminated public rhetoric, or, as he put it, "slogans, . . . rallies, radio panhandlers, government propagandists" (*L* 730; see Steinman, "Re-figuring" 55–58). While the work done by Crenshaw and by many of those who have built on it within legal or sociological contexts is decidedly not sloganeering, the popularized use of the term would involve the kind of use of unexamined catchphrases to which Stevens objected.

At the same time, more critical uses of intersectional theory are explicitly connected with the power relations at play in actual lived experiences and especially with issues of race, class, and gender – that is, with social and cultural power relations – that did inform Stevens's perspective and so inflect Stevens's writings but are not overtly addressed as thematic concerns in his work. In most cases, those involved in intersectional studies explicitly hope to have an effect on power relations in the world, which is one reason why it cannot easily be determined how most studies of Stevens or of his work are specifically related to intersectional studies.

Still, the way poetry affects people's placement in the world arguably was one of Stevens's central themes, just not in the sociopolitical terms used by those now thinking about intersectionality. When Stevens said in "The Noble Rider and the Sound of Words," a lecture first given at Princeton in 1941, that poetry "helps us to live our lives," he was speaking about how the mind expressing itself in words (not laws or social action per se) could "[protect] us from a violence without. It is," he continued, "the imagination pressing back against the pressure of reality" (*CPP* 665). In context, Stevens presumably meant that people could imagine their worlds as other than the world of war and violence, which it was in 1941; tacitly, he suggests recognizing how social organizations, wars, and other forms of violence are the products of the human imagination. On the one hand, this is not unrelated to a point made in a recent article using intersectional studies published in the *Harvard Law Review*, which includes the authors' "view that how we theorize social problems . . . necessarily shapes the scope and content of our social justice imaginary" (Carbado and Harris 2193). (The reference to a social justice "imaginary" rests in part on Benedict Anderson's concept of a national imaginary, often used to denote the set of values, institutions, laws, and images held in common and the corresponding sense of a collective whole that people imagine.) On the other hand, there is little sense that many of those in the United States currently practicing intersectional studies would find Stevens's point about the power of the individual imagination – compelling though it may be – sufficiently grounded in social reality.

For example, when Stevens talks about the imagination pressing back against the pressure of reality, he ignores what Lisa DuRose notes as "one of the more pressing forces of reality," namely, "the struggle for racial equality" (4). In the same lecture, Stevens refers to "the comfortable American state of life of the eighties, the nineties and the first ten years of the present [twentieth] century" (*CPP* 658), a description one might convincingly argue unselfconsciously reflects his own privileged position by 1941 as a vice president at The Hartford and his relatively privileged position even earlier, despite his anxieties in the first decades of the twentieth century about finding a job that would allow him to provide for himself and his family. One gets a similar sense of Stevens's perspective from a 1937 letter he wrote to one of his publishers, saying that when he was young he "really was a poet in the sense that [he] was all imagination," adding that he gave up writing for a while because he "didn't for a moment like the idea of poverty" (*L* 320). The letter implies, first, that both being a poet and making a living were choices he had available to him, and, second, that he had little sense of his relative privilege. That is, on-the-ground issues of how race, class, and gender might affect the choices available to other people were not Stevens's central or conscious concerns, although his views of others are reflected in his poems.

Over the past forty years or so, various critics have written about how race, class, and gender are represented in Stevens's work, without, however, for the most part thinking about such categories as interrelated. Critics have also raised questions about the way Stevens's tacit assumptions about race, class, and gender inform the poems. Relatedly, as suggested earlier about the assumptions implicit in "The Noble Rider and the Sound of Words," some critics have taken note of Stevens's own position as a white, bourgeois, heterosexual, male American – as someone who himself occupied an intersectional social position – which is to say that intersectional theory could be and in some ways already has been brought to bear on Stevens and his work.

At the very least, articles and books that seem closely related to intersectional studies, because they consider what we would now call intersectionality, have appeared over the past three or more decades. For example, in 1988 – a year before Crenshaw's article was published in the *University of Chicago Legal Forum* – Frank Lentricchia's book *Ariel and the Police* included a lengthy section titled "Patriarchy against Itself," in which he considers how both class and gender affected Stevens's theories of poetry as well as rooting his discussion in an analysis of a few of Stevens's poems, notably "Sunday Morning" and "A Postcard from the Volcano" (136–95). Along with Lentricchia, Alan Filreis and James Longenbach have both written books that consider Stevens and class. Those who have written about Stevens and race, class, or gender (again, even while not strictly speaking doing intersectional studies) often also consider historical context and, in particular, the ways in which social imaginations interact with historical particulars and cultural norms, another way in which studies of

Stevens, his poetry, and his poetics have anticipated, or participated before the fact in, intersectional studies.

To illustrate how this works, one might turn to studies of Stevens's ideas about poetry and gender that take into account the fact that in 1899, while a student at Harvard, Stevens wrote in his journal under the heading "Poetry and Manhood," "Those who say poetry is now the peculiar province of women say so because ideas about poetry are effeminate" (*L* 26). The journal entry reflects the way that the production of or interest in poetry was typically gendered as feminine in the years during which Stevens first formed his ideas about and began to dedicate himself to writing poems, a commonplace evident in a 1913 letter Stevens wrote to his wife characterizing his "writing of verses" as "positively lady-like" (*L* 180). Early in his career, then, he seems to have internalized, even as he resisted (among other things, early on, by continuing to write), the construction of poetry as feminine. By 1923, Stevens's first volume of poetry, *Harmonium*, appeared and included poems like "Sunday Morning" (first published in a different form late in 1915 in *Poetry*), which opens with a portrait of a woman enjoying "Complacencies of the peignoir, and late / Coffee and oranges in a sunny chair" (*CPP* 53), a figure that Lentricchia has called "the author as economic as well as sexual transvestite" (153). Sandra Gilbert and Susan Gubar took issue with Lentricchia's criticism of their 1979 book on women and Victorian literature, *The Madwoman in the Attic*, which he saw as too essentialist, that is, as not sufficiently taking into account how culturally constructed gender roles change over time. Gilbert and Gubar then continued the consideration of Stevens and gender by pointing to the rather different financial and psychological handicaps women poets in the United States from the nineteenth century on (unlike Stevens) faced. Both sides in this argument primarily consider the cultural circumstances of authorship.

Perhaps not surprisingly – and well before most literary critics were thinking about intersectionality per se – various critics focused on and disagreed even about how to analyze the place of the feminine in Stevens's poetry and poetics, a sign that critical approaches, as well as cultural commonplaces, change over time. How to define Stevens's relationship to questions of gender has been widely, sometimes acrimoniously (as in the debates between Lentricchia and Gilbert and Gubar), treated in scholarship about the poet, without including much agreement about how to define what counts as gender in Stevens, let alone how to think about the relationship between gender as it manifests in poems and in the lives lived outside of poems. Melita Schaum's important 1993 collection, *Wallace*

Stevens and the Feminine, for instance, includes essays that consider Stevens's biography; others consider the point of view or the speaking voice in the poems; still others focus on how feminine voices or "characters" – although most of Stevens's poems contain nothing like fleshed-out portraits of actual people – are represented in the poems. The approaches taken range from comparing Stevens's work with that of some women poets of his day to psychoanalytic readings of the poems or of Stevens as his attitudes changed over time, with the critical discourse not always clearly distinguishing between sexed bodies and gender as either culturally or internally defined (Steinman, "Feminine" 344–52).

A little over twenty years after Schaum's book appeared, Rachel Blau DuPlessis, addressing the question of Stevens and gender from another angle, argued (building on Barbara Johnson's work) that part of "male privilege" can be "the right to play femininity," even though DuPlessis concluded that Stevens's poetry is finally "gender neutral" ("Virile" 20, 32). The idea of "playing femininity" suggests the possibility of thinking both about the multiple subject positions opened in the poems, that is, about how they constantly shift perspectives, and about why Stevens, as a poet, imagined many of those positions as feminized, as well as what the implications of such an imagination might be for actual women, including his wife and his daughter (Steinman, "Houses" 200–02). Again, few of the approaches to Stevens or to his poetry on issues of class or gender rigorously consider how class, race, and gender might intersect, even if they provide a foundation on which such analyses might be constructed.

I have said less about Stevens and race because until quite recently less has been written on this topic. Aldon Nielsen's *Reading Race: White American Poets and the Racial Discourse in the Twentieth Century* was among the earliest full-length studies to include a consideration of Stevens and race. Nielsen argues that Stevens in his letters viewed those who were not white (and those who were not economically advantaged) as "brutish" and lacking "finer" feeling; in the poetry, Nielsen notes a "generalized exoticism of the black subject," pointing to poems such as "Exposition of the Contents of a Cab" and "The Greenest Continent," a section of "Owl's Clover" (60–65). Ten years later, DuRose drew on both Lentricchia and Nielsen to examine more closely the power dynamics involved in Stevens's often celebratory use of blackface – or "declaring in his poetry that he is just like African Americans" (8) – in more than twenty of his poems, seeing the strategy as a bid for freedom from the circumstances imposed on middle-class white men in the early twentieth century without acknowledging the actual powerlessness of those he represents in his work (12). That is, Stevens imagines freedom and creative power as the prerogative of outsiders, which bears some relationship to the way in which both Lentricchia and DuPlessis discuss Stevens's cross-dressing in the poems, namely as opening a space for Stevens's writing of poetry.

DuRose concludes that Stevens ultimately, if unwittingly, thus widens racial disparities, because no matter how he valorizes racial others in many of the poems, he does so by using racial stereotypes of those others as "exotic, primitive, and sexualized" (3); DuPlessis, borrowing from Alain Locke, dubs this "romantic racism" ("Darken" 52). Both critics offer critiques of Stevens's poems. Jacqueline Brogan, on the other hand, has argued that during and after the Second World War, Stevens's views about and uses of images of racial others (and of women) changed (Brogan ch. 8). DuRose, DuPlessis, and Brogan are all concerned primarily with questions of how race – and to a lesser extent class and gender – are represented in Stevens's work, as well as with how representations of "others" are related to actual, historical power relations.

These critical approaches opened important new ways of thinking about poetry like Stevens's that for earlier critics had appeared quite disconnected from the world. One nevertheless can see how some of Stevens's poems would yield to but also cause problems for such intersectional studies approaches. One might take, for instance, "The Virgin Carrying a Lantern," which first appeared in *Harmonium* in 1923 (*CPP* 56–57). It looks, at first glance, like many of Stevens's short "anecdotes," a nine-line poem consisting of three tercets: the first two lines of each tercet rhyme, with a steady tetrameter beat; the final line of each stanza is shorter (four words each, with end rhymes – "wrong," "long," and "strong" – across the stanzas). The poem sounds, again at first blush, like a whimsical ditty. It opens, "There are no bears among the roses, / Only a negress who supposes / Things false and wrong ..." "Negress," unlike some of the language Stevens used in poems and in person, would have been a relatively polite racial term in 1923, although the way it is used to rhyme with the Latinate "egress" in the final stanza may help make the whole poem and its characters "parodic" and "close to nursery rhyme" (Cook 65).

It also seems that the "negress" embodies several of the racial stereotypes – "brutish," lacking "finer" feeling, exotic, and sexualized – that critics see Stevens using. At the same time, the poem is syntactically ambiguous: is the "negress" mistaken for a bear by the speaker of the poem? Or is that first stanza using free indirect discourse to offer the perspective of the "negress" who falsely supposes there are bears in the flowers? The latter interpretation really only persists for a moment in the reader's mind, as the second stanza proceeds to describe what the false assumptions are about, making clear that the "negress" supposes false things not about a bear but about the lantern of a virgin who is carrying it (presumably not like Diogenes looking for an honest man). Yet the break between stanzas more or less ensures both readings linger; moreover, after reading the second stanza it is unclear who thinks there might be bears in the roses. The sentence is what is called a "garden path sentence," in which a grammatically correct sentence starts in such a way that a reader's most likely first reading will be incorrect; the reader is lured into what turns out to be a dead end or a clearly unintended meaning. In short, the poem has both us and the "negress" seeing and not seeing bears, as we wrongly suppose what it is she is wrongly supposing.

Does this make the "negress," then, "brutish" or bear-like? Unaware of "finer" feelings? A romantically racialized stereotype? This seems both plausible and implausible. That is, although the poem clearly exoticizes and eroticizes the representation of the "negress" (whose "vigil" is said to be filled with "heat" in the final stanza, as she presumably sees the virgin seeking or emerging from or perhaps inviting a tryst), she nonetheless becomes a figure of strong poetic imagination. Most, though not all, critics have noticed the poem's identification with the "negress," but few say much about the fact that the bear seems to come from *A Midsummer Night's Dream*, act V, scene 1, where Theseus tells Hippolyta,

> Lovers and madmen have such seething brains,
> Such shaping fantasies, that apprehend
> More than cool reason ever comprehends.
> The lunatic, the lover, and the poet
> Are of imagination all compact.
> . . . .
> Such tricks hath strong imagination,
> That if it would but apprehend some joy,
> It comprehends some bringer of that joy.
> Or in the night, imagining some fear,
> How easy is a bush supposed a bear! (lines 4–8, 18–22)

Not only does this align the "negress" with the poet, but it also suggests that fear, not joy, impels the imagination of bears. For whom? It is, once again, impossible to say for certain: maybe for us, by virtue of the praeter-itio (the trope by which one calls attention to what one seems to dismiss); perhaps, briefly, in that (rose) garden path sentence – it is difficult to believe that the pun is not Stevens's – for the "negress." Still, it seems unlikely that the poem, with its lightness of tone, is calling attention to the actual fear that loitering outside and spying in a white neighborhood might occasion in an actual African American woman. As mentioned, it could even be suggested that what first looked like a bear, an animal, turns out to be the "negress" herself, another racial stereotype, although Helen Vendler hears the voice of the poem as that of a "simpering Victorian" woman (18), presumably like the titular pious virgin carrying a lantern who seems to be a proper or prudish stereotyped white woman mocked by the poem. If so, the conflation of the "negress" and the bear in the roses is repudiated, which reinforces the sense, however "false and wrong," that the "negress," like the reader, is the imaginative one, Shakespeare's "lover" and "poet." Saying this does not counter the suggestion that Stevens used women and racial others to open space for his own resistance to Victorian cultural attitudes from a position that empowered him but did not consider actual power relations. In other words, the Shakespearean validation of the "negress" is not about the cultural authority of the character. However, like the poem's syntax, it does complicate intersectional readings of the poems in a few ways.

First, one might consider the confluence of gender and race. There are two women characters – both, one might add, stereotypes – in the poem. That the "negress" is both African American and a woman may well strengthen Stevens's ability to use her perspective to imagine a kind of poetic transgressiveness; the virgin carrying the lantern, on the other hand, opens a different kind of space, one that allows the poem more easily to flout cultural norms (DuRose 5, 8, 15–16; DuPlessis 50). The readings of the poem by DuPlessis, Vendler, and DuRose mentioned earlier focus on the differences between the representation of the (presumably) white woman and of the African American woman – arguably an intersectional approach – to suggest that such representations can affect and reinforce social imaginaries, at least for readers of poetry. Moreover, DuRose, in particular, argues that the poem tacitly assumes a white readership (19).

Stevens's assumptions about his readers may indeed have been just that; he did not pay attention to African American writers who were his contemporaries – Langston Hughes, Countee Cullen, and others – and his racially charged remarks about Gwendolyn Brooks at a meeting of the National Book Award committee (Richardson 387–88) reached a wider readership and elicited many comments when Major Jackson returned to the episode in his 2008 post – titled "Wallace Stevens after 'Lunch'" – on the Poetry Foundation's literary blog, *Harriet*. However, Jackson's post helps underline that whatever Stevens may have assumed about his future readers, they decidedly have included those who are not white. Rachel Galvin also details responses to Stevens from a range of poets of color (Olive Senior, Terrance

Hayes, Rafael Campo, and Richard Blanco), concluding that such responses can "fuel incisive ideological critique" and persuasively repeating the claim that "literary representations instantiate culture" (293, 287).

Galvin's project is primarily concerned with representation and aims more to reconsider intertextuality than intersectionality, yet it is in keeping with how, on Jackson's *Harriet* post and in various other forums, poets of color – such as Jackson, Reginald Shepherd, Carl Phillips, Thylias Moss, Vivek Narayanan, Hayes, and C. S. Giscombe – have read and voiced ambivalent responses to Stevens's work that focus on Stevens's style (Steinman, "Unanticipated" 218–20). As Hayes's poem "Snow for Wallace Stevens," framing his view of Stevens as involving "love without / forgiveness," puts it: Stevens knew how "to bring a sentence to its knees" (57). Returning to the use of language in "The Virgin Carrying a Lantern," one might recall the ambiguity, the garden path sentence, the shifting subject positions (the suspect speaking voice; the implicit, possibly false but imaginative perspective of the "negress"; the at least tacit suggestion that the lantern-carrying "beauty" is mourning "as a farewell duty"), all in nine lines. Carl Phillips has called Stevens a "poet of the lack of closure," admiring the suppleness of his syntax; Narayanan, noting that reading Stevens makes him feel like an "interloper," finds that very stance "productive and even enabling," while Shepherd has said that reading Stevens is "complicated and ambiguous," but that, although he struggled with Stevens as a poet, Stevens's writing made him "possible as a writer" (qtd. in Steinman, "Unanticipated" 219–20). Ambiguity and ambivalence are not the same thing; the first presumably marks the slipperiness of Stevens's language as well as the shifting perspectives that such language makes available; the second marks how the poets just quoted feel about the perspectives represented. Still, it seems that the complexity of Stevens's style allows for or even requires ambivalent responses. And both ambiguity and ambivalence have a central place in African American literary traditions, as well, as described by Henry Louis Gates Jr.'s *The Signifying Monkey* (1988) or featured in Ralph Ellison's *Invisible Man* (1952), which may be why those dismayed by Stevens's racism nonetheless, ambivalently, admire how his use of language – resisting closure, full of complication, resulting in productive watchfulness – allows African American writers to position themselves and reposition Stevens rather than being positioned by Stevens. Such readings may define a different kind of intersectionality, an intersection between past, present, and future readers and writers, between reading communities and poetic – and so social – imaginaries, than has been explored in intersectional studies so far.

WORKS CITED

Anderson, Benedict. *Imagined Communities: Reflections on the Origin and Spread of Nationalism*. Verso, 1983.

Brogan, Jacqueline. *The Violence Within / The Violence Without: Wallace Stevens and the Emergence of a Revolutionary Poetics*. U of Georgia P, 2003.

Carbado, Devon W., and Cheryl I. Harris. "Intersectionality at 30: Mapping the Margins of Anti-Essentialism, Intersectionality, and Dominance Theory." *Harvard Law Review*, vol. 132, no. 8, 2 June 2019, pp. 2193–239.

Collins, Patricia Hill. *Intersectionality as Critical Social Theory*. Duke UP, 2019.

Constable, Marianne. "The Facts of Law." *PMLA*, vol. 134, no. 5, Oct. 2019, pp. 1121–28.

Cook, Eleanor. *A Reader's Guide to Wallace Stevens*. Princeton UP, 2007.

Crenshaw, Kimberlé Williams. "Demarginalizing the Intersection of Race and Sex: A Black Feminist Critique of Antidiscrimination Doctrine, Feminist Theory and Antiracist Politics." *University of Chicago Legal Forum*, vol. 1989, issue 1, 1989, Article 8, chicagounbound. uchicago.edu/uclf/vol.1989/iss1/8.

DuPlessis, Rachel Blau. "'Darken Your Speech': Racialized Cultural Work of Modernist Poets." *Reading Race in American Poetry: "An Area of Act,"* edited by Aldon Lynn Nielsen, U of Illinois P, 2000, pp. 43–83.

"'Virile Thought': Modernist Maleness, Poetic Forms and Practices." *Modernism and Masculinity*, edited by Natalya Lusty and Julian Murphet, Cambridge UP, 2014, pp. 19–37.

DuRose, Lisa. "Racial Domain and the Imagination of Wallace Stevens." *The Wallace Stevens Journal*, vol. 22, no. 1, Spring 1998, pp. 3–22.

Ellison, Ralph. *Invisible Man*. Vintage, 1980.

Galvin, Rachel. "Race." *Wallace Stevens in Context*, edited by Glen MacLeod, Cambridge UP, 2017, pp. 286–96.

Gates, Henry Louis, Jr. *The Signifying Monkey: A Theory of African-American Literary Criticism*. Oxford UP, 1988.

Gilbert, Sandra, and Susan Gubar. *The Madwoman in the Attic: The Woman Writer and the Nineteenth-Century Literary Imagination*. Yale UP, 1979.

"The Man on the Dump versus the United Dames of America; Or, What Does Frank Lentricchia Want?" *Critical Inquiry*, vol. 14, no. 2, Winter 1988, pp. 386–406.

Hayes, Terrance. *Lighthead*. Penguin, 2010.

"Intersectionality." *Merriam-Webster Dictionary*, www.merriamwebster.com/dictionary/intersectionality?src=search-dict-box.

"Intersectionality, n." *OED Online*, Oxford, Sept. 2019, www.oed.com/view/Entry/429843.

Jackson, Major, Reginald Shepherd, and Vivek Narayanan. "Wallace Stevens after 'Lunch.'" *Harriet*, Poetry Foundation, 4–16 Feb. 2008, www.poetryfoundation.org/Harriet/2008/02/wallace-stevens-after-lunch.

Joseph, Lawrence. "Law." *Wallace Stevens in Context*, edited by Glen MacLeod, Cambridge UP, 2017, pp. 297–305.

Lentricchia, Frank. *Ariel and the Police: Michel Foucault, William James, Wallace Stevens*. U of Wisconsin P, 1988.

Nielsen, Aldon Lynn. *Reading Race: White American Poets and the Racial Discourse in the Twentieth Century*. U of Georgia P, 1988.

Richardson, Joan. *Wallace Stevens: A Biography; The Later Years, 1923–1955*. William Morrow, 1988.

Robertson, Eleanor. "Intersectional – what? Feminism's problem with jargon is that any idiot can pick it up and have a go." *The Guardian*, 30 Sept. 2017, www.theguardian.com/world/2017/sep/30/intersectional-feminism-jargon?CMP=share_btn_link.

Steinman, Lisa M. "The Feminine." *Wallace Stevens in Context*, edited by Glen MacLeod, Cambridge UP, 2017, pp. 344–52.

"The Houses of Fathers: Stevens and Emerson." *Wallace Stevens and the Feminine*, edited by Melita Schaum, U of Alabama P, 1993, pp. 190–202.

"Re-figuring Stevens: The Poet's Politics." *The Wallace Stevens Journal*, vol. 16, no. 1, Spring 1992, pp. 53–63.

"Unanticipated Readers." *Poetry and Poetics after Wallace Stevens*, edited by Bart Eeckhout and Lisa Goldfarb, Bloomsbury, 2017, pp. 217–28.

Stevens, Wallace. *Letters of Wallace Stevens*. Edited by Holly Stevens, Alfred A. Knopf, 1966.

Wallace Stevens: Collected Poetry and Prose. Edited by Frank Kermode and Joan Richardson, Library of America, 1997.

Vendler, Helen. *Wallace Stevens: Words Chosen Out of Desire*. Harvard UP, 1986.

CHAPTER 11

Cognitive Literary Studies

G. Gabrielle Starr

Stevens and Cognitive Perspectives on Aesthetics

Across the multiple versions of aesthetic experience Wallace Stevens engages, two differing aesthetic modes take on compelling shape through a cognitive lens. Broadly speaking, understanding aesthetics involves paying close attention to the complex connections, both positive and negative, between thoughts, feelings, knowledge, and action that may begin with sensory or imagined contemplation of works of art and the natural world. However, a cognitive approach to aesthetics, in particular, starts with the understanding that aesthetic experiences aren't "in your head" or even "in your mind." They are embodied. While they vary across individuals, there are both biological and social parameters that constrain as well as enable us as humans to engage aesthetically with the world and with the objects humans create. Such an approach is well suited to Stevens's poetry, for his writing is deeply concerned with key areas in the study of cognition, from perception and imagination to distinctions between putatively internal and external experience. Indeed, Stevens's poetic techniques, particularly in deploying sound, meter, and imagery, fully repay engagement with the tools of cognitive science, as he weaves aesthetic experiences that powerfully manipulate human cognitive architecture.

One mode of aesthetic experience that matters for Stevens's poetry involves disruption, and it can take two forms: a mismatch between expectations and experience or a disruption of a reader's everyday experience by an overlay of imagery. The second key mode depends on effects of pleasure: under certain conditions, elements of a poem that might defy normative concepts of poetic form emerge instead as salient formal features because they take on the weight given by pleasure. This mode of aesthetic experience relies on possibilities of redefinition, sketching out new versions of form by freighting experience with

I would like to thank colleagues who helped me in thinking through this piece: Kevin Dettmar, Elaine Freedgood, Christopher Miller, and John Seery.

sensation that has been given a value – not just sensation but sensation combined with pleasure.

Aesthetic Disruption as Mismatch

Let's take the first kind of aesthetic experience, which is linked to the concept of "expectation mismatch." This concept is an important one in cognitive neuroscience, and especially in understanding learning. Animals thrive in an environment where they have some reasonable ability to extrapolate about what the future holds. We have expectations about what will happen next in life, on a walk; in a relationship; or in stories, music, and poems. Those expectations are often learned. When we predict correctly, we are rewarded by the outcome in the world as well as by means of neural signals that correlate with felt pleasure or displeasure (see, e.g., Kringelbach). A mismatched expectation is generally not associated with positive outcomes, but humans, like other animals, learn from those mistakes, through both negative outcomes and the pains or displeasures that emerge.

In aesthetic terms, a simple way to conceive of the power of violated expectations is a wrong note; indeed, as Stevens wrote, "Personally, I like words to sound wrong" (*L* 340). If in a piece of music, the sound you expect to come next doesn't appear – you yourself played the wrong note, or maybe the composer is playing a game with your expectations – something happens. It is probably not pleasurable on the first go. If it is truly a mistake – you hit the wrong key, or your fingers just didn't do what you needed them to – it probably never produces a positive experience. But if, say, you begin to understand what John Coltrane is doing and why, or why Wallace Stevens just won't satisfy your expectations about rhythm in a particular line, word, or poem, then pleasure may emerge. Yet this remains to be seen: in and of itself, the missed expectation produces a disruption that may or may not be pleasurable.

Nicholas Myklebust describes disruption of expectations around metrical violations in "The Comedian as the Letter C," where Stevens schools the reader over many lines to expect iambic pentameter as the dominant pattern of stress, yet in "an instance of organized violence" the poet presents "a deviation from the norm: 'Inscrutable hair in an inscrutable world'" (146). The line sounds wrong to the inner ear – or the outer one – if only because there are eleven syllables where there should be no more than ten. Ultimately, however any particular reader assigns stresses in this line, "What . . . matter[s] is the *felt* need to repair the line, to make it fit prior expectations" (146). Something has got to give when the pattern has been violated, and following the work of Reuven Tsur, Myklebust argues that the poem "exploits this violence by turning interference into pleasure" (146). Mending the line, figuring out what the deviation from the poem's past patterns might mean, generates a kind of satisfaction for readers who solve the metrical puzzle in a way that makes sense to them. This is not to say there is only one solution: there are different ways to "hear" the stress of the line (Myklebust suggests either scanning with two anapests or using syncope to elide one syllable), but finding the poem pleasurable means finding a pleasurable solution.[1]

The patterns of sound in Stevens may richly vary; "Bouquet of Roses in Sunlight" utilizes that richness effusively to violate a different kind of expectation. The stress pattern in this poem is not so much governed by a regular rhythm as guided by a rhetorical precision, a sense of linguistic propriety that seems to belong more to emphasizing an argument than to effecting the beat of a poem:

> Sáy that ít is a crúde efféct, bláck réds,
> Pínk yéllows, órange whítes, tóo múch as they áre
> To be ánything élse in the súnlight of the róom,
> . . . .
> And yét this efféct is a cónsequénce of the wáy
> We féel and, thérefore, is not réal, excépt
> In our sénse of it, our sénse of the fértilest réd. . . . (CPP
> 370)

The stress sweeps across the line to emphasize the points of argument, the key elements of contention in a philosophical and phenomenological statement about perception and reality. Thus, from the very beginning, Stevens uses sound to unsettle the poem's status as poetry, an irony made clear in the final lines, where he writes that the very sensual nature of the "roses" (roses we readers can never see) makes them resistant to "the rhetorician's touch" (CPP 371). However, the sensory frame of the poem – the sounds of stress – emphasizes the rhetorician's skill at argument, using aesthetic power to blend genres of speech (poetry and rhetoric), to disrupt generic expectations, and to render poetry's effect as that of evoking conviction as well as piquing imagination. Still, effects proper to poetry at times explode onto the page, as with the sudden shift from everyday argument and rhetorical emphasis to a changed beat that comes with florid color: "fertilest red." An explosion of poetry thus paradoxically interrupts the poem, cascading visual brilliance into a fluid background of sound. As Stevens jots down in his "Adagia," "The poet comes to words as nature comes to dry sticks" (CPP 909): poetry refreshes language; as language is made new, we might find startling pleasure in a sudden vividness, when one rose, even against a riotous background of others, stands out with sharp virility.

Aesthetic Disruption as Disorientation

Stevens elsewhere specializes in using disruption to signal a kind of minimalist aesthetic effect, a disorienting brush between embodied sensation and imagination. This happens as an effect of imagery or words that can lead a reader to feel simultaneously present in the moment of reading and estranged from that present moment. There are numerous opportunities for such felt registration of the effects of poetry in Stevens. They are opportunities, however, not givens, because as "Bouquet of Roses in Sunlight" contends, "Our sense of these things changes" (*CPP* 370).

In some of Stevens's work, disorientation emerges when perceptual discomfort is combined with semantic confusion. As I have argued elsewhere, one of the clearest examples of this combination comes in "The Auroras of Autumn" (Starr 167–71). There, sensation begins to eat its way into consciousness: "A cold wind chills the beach. / The long lines of it grow longer, emptier, / A darkness gathers though it does not fall" (*CPP* 356). This pause in sensation corresponds with a lack of comprehension: after all, this canto opens with a "Farewell to an idea" (*CPP* 355). These words point toward a double discomfort. On the one hand, there is the discomfort that comes when a puzzle just won't resolve, where all that one can achieve is not remembrance, but "trying to remind" (*CPP* 356). On the other hand, sight is troubled as the viewer strives to see; the aurora borealis emerges with clarity only after a moment of blinding whiteout suddenly retreats:

> And the whiteness grows less vivid on the wall.
> The man who is walking turns blankly on the sand.
> He observes how the north is always enlarging the change,
>
> With its frigid brilliances, its blue-red sweeps
> And gusts of great enkindlings, its polar green,
> The color of ice and fire and solitude. (*CPP* 356)

This moment in the second canto depicts a discomfort – the blankness of sight, the failing of sensation and sense – that resolves into a poetic optimum: sheer sensory brilliance, brought to you from the blankness of the page.

Stevens finds this kind of disruption in search of resolution generative; in a wide variety of poems, he sketches disruptive contact that joins physical or sensory discomfort with semantic confusion, pointing out the fundamental instability between what we know and what we sense. Myklebust suggests that disorientation may emerge as an aesthetic experience because "aesthetic experience arises from organized interference with default cognitive processes" (143). Or to put it from a neurological perspective, powerful aesthetic experience involves the engagement of networks that underpin default modes of cognition in atypical ways.

One set of regions known as the default mode network (see Raichle) has been implicated in a set of key everyday occurrences, from daydreaming to mind wandering, imagining the future and the past, imagining others, monitoring self-presence (feelings of self-awareness and awareness of one's surroundings), as well as registering what is particularly relevant to a particular individual (Andrews-Hanna et al.) and even in musical creativity (Bashwiner et al.). What is unusual about powerful aesthetic experience (rather than what might be called merely liking or appreciating something in an aesthetic sense) is that the default mode network, which is usually anti-correlated with sensory and attention networks, is not negatively correlated with an intense focus on an object in the external world. In other words, when individuals look at and evaluate objects that they find only mildly or moderately aesthetically appealing, the default mode network ramps down. When the object calls to one powerfully, however, the default mode network re-engages.[2]

The entire range of cognitive processes that aesthetic experiences may engage or disrupt is not yet clear, even as we learn more (see, e.g., Brielmann and Pelli). However, one set of default cognitive processes important in aesthetics probably involves the feelings that come with bodily awareness. We are only weakly aware of much of our bodily experience, from, for example, the exact sensations of sitting in a chair to the feel of the back of one's hand as it holds a book (de Vignemont; cf. Clune). Given the faintness of our awareness of much of the sensory data generated by our bodies, it becomes somewhat easy (if you are a gifted poet) to manipulate imagery so that a reader is disoriented, pushed by the strength of imagined sensation to feel both present in the here and now and impossibly absent from it, touched by a poem's light motions, and moved to feel something extraordinary. It is the gossamer of "Final Soliloquy of the Interior Paramour": "Within a single thing, a single shawl / Wrapped tightly round us, since we are poor, a warmth, / A light, a power, the miraculous influence" (*CPP* 444).

Stevens repeatedly figures the light yet confusing encounter between the space in which we read – rooms, terraces, gardens – and the space we imagine as we read, whether it is in "Sunday Morning," "Things of August," or "To an Old Philosopher in Rome." In these poems, the imagined or contemplated and the real rub against each other in ways that need resolution. Take the old philosopher who sits in his chamber: "The bed, the books, the chair, the moving nuns, / The candle as it evades the sight," contrast with "The newsboys' muttering" outside (*CPP* 432). The philosopher – an analogue for the reader (even as much as he is a figure for George Santayana) – is quieted, "Your dozing in the depths of wakefulness, / In the warmth of your bed, at the edge of your chair, alive / Yet living in two worlds" (*CPP* 433). The sensations of an outer world penetrate and disrupt the sensations of an inner world; one is an analogue for poetry, one is not. It's not clear, however, which is which. Is the peaceful world inside the reader's head disturbed by the world rendered vivid in poetry? Is the space of contemplation or imagination (the place of poetry) disturbed by an obtrusive reality (the mundane world)? Or is poetry maybe somewhere in the middle, mediating this exchange, conflict, or synthetic cumulation? Nonetheless, between the two worlds something amazing happens:

> It is a kind of total grandeur at the end,
> With every visible thing enlarged and yet
> No more than a bed, a chair and moving nuns,
> . . . .
> Total grandeur of a total edifice,
> Chosen by an inquisitor of structures
> For himself. He stops upon this threshold,
> As if the design of all his words takes form
> And frame from thinking and is realized. (*CPP* 434)

This moment of contact between two worlds generates an aesthetic sensation that is paradoxically minimal even as it is extremely moving, because it tingles only at the edges of awareness, blurring the lines between everyday experience and what life lived under the influence of poetry can be. We stop upon the threshold but do not cross.

Pleasure as Index of Form

Stevens creates aesthetic possibilities in various other ways by using tactics of disruption or disorientation. One key method is to employ disruption to point out elements of a poem that define its overall formal structure.

I return to "Bouquet of Roses in Sunlight": another way of reading the poem's opening stanzas is as an intimate colloquy or conversation. Such a colloquy evokes one paradigm central to the idea of the lyric poem (especially the idea of poetry honed as early twentieth-century poets reconnected with the work of John Donne; cf. Jackson). In reading the poem, one might find the intimacy of (imagined) shared sight to be intense. What is "real" in this poem is perception, and perceptions change with us as we settle in together with the poem's speaker "in a completing of . . . truth" (*CPP* 370). However, such readerly intimacy is threatened in the final stanza. Throughout the earlier lines, the speaker of the poem has emphasized the strength of sensation: those percepts generated by the roses are "Too actual, things that in being real / Make any imaginings of them lesser things" (*CPP* 370). Reality is sensual.

The paradox is obvious. Glaring, even. So what? Well, take the final lines: "We are two that use these roses as we are, / In seeing them. This is what makes them seem / So far beyond the rhetorician's touch" (*CPP* 371). The challenge is that the scene the poem plots can be seen in two ways: an actual room in which two people look at the bouquet and "use these roses" as paradigms of sensation and aesthetic pleasure and, alternatively, a space marked out by the reader's and poet's imaginations, in which the reader is part of the "we" and is the addressee of Stevens's first lines.

The double scene of the poem is thus at the end made disorienting – who gets to use the roses? And which "roses" are they – the real ones, which are "Too much as they are" or the imagined ones, which also are "Too much as they are"? This disorientation points out a feature of literary form: the instability of the colloquy as genre. Who is really listening to the conversation the poem evokes or implies? And how is the intimacy of conversation constructed? The discomfort of attending to the split perspective ultimately calls attention to the poem as a formal object. Yet, because the "use" of the roses is to revel in sensation, pleasure here is the marker of aesthetic form. "Wait – did I feel it?" a reader might ask. "Was I supposed to?" Thus, the end of the poem in both the interpretations I offer enables violated or altered expectations to lead to a shift in how a reader might interpret the formal structure that is genre. Such violation and reinterpretation depend in part on pleasure as a means of guiding attention to formal features.

The idea that pleasure is a marker of aesthetic form makes particular sense in the context of cognitive psychology. Pleasure, in this framework, assigns hedonic value to an experience, and it has two basic functions. It can be a sign of success – having achieved a goal. It also may be, as Charles Carver points out, something of an error signal, alerting us that we have not only achieved what we wanted, but maybe we have even overdone it. In this way, pleasure signals that it is time to free our mind, senses, and attention so that we notice or explore the world more openly. Pleasure allows us to "broaden and build" (Fredrickson).

Elsewhere, Amy Belfi and I argue that pleasure in reading can enable one to widen one's focus to see the broader shape of the formal presence of a poem. While some elements of poetic form emerge by definition (e.g., the fourteen lines that make a sonnet) or by content (as with the shepherd of pastoral poetry), others emerge not by definition but by subjective experience. In this sense, I understand form to be something like Samuel Taylor Coleridge's "organic" form, or the totality of marks that make up the aesthetic stamp of an artwork (see ch. 14 of *Biographia Literaria*; also Bell). Coleridge argues that the reader must be drawn on by pleasure, but it is puzzling that this is a fundamental principle of engagement, because pleasures in the written word – or in the arts more broadly – are not universal. If pleasure is to be a standard of poetic achievement, it makes for a risky bet.

It is empirically true that human beings diverge in their taste. But remarkably, we diverge far less in the pleasures we take in objects that are more fully natural (human faces or physical landscapes) than we do in pleasures that arise from objects that are more fully artifactual (architecture, paintings, and poems). The difference is quite striking. For faces, for example, mean minus-one agreement (average agreement of one observer in a study compared with all other observers) in how pleasurable one finds a human face is 0.85; for landscapes, it is about 0.6. For architecture, it is radically lower, at 0.38; and for visual art, pleasures are still more divergent, with the mean minus-one agreement at 0.31 (Vessel et al., "Stronger"). With sonnets and haiku, disagreement about how pleasing readers find a poem is also extremely high, with interclass correlations (another measure of agreement between individuals) below 0.2 (Belfi et al.). Such stunning divergence in pleasures is truly noteworthy, and it suggests that a hallmark of the aesthetic experience of artifacts of human culture is the degree to which individuals diverge in the pleasures they take in them. Thus, the divergence in pleasures may be interpreted as a sign of form: an indication of the ways in which an art object – whether painting or poem – has been shaped for aesthetic engagement (Starr and Belfi).

Pleasures can clarify or lead to the reinterpretation of form – or even of a poetic career – as I offer in engaging one of Stevens's late poems, "Banjo

Boomer." This poem is unusual in many ways for Stevens: formally intricate in a quite traditional way, rhymed through repetition, and with a gentle refrain that is reminiscent of a children's rhyme. As Tim Armstrong argues, "Mulberry, shade me, shade me awhile" (*CPP* 475) is the older man's version of a play yard song, "Here we go round the mulberry bush" (Armstrong 36), even matching its meter, singing its song. That the poem might be two things at once is clear from the very first line, which states, "The mulberry is a double tree"; that those two things might be youth and old age is signaled by the somewhat exhausted repetition at the end of the lines. The poet can't find a rhyme, and why try anyway, when the same word or phrase is just as good: "tree," "awhile," "as well," and even just "word" (*CPP* 475).

However, again in this poem, Stevens suddenly shifts the frame, forgoing the straightforwardness of repetition, and the dominating dactyls of the refrain, by introducing near rhyme and altering the beat: "It is a shape of life described / By another shape without a word." The poem breaks its shape, to signal that something has to change for the poem to close, and the final two lines return to the fascination that is repetition: "With nothing fixed by a single word. / Mulberry, shade me, shade me awhile" (*CPP* 475). The refrain evokes the search for comfort, the return to gentle rhythmic rocking that is the heart of a lullaby.

Importantly, late in his career, Stevens offers clarification, even simplicity, and not mystery. The poem-as-lullaby recalls a child's experience, that of family, home. Indeed, one needn't know the world of poetry intimately to hear the children's song, or to hear it broken; the song is so familiar that any deviation may be clear. Thus, when the comfortable, simple, and shared (cultural) knowledge of the rhythm or the sense of the lullaby begins to falter, that's not an effect of expertise, remarkable for a poet who often foregrounds expert knowledge. The bough breaks, and the cradle might fall. But here there may be backup. At the end of the poem, a reader might discover that the overall rhythm of the poem – not only the scansion of meter but also the larger repetitions and returns – is not just about the circularity of children moving around a tree. If disruption of expectation can signal pleasure, confirmation of expectation can bring pleasure too. The repetition of the refrain as a phrase means that nothing can be fixed by a single word, nor understood by a single beat: "By anóther shápe withóut a wórd." With the return of the refrain at the poem's close, something – poetry, life, joy – has been remade.

What matters, ultimately, is the circularity of life and of the search for comfort – the comfort of old age returning to childhood and dependence, and the pleasure of a poet who mixes the rocking rhythm of a lullaby, seeking shade and rest, with the beat of American music. It is the hand knocking out an extra rhythm as the banjo player adds an extra beat on the board of the instrument, even as the fingers pursue the complicated rhythm of the song: the banjo boomer of the title.[3]

Notes

1 For a different cognitive approach to sound in Stevens, see Tartakovsky.
2 See Belfi et al. and the four entries under Vessel et al.
3 The deep irony here is that the banjo is an invention of African American music, and given Stevens's generally dismissive stance toward Black people, it is remarkable that an African American beat shapes some of his last work.

WORKS CITED

Andrews-Hanna, J. R., et al. "Functional-Anatomic Fractionation of the Brain's Default Network." *Neuron*, vol. 65, no. 4, 25 Feb. 2010, pp. 550–62.

Armstrong, Tim. "Stevens' 'Last Poem' Again." *The Wallace Stevens Journal*, vol. 12, no. 1, Spring 1988, pp. 35–43.

Bashwiner, David M., et al. "Musical Creativity 'Revealed' in Brain Structure: Interplay between Motor, Default Mode, and Limbic Networks." *Nature Scientific Reports*, vol. 6, no. 20482, 2016, www.nature.com/articles/srep20482.

Belfi, Amy M., et al. "Dynamics of Aesthetic Experience Are Reflected in the Default-Mode Network." *NeuroImage*, vol. 188, 2019, pp. 584–97.

"Individual Ratings of Vividness Predict Aesthetic Appeal in Poetry." *Psychology of Aesthetics, Creativity, and the Arts*, vol. 12, no. 3, 2017, pp. 341–50.

Bell, Clive. *Art*. Chatto and Windus, 1914.

Brielmann, Aenne A., and Denis G. Pelli. "Beauty Requires Thought." *Current Biology*, vol. 27, no. 10, 22 May 2017, pp. 1506–13.

Carver, Charles S. "Pleasure as a Sign You Can Attend to Something Else: Placing Positive Feelings within a General Model of Affect." *Cognition and Emotion*, vol. 17, no. 2, Mar. 2003, pp. 241–61.

Clune, Michael. *Writing Against Time*. Stanford UP, 2013.

Coleridge, Samuel Taylor. *Biographia Literaria*. Edited by James Engell and W. Jackson Bate, Princeton UP, 1983.

de Vignemont, Frédérique. "Habeas Corpus: The Sense of Ownership of One's Own Body." *Mind and Language*, vol. 22, no. 4, 2007, pp. 427–49.

Fredrickson, Barbara L. "The Role of Positive Emotions in Positive Psychology: The Broaden-and-Build Theory of Positive Emotions." *The American Psychologist*, vol. 56, no. 3, Mar. 2001, pp. 218–26.

Jackson, Virginia Walker. *Dickinson's Misery: A Theory of Lyric Reading*. Princeton UP, 2005.

Kringelbach, Morten L. "The Human Orbitofrontal Cortex: Linking Reward to Hedonic Experience." *Nature Reviews Neuroscience*, vol. 6, no. 9, Sep. 2005, pp. 691–702.

Myklebust, Nicholas. "'Bergamo on a Postcard'; or, A Critical History of Cognitive Poetics." *The Wallace Stevens Journal*, vol. 39, no. 2, Fall 2015, pp. 142–56.

Raichle, Marcus E. "The Brain's Default Mode Network." *Annual Review of Neuroscience*, vol. 38, no. 1, 8 July 2015, pp. 433–47.

Starr, G. Gabrielle. "Aesthetics and Impossible Embodiment: Stevens, Imagery, and Disorientation." *The Wallace Stevens Journal*, vol. 39, no. 2, Fall 2015, pp. 157–81.

Starr, G. Gabrielle, and Amy M. Belfi. "Pleasure." *Further Reading*, edited by Matthew Rubery and Leah Price, Oxford UP, 2020, pp. 282–93.

Stevens, Wallace. *Letters of Wallace Stevens*. Edited by Holly Stevens, U of California P, 1996.

Wallace Stevens: Collected Poetry and Prose. Edited by Frank Kermode and Joan Richardson, Library of America, 1997.

Tartakovsky, Roi. "Acoustic Confusion and Medleyed Sound: Stevens' Recurrent Pairings." *The Wallace Stevens Journal*, vol. 39, no. 2, Fall 2015, pp. 233–48.

Tsur, Reuven. *Poetic Rhythm: Structure and Performance; An Empirical Study in Cognitive Poetics*. Peter Lang, 1998.

Vessel, Edward A., et al. "Art Reaches Within: Aesthetic Experience, the Self and the Default Mode Network." *Frontiers in Neuroscience*, vol. 7, no. 258, 30 Dec. 2013, p. 258.

"The Brain on Art: Intense Aesthetic Experience Activates the Default Mode Network." *Frontiers in Human Neuroscience*, vol. 6, 20 Apr. 2012, p. 66.

"The Default-Mode Network Represents Aesthetic Appeal That Generalizes across Visual Domains." *Proceedings of the National Academy of Sciences*, vol. 116, no. 38, 17 Sep. 2019, pp. 19155–64.

"Stronger Shared Taste for Natural Aesthetic Domains Than for Artifacts of Human Culture." *Cognition*, vol. 179, Oct. 2018, pp. 121–31.

PART III

Revisionary Readings of Stevens

CHAPTER 12

Poetic Responses

Andrew Epstein

In 1959, the poet James Schuyler wrote a letter to the editor Donald Allen, who was then compiling *The New American Poetry, 1945–1960*, the landmark anthology that would do so much to codify the postwar avant-garde by gathering together works by the Beats, the Black Mountain school, and other "anti-academic" movements. Allen had invited Schuyler to contribute some poems to the volume, where he would be placed within one of the most important groupings, the New York School of poets. This group, centered on Frank O'Hara, John Ashbery, Kenneth Koch, Barbara Guest, and Schuyler himself, would go on to become one of the most lasting and influential poetry movements of the second half of the twentieth century. In response to Allen's curiosity about the most salient influences on the new poetry of the era, Schuyler offered a list of predecessors who had been most instrumental for his own coterie: "For the greats: Williams, Moore, Stevens, Pound, Eliot," Schuyler told Allen. "Eliot made the rules everybody wants to break. Stevens and Williams both inspire greater freedom than the others, Stevens of the imagination, Williams of subject and style" (*Just* 109).

It may seem rather surprising that Schuyler gives pride of place to Stevens in this rundown of the major influences on his group of friends, because literary history has tended to minimize, or even dismiss, the significance of Stevens to the movements gathered together under the "New American Poetry" umbrella, and to the New York School in particular. A narrative quickly took hold that divided the period's poetry into two sharply opposed camps, the "raw" versus the "cooked" (to use the paired terms Robert Lowell made famous in his speech upon receiving the National Book Award in 1960). According to this view, the "raw" New American poets mounted a fierce challenge to the reign of T. S. Eliot and his disciples, the formalist New Critics, who had installed a brand of "cooked," formal, polished, erudite, and "academic" verse as the dominant mode in postwar American poetry. To fuel their revolution, the leading

New American poets – figures like Charles Olson, Robert Creeley, Allen Ginsberg, and Frank O'Hara – turned away from Eliot and toward less-sanctioned modernist poets, chiefly Ezra Pound and William Carlos Williams. The framing and preface to Allen's anthology did a good deal to lock this narrative in place: he announces that the rebel poets in his collection – united in "their total rejection of all those qualities typical of academic verse" – follow "the practice and precepts of Ezra Pound and William Carlos Williams" (xi).

While it is certainly accurate to view Pound and Williams as towering influences for postwar avant-garde poetry, the omission of Stevens from this story – despite his sense that "All poetry is experimental poetry" (*CPP* 918) – has always seemed rather curious and misleading, given his import-ance to many of the poets involved. Nonetheless, following the lead of Allen's anthology, scholars have long downplayed or ignored Stevens's crucial role in the history of experimental poetics, from Objectivism to the various movements of the "New American Poetry," to Language poetry, and beyond. This is in part due to the work of major scholars like Hugh Kenner and Marjorie Perloff in the 1970s and 1980s, who placed Pound and Williams at the head of this avant-garde poetic tradition and often pitted them against Stevens, whose work they deemed more late Romantic than truly modernist, less experimental in form, more conserva-tive and old-fashioned.[1] For example, Perloff's influential essay "Pound/ Stevens: Whose Era?" elevates Pound as the forward-looking, modernist avant-garde innovator who declared "MAKE IT NEW!" over Stevens, a poet "who carries on the Symbolist tradition" and is admired "for his ability to MAKE IT OLD" (14).

Scholars have noted the persistence of this division: as Alan Golding observes, "Critics still tend to see Stevens, on the one hand, and Pound and Williams, on the other, as representing the divergence of the Symbolist and Imagist traditions in twentieth-century American poetry" (*From Outlaw* 136). This overly schematic binary has left us with a general sense that Stevens's progeny, his most visible and important descendants, are poets associated with the "mainstream" – such as Elizabeth Bishop, Theodore Roethke, James Merrill, Richard Wilbur, John Hollander, Mark Strand, or Jorie Graham – rather than from the "experimental" fringes. One figure who bucks this trend is Ashbery, whose connections to Stevens *have* been widely, exhaustively discussed, but often with the goal of removing Ashbery from the avant-garde tradition, and positioning him as the inheritor of a grand poetic lineage that descends from Romanticism.

This image of Stevens as a formalist favorite and latter-day Romantic or neo-Symbolist poet, of marginal importance to avant-garde poets who follow him, has begun to change somewhat. For example, Alan Filreis has argued that the more avant-garde side of Stevens – which he refers to as the "languaged Stevens," and defines as "theoretical, serial, and nonnarra-tive, metapoetically radical" – has quietly served as a powerful force within contemporary innovative poetry, even if the more conservative "medita-tive-lyric" Stevens still has more visibility and dominance ("Stevens Wars" 191).[2] Nevertheless, the latter still clouds our understanding of the import-ant role Stevens plays for figures like Louis Zukofsky, Robert Creeley, Susan Howe, and many other younger poets who find Stevens's work energizing and provocative.

In the particular case of the New York School, the neglect of Stevens as an important precursor causes problems in both directions: it unnecessarily limits our sense of New York School poetry, simultaneously hindering our understanding of Stevens and his legacy.[3] For one thing, it gives us a misleading picture of the aesthetic and philosophical complexity of New York School poetics, which can too easily be reduced to a chatty, pop-culture-infused poetry of urban daily life. On Stevens's side of the equa-tion, this neglect reinforces the distorted image of Stevens as a stuffy, backward-looking aesthete, devoted solely to abstraction and imagination, disdainful of the concrete, everyday realities so dear to the New York School, and perpetuates the notion that he has been of minimal import-ance to the avant-garde strain in American poetry.

In what follows, I trace some of the reasons why Stevens's influence on the New York School has been overlooked and misconceived and examine his importance not only to Ashbery but also to O'Hara, Schuyler, Guest, Koch, and members of the New York School's second generation, like Ted Berrigan. Ultimately, this chapter will suggest that, for all their differences, Stevens and the New York School poets share a great deal: an obsession with painting and a passion for all things French; a delight in wordplay and the sensuous surfaces of language; an anti-foundational skepticism toward fixity in self, language, or idea; and, perhaps most of all, an embrace of the imagination and deep attraction to the surreal combined with a devotion to the ordinary and everyday.

***

As I have suggested, most general assessments of the New York School stress that these young poets, like other New American poets, felt stifled by the poetic doctrines of Eliot and New Critical orthodoxy at mid-century and defiantly turned elsewhere, to alternative sources of inspiration – in their case, to the European avant-garde (Cubism, Dada, Surrealism, French, and Russian poetry); Abstract Expressionist painting; the vitality and absurdity of popular culture; and a lineage of American poets outside of the Eliotic canon, especially Whitman, Williams, Stevens, Stein, and Moore, along with early Auden.[4] While Stevens is mentioned in such tallies of influence, his importance is usually downplayed, except in the case of Ashbery.[5] And it is not hard to see why: in some ways, the New York School's reputation for having perfected a mode of conversational, gossipy, formally experimental, coterie-focused social poetics founded on personal experience, proper names of friends, materials drawn from pop culture and the banal stuff of daily life can seem a world away from the elegant, rarefied, impersonal, and philosophical meditations associated with Stevens.

But this view rests on a reductive sense of New York School poetry – its range, its seriousness, and its philosophical investments – as well as a limited understanding of Stevens's presence and ubiquity for young, rebellious poets coming of age in the late 1940s and early 1950s. This is particularly problematic because Stevens's influence was quite pervasive and profound – not only for Ashbery but also for virtually all the poets associated with this movement. Take the case of Frank O'Hara: while critics have perhaps overemphasized the extent of Stevens's influence on Ashbery, they have gone the other direction in the case of O'Hara, often assuming he either ignored or disliked Stevens, while locating the roots of his plainspoken everyday poetics instead in Williams and other poets. In her groundbreaking 1977 study *Frank O'Hara: Poet Among Painters*, Perloff argues, "O'Hara's view of Wallace Stevens is respectful but somewhat distanced. . . . A great poet, in short, but one who looks to the past rather than to the future" (61). She claims O'Hara never seemed "to have much interest in . . . Stevens" – and later O'Hara critics have mostly followed this lead (62). However, we must be careful not to underestimate O'Hara's early and lasting enthusiasm for Stevens, as well as his subtle responses to Stevensian motifs and ideas in his poetry.

Far from viewing Stevens as a fossil of an earlier epoch or a poet who "looks to the past rather than to the future," O'Hara and the other young New York poets saw Stevens as very much alive and kicking, writing some of his most powerful poetry during the movement's formative years of the late 1940s and early 1950s. On February 11, 1947, Stevens gave a rare public reading at Harvard, where O'Hara, Ashbery, and Koch were students, an event that made a strong impression on the aspiring poets.[6] Ashbery had already fallen for Stevens's work several years earlier, when he had discovered "The Emperor of Ice-Cream" (Roffman 144). While at Harvard, Ashbery took a class on twentieth-century American poetry with the famous scholar F. O. Matthiessen, which, Ashbery recalled, "is where I really began to read Wallace Stevens" (Stitt 42); Ashbery even wrote a paper for Matthiessen on Stevens's poem "Chocorua to Its Neighbor" (Gooch 137). In a 1950 letter to O'Hara, Ashbery quipped that Stevens's work was so intimidatingly brilliant that it made him want to quit writing altogether: "Please open *Parts of a World* this instant and read a poem called 'Yellow Afternoon.' That poem has completely floored me with its greatness – every time I read it I am ready to turn in my chips and become an osteopath" (qtd. in Gooch 173).

Nearly every commentator on Ashbery has noted that Stevens quickly became one of the primary influences on his developing aesthetic. Although space prohibits a detailed discussion of the specifics of their dialogue, it is important to note that Ashbery's complex and evolving relationship to Stevens has been central to the younger poet's reception from the beginning, and that Ashbery is "perhaps the poet most frequently anointed as Stevens' great heir" (Eeckhout and Goldfarb, "Introduction" 8).[7] O'Hara himself was one of the first to highlight this connection: in his glowing review of his friend's first book, *Some Trees*, O'Hara called it "the most beautiful first book to appear in America since *Harmonium*" (*Standing* 78). The strong link between the poets became unshakable when Harold Bloom began to champion Ashbery in the 1970s as the main inheritor of the visionary tradition of Romantic poetry and to hail him as "the most legitimate of the sons of Stevens" (*Anxiety* 143). "Since the death of Wallace Stevens in 1955," one characteristic Bloom blurb declares, "we have been in the Age of Ashbery" (qtd. in Harvey).

But Ashbery wasn't alone among his friends in falling for Stevens's work: soon after meeting in college and becoming fast friends, Ashbery and O'Hara bonded over their mutual passion for Stevens, which may seem surprising, given the general consensus that O'Hara never warmed to his poetry. The writer Harold Brodkey, who was also at Harvard at the same time, recalled that both Ashbery and O'Hara tried to convince him to become a follower of Stevens rather than the mandarin traditionalist Eliot: "One day I ran into John and Frank on Massachusetts Avenue and they started saying that Stevens was a more important poet to them than Eliot, who was a huge influence on half the professors at Harvard.... They wanted to abandon Eliot for Stevens and they wanted me to go along with them" (qtd. in Gooch 138).

A few years later, in 1952, O'Hara gave a talk in New York at The Club, the legendary hangout of the Abstract Expressionist painters he revered, in which he praised Stevens's work, including his more recent poetry, while admiring the poet's stubborn refusal to bend to the dictates of fashion: "Never making concessions to styles or public comments he has remained austere without becoming cold and finicky; his work has grown steadily in beauty and wisdom while never thickening into mere fuss and elegance nor hardening into theory" (qtd. in Perloff, *Frank* 61). Furthermore, far from dismissing him entirely, O'Hara retained a reverence for Stevens throughout his career. As late as 1965, in an interview he gave shortly before his tragic early death, O'Hara praised the younger poet Tony Towle for having "this marvelous diction which is out of Wallace Stevens" and mentioned he had even recently incorporated a poem by Stevens into a poetry reading he gave: "And finally I was so tired of reading my own work, I read all Auden's things and some MacNeice and, let's see, one poem of Wallace Stevens" (*Standing* 22, 24).

At the same time, there are signs that O'Hara occasionally sought to distance himself and his work from Stevens. Even in his remarks at The Club, O'Hara pointed out (perhaps a tad defensively) that Stevens "has had very little influence when one considers his stature" (qtd. in Perloff, *Frank* 61). And, as critics have often noted, O'Hara makes a handful of cutting, if rather ambiguous, remarks about Stevens in some important later works. For instance, in his most famous essay, O'Hara writes that "Personism," the mock avant-garde movement he has just created, "is to Wallace Stevens what *la poésie pure* was to Béranger" (*Collected* 499) – apparently aligning Stevens with Béranger, "whose popular ballads initiated the scorn of Baudelaire" (Ragg 2).[8] Similarly, in his late long poem "Biotherm," O'Hara seems both to pay tribute to the older poet (mentioning an "hommage au poète américain / lyrique et profond, Wallace Stevens") and to chide him for his perceived failings: "but I don't get any love from Wallace Stevens no I don't" (*Collected* 439).[9]

While these moments certainly display some ambivalence, O'Hara repeatedly returns to Stevens not out of dislike, nor to signal his indifference to a poet he deems irrelevant, nor even from a sense that their projects are diametrically opposed. Rather, he does so out of deep fascination, a mingling of attraction and repulsion. As I have argued elsewhere, O'Hara's relationship to Stevens is inextricable from his complicated friendship with Ashbery, one of his closest friends and rivals – indeed, the figure of Stevens becomes a key element in O'Hara's efforts to separate his own poetic identity from Ashbery's.[10] This helps explain why the poets' shared commitment to Stevens was short-lived, as O'Hara soon fell in love with the work of Williams. When O'Hara informed Ashbery about his new passion for Williams, Ashbery wrote back, "I'm glad W. C. Williams has made a hit with you. By a strange and no doubt explainable coincidence, I've been reading tons of Wallace Stevens" (qtd. in Gooch 173). This "strange and no doubt explainable coincidence" is no accident, as Ashbery wryly hints. As their friendship and rivalry develops, O'Hara and Ashbery continually align themselves with contrasting poetic models – especially Williams and Stevens – as part of their bid to establish their difference from each other.[11]

One could argue that Stevens and all he represents for O'Hara – including various things he also associates with Ashbery, like imagination, abstraction, philosophical meditation, elevated diction – seem to haunt O'Hara's poetry from beginning to end. O'Hara's entire body of work, written under the motto "How I hate ... all things that don't change" (*Collected* 275), takes off from Stevens's fundamental belief that "Life Is Motion" and his proclamation that "It Must Change" (*CPP* 65, 336). O'Hara seems especially drawn to Stevens's key vocabulary, tropes, and intellectual obsessions in those frequent moments when he grapples with philosophical questions – about the fluid nature of selfhood, for example, or the blurry relationship between reality and dream, or the notion that experience is defined by change, movement, and flux. Stevens hovers in the background of O'Hara's writing, such as when he echoes Stevens's conviction that "There would still remain the never-resting mind" (*CPP* 179) when he dismisses the idea of "a rest for the mind no such / things available" (*Collected* 394). Or when he writes deeply Stevensian poems like "Sleeping on the Wing" that fuse dream and reality. Or in his major statement on the self as protean and multivalent, "In Memory of My Feelings," which directly echoes Stevens's "The Auroras of Autumn" by centering on the same trope of a serpent to embody its guiding theme of ceaseless transformation and mutability.[12]

Stevens was a catalyst not only for Ashbery and O'Hara but also for the other central members of the New York School's first generation. Barbara Guest's writing is suffused with Stevens's characteristic vocabulary and obsession with "reality" and "imagination," as can be seen in her probing meditations of *Fair Realism* and the *Forces of Imagination* (to name two of her book titles). As David Jarraway has recently argued, it is Stevens once again who helped bring the New York poets together in the first place: "it was the poetry of Wallace Stevens that truly forged the intimate association between Guest and O'Hara in the New York School context" (160). Guest suggested as much herself when she told an interviewer, "This is what Frank and I once talked about, how mysterious Wallace Stevens was to us. Then we started writing our own poetry, really writing it, and Wallace Stevens became simpler to understand" (qtd. in Jarraway 160). As Jarraway argues, many of the defining features of Guest's writing echo Stevens, including her devotion to an open-ended poetics, her aversion to the fixed and definitive, her unwillingness to stay rooted, whether in houses, places, or identities.

Stevens served as an equally important touchstone for James Schuyler. Stevensian obsessions with the relationship between realism and abstraction, change and stasis, and the nature of the ordinary undergird virtually all of Schuyler's writing.[13] Ashbery noted the connection in a warm introduction he gave to Schuyler's work when he said that his friend "somehow managed to draw on the whole arsenal of modernism, from the minimalism of Dr. Williams to the gorgeous aberrations of Wallace Stevens and the French Surrealists" (qtd. in Lehman 264). References to Stevens crop up throughout Schuyler's writing, whether through his use of a phrase from Stevens as an epigraph (for the poem "I sit down to type") or in the many lines from Stevens that fill "The Fauré Ballade," a commonplace book of favorite quotations in the form of a poem (*Collected* 240, 206–13). Stevens makes appearances in his diary as well: in one entry Schuyler quotes from "Sunday Morning" and in another he notes that "a line of Stevens kept coming into my mind" (*Diary* 241, 276). Furthermore, many Schuyler poems are implicitly in dialogue with Stevens and his major concerns – for instance, when Schuyler writes in "Dec. 28, 1974" that "I don't want to be open, / merely to say, to see and say, things / as they are" (*Collected* 234), it is impossible not to hear the refrain of Stevens's "The Man with the Blue Guitar": "Things as they are / Are changed upon the blue guitar" (*CPP* 135).[14]

Like the rest of the poets in this circle, Kenneth Koch found Stevens endlessly inspiring. In his 1956 poem "Fresh Air," a hilarious and forceful manifesto for the New York School's own aesthetic, Koch lists Stevens among other "great poets of our time" alongside Williams, Rilke, Lorca, and Apollinaire (*Collected* 123). For Koch, Stevens may have been most valuable for granting poets the intoxicating permission to fill their poems with wonderful, weird music and odd, unexpected words, and to imaginatively transform the real into something strange and wild. Late in life, Koch used an unforgettable line by Stevens to illustrate how he personally experienced the powerful force of poetic inspiration: "Stevens writes 'Catches tigers / In red weather' and I can't be contented until I get that much noise into two short lines" (*Making* 83). Stevensian motifs and gestures can be found throughout Koch's large body of work, whether in the echo of word-drunk poems like "Bantams in Pine-Woods" that one finds in Koch's radical foray into the sensual materiality of language in an early book-long poem like *When the Sun Tries to Go On*, or in his frequent use of the same kind of "theme and variations" structure one encounters in Stevens poems such as "Sea Surface Full of Clouds" or "Someone Puts a Pineapple Together" for poems like "Thank You," "The Magic of Numbers," or "In Bed."

In addition, Koch wrote about Stevens with infectious enthusiasm in his books about the teaching and writing of poetry, like *Sleeping on the Wing* and *Making Your Own Days*. A renowned and inspiring teacher, he spread the gospel of Stevens to his legions of pupils and disciples, many of whom went on to become central figures in the New York School's later incarnations. For example, one of his earliest protégés, Ted Berrigan, wrote in a 1962 letter about the moment Koch turned him on to the poet: "Koch lectured on Wallace Stevens, and it was the best lecture I have ever seen or heard on a poet. He read selections from 'Le Monocle de Mon Oncle,' and from 'The Comedian as the Letter C,' and also a few shorter poems, and he read with such verve and enthusiasm that the lines just leaped off the page" (*Dear Sandy* 117).

As this suggests, even Berrigan, the scruffy bohemian radical and arch disciple of O'Hara, revered Stevens and placed him at the front rank of all poets. In another letter, Berrigan wrote, "I'm reading Wallace Stevens's poems again, and he is such a great writer. He uses language in a way that very few writers can, and he illustrates that English is as beautiful a language as any poetic language.... There are times when Stevens is my favorite poet in the whole world. Only Shakespeare, and a rare few others, can write the English language like Stevens does" (*Dear Sandy* 138–39). According to Siobhan Phillips (94), Berrigan may even have taken the title for his now-legendary small literary magazine *C* from Stevens's poem "The Comedian as the Letter C," which would mean that Stevens, of all poets, underwrote one of the more influential underground, experimental magazines of the 1960s. Stevens also pops up in Berrigan's poems, which often track his own reading and appropriations: for example, in "Personal Poem #7" he, too, brings together Williams and Stevens when he writes, "had 17 ½ milligrams of desoxyn / last night 1 Miltown, read Paterson, parts / 1 & 2, poems by Wallace Stevens ..." (*Collected* 117). In his groundbreaking avant-garde sequence *The Sonnets*, Berrigan self-consciously constructs a lineage for himself that embraces both Stevens and first-generation poets of the New York School: "Back to books. I read / poems by Auden Spenser Pound Stevens and Frank O'Hara" (68). Berrigan's fascination with Stevens provides yet another sign that Stevens's legacy reaches deep into the New York School and the avant-garde precincts of contemporary poetry.

For too long, literary history has viewed postwar American poetry through a binary, "raw versus cooked" framework that has created a misleading image of Wallace Stevens and his poetic legacy and obscured his very real and tangible influence on a wider range of poets than is often assumed. If we take seriously the abundant connections between Stevens and these overlooked offspring, the work of the postmodernist New York School poets starts to look more philosophical, more weighty and serious, as it wrestles with Stevensian questions about language, epistemology, consciousness, and subjectivity. Conversely, if his impact on the New York School is better understood, a different Stevens can flicker into view: a poet firmly grounded in the daily, responsive to "the pressure of reality" (*CPP* 665), deeply attuned to contemporary philosophical currents, and "wildly experimental" in his language, in Susan Howe's phrase (qtd. in Filreis, "Later" 120). The dialogue between Stevens and the New York School makes it clearer than ever that the time has come to finally recognize Stevens as a major figure for the long tradition of avant-garde aesthetics that stretches from modernism to the postwar "New American Poetry," to Language poetry and its offshoots, down to the diverse array of innovative contemporary poets who continue to find Stevens's work endlessly inspiring and generative.

Notes

1 See Kenner's *The Pound Era* and *A Homemade World* and Perloff's "Pound/ Stevens." See also Perloff's reconsideration of her earlier views in "'Pound/ Stevens: Whose Era?' Revisited."
2 For further examples, see Golding; Richardson; Filreis, "Later"; and Epstein, "Rhapsody."
3 Aside from Ashbery, the New York School poets have rarely appeared in major critical studies of Stevens, including the excellent recent collection devoted to Stevens's influence on a wide range of poets, Eeckhout and Goldfarb's *Poetry and Poetics after Wallace Stevens*, or gatherings of contemporary Stevens criticism (such as the collections edited by Serio and MacLeod). By the same token, most studies of the New York School and its individual poets (other than Ashbery) generally downplay or omit discussions of Stevens, though there are notable exceptions, as I mention in note 5.

4 For a comprehensive group portrait of the New York School poets, see Lehman. For other discussions of the New York School as a whole, see Ward and Silverberg.

5 For recent exceptions to this general critical trend, see Phillips; Janssen; Jarraway; and Ragg. See also Filreis's "Coda: Wallace Stevens of the New York School," a "brief, whimsical" piece (163) in which Filreis (in the words of the volume's editors) "experimentally reads the aging Stevens as himself part of that literary cohort" (Goldfarb and Eeckhout 19).

6 According to Roffman, Ashbery was in the front row and loved Stevens's reading (144). Gooch mentions that O'Hara attended as well and it inspired him to try his hand at a Stevens imitation (109).

7 The list of critics who have discussed the connections, similarities, and disjunctions between Ashbery and Stevens is by now rather vast, but in addition to Bloom ("Charity"), some of the most important include Keller; Shapiro; Shoptaw; Herd; and Altieri.

8 For more on this passage as a slap at Stevens, see Ragg 2 and Phillips 96.

9 For more on this passage as illustrative of O'Hara's distance from Stevens, see Perloff, *Frank* 61; Janssen 997; and Phillips 96.

10 See *Beautiful Enemies*, especially 233–74.

11 In a 1950 letter to O'Hara, Ashbery grumbles, "You always disagree with everything I say.... Such as when I liked Lyon [Phelps] you didn't and now vice versa, and the similar business with Stevens and Williams, and you liking Shelley and Shostakovitch, while I preferred Keats and Prokofiev, etcetera" (qtd. in Gooch 174).

12 For an extended discussion of this poem in relation to Stevens and "The Auroras of Autumn," see Ladkin.

13 See Phillips for a discussion of "Stevens' presence in Schuyler's poetry" (97).

14 For another example, see my discussion of Schuyler's "June 30, 1974" as a response to Stevens's "Sunday Morning" (*Attention* 107–08).

WORKS CITED

Allen, Donald M., editor. *The New American Poetry, 1945–1960.* Grove, 1960.

Altieri, Charles. "How John Ashbery Modified Stevens' Uses of 'As.'" *Poetry and Poetics after Wallace Stevens*, edited by Eeckhout and Goldfarb, pp. 183–200.

Berrigan, Ted. *Collected Poems.* U of California P, 2007.

Dear Sandy, Hello: Letters from Ted to Sandy Berrigan. Coffee House Press, 2010.

The Sonnets. Penguin, 2000.

Bloom, Harold. *The Anxiety of Influence: A Theory of Poetry.* 1973. 2nd ed., Oxford UP, 1997.

"The Charity of the Hard Moments." *John Ashbery: Modern Critical Views*, edited by Bloom, Chelsea House, 1985, pp. 49–80.

Eeckhout, Bart, and Lisa Goldfarb. "Introduction: *After* Stevens." *Poetry and Poetics after Wallace Stevens*, edited by Eeckhout and Goldfarb, pp. 1–11.

editors. *Poetry and Poetics after Wallace Stevens*. Bloomsbury, 2017.

Epstein, Andrew. *Attention Equals Life: The Pursuit of the Everyday in Contemporary Poetry and Culture*. Oxford UP, 2016.

Beautiful Enemies: Friendship and Postwar American Poetry. Oxford UP, 2006.

"'The Rhapsody of Things as They Are': Stevens, Francis Ponge, and the Impossible Everyday." *The Wallace Stevens Journal*, vol. 36, no. 1, Spring 2012, pp. 47–77.

Filreis, Alan. "Coda: Wallace Stevens of the New York School." *Wallace Stevens, New York, and Modernism*, edited by Lisa Goldfarb and Bart Eeckhout, Routledge, 2012, pp. 163–69.

"Later Poets." *Wallace Stevens in Context*, edited by MacLeod, pp. 120–30.

"The Stevens Wars." *Boundary 2*, vol. 36, no. 3, Fall 2009, pp. 183–202.

Goldfarb, Lisa, and Bart Eeckhout. "Introduction: Back at the Waldorf?" *Wallace Stevens, New York, and Modernism*, edited by Goldfarb and Eeckhout, Routledge, 2012, pp. 1–20.

Golding, Alan. "The 'Community of Elements' in Wallace Stevens and Louis Zukofsky." *Wallace Stevens and the Poetics of Modernism*, edited by Albert Gelpi, Cambridge UP, 1985, pp. 120–40.

From Outlaw to Classic: Canons in American Poetry. U of Wisconsin P, 1995.

Gooch, Brad. *City Poet: The Life and Times of Frank O'Hara*. Alfred A. Knopf, 1993.

Harvey, Giles. "Fall Preview: Poet John Ashbery Makes His Elliptical Way into Library of America." *The Village Voice*, 4 Sep. 2008, www.villagevoice.com /2008/09/04/fall-preview-poet-john-ashbery-makes-his-elliptical-way-into-library-of-america/.

Herd, David. *John Ashbery and American Poetry*. Manchester UP, 2000.

Janssen, Lesley. "Triangulating Poetics: Late Wallace Stevens and a New York School." *Modern Language Review*, vol. 110, no. 4, Oct. 2015, pp. 992–1010.

Jarraway, David. *Wallace Stevens Among Others: Diva-Dames, Deleuze, and American Culture*. McGill-Queens UP, 2015.

Keller, Lynn. *Re-Making It New: Contemporary American Poetry and the Modernist Tradition*. Cambridge UP, 1987.

Kenner, Hugh. *A Homemade World: The American Modernist Writers*. Alfred A. Knopf, 1974.

The Pound Era. U of California P, 1973.

Koch, Kenneth. *The Collected Poems of Kenneth Koch*. Alfred A. Knopf, 2007.

Making Your Own Days: The Pleasures of Reading and Writing Poetry. Simon & Schuster, 1998.

Ladkin, Sam. "Frank O'Hara's Ecstatic Elegy: 'In Memory of My Feelings' in Memory Wallace Stevens." *Blackbox Manifold*, vol. 10, 2013, pp. 1–43.

Lehman, David, editor. *The Last Avant-Garde: The Making of the New York School of Poets*. Doubleday, 1998.

MacLeod, Glen, editor. *Wallace Stevens in Context*. Cambridge UP, 2017.

O'Hara, Frank. *Collected Poems*. U of California P, 1971.

Standing Still and Walking in New York. Edited by Donald Allen, Grey Fox, 1975.

Perloff, Marjorie. *Frank O'Hara: Poet Among Painters.* U of Texas P, 1977.

"Pound/Stevens: Whose Era?" 1982. *The Dance of the Intellect: Studies in the Poetry of the Pound Tradition*, Northwestern UP, 1996, pp. 1–32.

"'Pound/Stevens: Whose Era?' Revisited." *The Wallace Stevens Journal*, vol. 26, no. 2, Fall 2002, pp. 135–42.

Phillips, Siobhan. "Stevens and an Everyday New York School." *The Wallace Stevens Journal*, vol. 36, no. 1, Spring 2012, pp. 94–104.

Ragg, Edward. *Wallace Stevens and the Aesthetics of Abstraction.* Cambridge UP, 2010.

Richardson, Joan. "'Ghostlier Demarcations, Keener Sounds': Stevens, Susan Howe, and the Souls of the Labadie Tract." *Poetry and Poetics after Wallace Stevens*, edited by Eeckhout and Goldfarb, pp. 171–82.

Roffman, Karin. *The Songs We Know Best: John Ashbery's Early Life.* Farrar, Straus, and Giroux, 2017.

Schuyler, James. *Collected Poems.* Noonday, 1993.

The Diary of James Schuyler. Edited by Nathan Kernan, Black Sparrow, 1997.

Just the Thing: Selected Letters of James Schuyler, 1951–1991. Edited by William Corbett, Turtle Point P, 2004.

Serio, John N., editor. *The Cambridge Companion to Wallace Stevens.* Cambridge UP, 2007.

Shapiro, David. *John Ashbery: An Introduction to the Poetry.* Columbia UP, 1979.

Shoptaw, John. *On the Outside Looking Out: John Ashbery's Poetry.* Harvard UP, 1994.

Silverberg, Mark. *The New York School Poets and the Neo-Avant-Garde: Between Radical Art and Radical Chic.* Ashgate, 2010.

Stevens, Wallace. *Wallace Stevens: Collected Poetry and Prose.* Edited by Frank Kermode and Joan Richardson, Library of America, 1997.

Stitt, Peter A. "The Art of Poetry XXXIII: John Ashbery." Interview. *The Paris Review*, no. 90, Winter 1983, pp. 30–59.

Ward, Geoff. *Statutes of Liberty: The New York School of Poetry.* St. Martin's P, 1993.

CHAPTER 13

Poetic Fiction

Lisa Goldfarb

Wallace Stevens's writing took many forms: we know him for his personal journals as a young man and letters throughout the years, his essays, aphorisms, and of course his poems. For publication, aside from three experiments with playwriting early on, his literary temperament was decidedly poetic. He positioned himself so firmly in the realm of poetry that scholars of modernist fiction have tended to bypass him, while Stevens criticism has paid but little attention to the aesthetic affinities he shares with certain fiction writers. Yet, in essays and letters he does comment on novelists intermittently and has high praise for a few modernist figures. Stevens's regard for Marcel Proust, in particular, is striking; in a 1948 letter to José Rodríguez Feo, he writes,

> The only really interesting thing about Proust that I have seen recently is something that concerned him as a poet. It seems like a revelation, but it is quite possible to say that that is exactly what he was and perhaps all that he was. He saw life on many levels, but what he wrote was always on the poetic level on which he and you and I live. (*L* 575)

This chapter amplifies Proust's presence in Stevens in three segments: the first briefly addresses Stevens's relation to modernist fiction; the second probes Stevens's insight into Proust's writing style, highlighting formal and thematic aspects of the novelist's poetic prose that might have spurred Stevens to pronounce him a poet; the third focuses on Proustian echoes in Stevens's verse, particularly on the interlacing themes of the senses, time, and memory in a number of his shorter poems across different volumes.

I

Although Stevens's reading habits were wide-ranging, he was remarkably little drawn to the genre of fiction, with its dimensions of narrative plot and character depiction. It is clear, however, that he read the work of novelists, and their names appear in his prose: Henry James, Willa Cather, Ernest

Hemingway, and William Faulkner are among the American novelists he mentions, and, in the French tradition, Stendhal, Gustave Flaubert, André Gide, and Proust. While he had a friend smuggle a copy of the first print run of James Joyce's *Ulysses* into the country in 1922, Stevens seems to have been unexcited by the prospect of also reading it: we know from the surviving copy that he never sat down to cut the pages.[1] Still, Stevens's occasional comments in letters demonstrate his interest in novels and what he wished to find in them. That he looked to the novel for diversion is clear from a letter to Henry Church in 1946: "I wish I could think of a good novel or two. If I could, I should send for them for myself because I am terribly in need of some such holiday" (*L* 521). That it was not conventional fiction that he preferred is also clear from his correspondence. "Stendhal," he writes in a 1946 letter to Rodríguez Feo, "is the embodiment of the principle of prose." He seems to favor Stendhal over Flaubert "because Stendhal is a point of reference for the mature, while Flaubert is a point of reference for the artist, and perhaps for the immature" (*L* 505). Of novelists on the American side of the Atlantic, Stevens favors Cather, as a letter to Leonard C. van Geyzel demonstrates. "[Y]ou may think she is more or less formless," he writes. "Nevertheless, we have nothing better than she is," and he reveals that it is Cather's subtle voice that he appreciates: "She takes so much pains to conceal her sophistication that it is easy to miss her quality" (*L* 381).

Stevens reserves his highest praise for novelists whom he deems "poetic." He singles out Hemingway and Faulkner as figures who, in addition to Proust, are modern writers of poetic fiction. Hemingway, in fact, was Stevens's first recommendation as a potential lecturer when his friend Henry Church was convening a series on poetry at Princeton: "Most people don't think of Hemingway as a poet, but obviously he is a poet and I should say, offhand, the most significant of living poets" (*L* 411). The same is true of Faulkner, Stevens's second choice: "For all his gross realism, Faulkner is a poet" (*L* 412). Stevens makes it clear in a letter to Rodríguez Feo later in the same year that writers of prose fiction can equally be poets. Of Hemingway he writes, "I haven't the slightest doubt that what Hemingway will be trying to get at is what everyone instantly recognizes to be poetry" (*L* 520). Poetry, for Stevens, then, covers a wider field than formal verse alone and can take markedly different forms.

II

When Stevens names Proust a poet in his letter to Rodríguez Feo, he explains a bit more what he means than when he graces Hemingway or Faulkner with the term. Perhaps especially given the French novelist's expansive multi-volume form and architectural scope, Proust is a "revelation" of a kind, for his poetic qualities may not be the most ready way of describing him. Stevens signals his importance in the way he associates Proust's writerly posture with his own and his Cuban friend's: like the two of them, "what he wrote" and how he lived were "always on the poetic level" (*L* 575).

Stevens's "revelation" also intrigued Rodríguez Feo, who asked him in a subsequent letter for the source of his conjecture: "I would like to know where you read about Proust, *le poète*, unless you divined that yourself" (*Secretaries* 117). While Stevens does not directly respond to his friend's query, his essay "The Relations Between Poetry and Painting" suggests that he might have been referring to the work of Professor Denis Saurat, an Anglo-French scholar with whom he was familiar. Stevens quotes from Saurat, who, he explains, describes "the poetry in the prose of Proust, taken from his vast novel. . . ." What is "poetic" in Proust, Stevens proposes, by way of Saurat, are Proust's "'description[s] of those eternal moments in which we are lifted out of the drab world. . . . The madeleine dipped in tea, the steeples of Martinville, some trees on a road, a perfume of wild flowers, a vision of light and shade on trees'" (*CPP* 744). Stevens thus highlights the heightened sensory moments that stand out from the narrative arc of Proust's novel, moments of intense awareness that lift the narrative outside the usual flow of time. It is, of course, Proust's narrator – the narrative voice of the novel – who directs our attention to those moments so that we can feel their significance within and beyond the tale. For Stevens, as for Proust, the voice to which we listen binds together poet and reader so that when Proust's narrator lingers over the madeleine, the steeples, the trees on the road, and the perfume of flowers, it is through the quality of his voice that we taste, see, hear, smell, and feel along with him the significance of those exceptional sensory moments.

Stevens's insight into Proust's poetic dimension is best formally illustrated by the way the novelist uses simile to extend his reach beyond the plot and deepen the reader's understanding of the scope of his protagonist's life. At the same time that the narrator takes us through his daily experience, guiding us through the world he inhabits – the routines of everyday life, the features of the town, and the sky and landscape through which he travels on his family walks – Proust's similes connect this quotidian life with aspects of the historical, social, natural, and physical worlds in which it unfolds.

Given the vastness of *Remembrance of Things Past*, a few examples must suffice. I draw passages from the first volume, *Swann's Way*, to render the discussion manageable, but also because it is likely that Stevens himself would have been most familiar with the opening volume. For Proust's narrator, the human, built environment is never too distant from the wider natural world. Even the opening pages of the novel demonstrate the resemblance Proust seeks to reveal. The adult Marcel awakens in a room in the middle of the night, and in a state between waking and dreaming he strains to situate himself geographically and temporally:

> I would ask myself what time it could be; I could hear the whistling of trains, which, now nearer and now farther off, punctuating the distance like the note of a bird in a forest, showed me in perspective the deserted countryside through which a traveller is hurrying towards the nearby station. . . . (3)

In his in-between state, the narrator can scarcely locate the sounds that he hears: Proust reminds us that they are alternately "nearer" and "farther," so that rather than resolving into clear tones that would define them, the sounds themselves shift and change to reflect his own disoriented state. In this condition, the narrator likens the train's fluctuating sounds in the distance to "the note of a bird in the forest." With this simile, Proust at once draws the reader into the narrator's confused state and stretches our understanding. The sounds of the human-made train are not distinct from those of the forest bird, for the narrator's apprehension of their difference is wholly dependent on the consciousness of the listener.

Proust's narrator describes his experience of the natural world using similes that imbue the moon and its light, the wind, rain, and flowers (much like Stevens will in poems) with a nearly human agency. Consider, for example, how early in the novel Marcel, determined to stay awake to await his mother's goodnight kiss, opens his bedroom window and describes the moonlight:

> Noiselessly I opened the window and sat down on the foot of my bed. I hardly dared to move in case they should hear me from below. Outside, things too seemed frozen, rapt in a mute intentness not to disturb the moonlight which, duplicating each of them and throwing it back by the extension in front of it of a shadow denser and more concrete than its substance, had made the whole landscape at once thinner and larger, like a map which, after being folded up, is spread out upon the ground. (35)

So silent is the night that the narrator describes how "things" first appear "frozen," yet he describes what he can see as "rapt in a mute intentness," almost as though the landscape possesses its own awareness. Proust describes the moon as if it were a character that should not be disturbed. His simile exquisitely renders the quiet of the night and suggests that the light itself possesses a vivifying and directive power.

Just as the moonlight sets the landscape "quivering" (35), so does the wind disperse its spirit over Combray, sometimes with the scent of the narrator's beloved hawthorns and lilacs. When the narrator describes his walk along the Méséglise Way, he refers to the windy hawthorns:

> Once in the fields, we never left them again during the rest of our Méséglise walk. They were perpetually traversed, as though by an invisible wanderer, by the wind which was to me the tutelary genius of Combray. Every year, on the day of our arrival, in order to feel that I really was at Combray, I would climb the hill to greet it as it swept through the furrows and swept me along in its wake. (158–59)

Proust describes the wind of Combray metaphorically as its "tutelary genius"; the wind functions as the narrator's guardian-like spirit. It is hard not to think of the wind that blows so often through Stevens's verse in reading Proust's descriptions, for his landscape, like that of Proust, is "perpetually traversed . . . by an invisible wanderer," sometimes gently and sometimes bitingly.

Stevens writes in his "Adagia," "Weather is a sense of nature. Poetry is a sense" (*CPP* 902). In doing so, he gestures to the role sensation plays in his own poems, and simultaneously to another poetic aspect of *Combray* for which the novelist is well known. For Proust, it is the senses that awaken consciousness and, crucially, memory and an understanding of time – the all-important themes of his work. While we are most familiar, as Stevens must have been, with the culminating scene of *Combray*, when the grown-up Marcel dips his madeleine in tea and inadvertently summons his entire childhood – that "vast structure of recollection" sparked by his involuntary memory (51) – Proust's emphasis on the senses as a gateway to consciousness and knowledge is apparent on the novel's every page. In the early pages, the narrator is attuned to bells of various kinds that alert the reader to the significance of their sounds. Proust announces the auditory importance of the bells that will sound through the novel when the narrator describes his family's retiring to the summer garden after dinner:

> On those evenings when, as we sat in front of the house round the iron table beneath the big chestnut-tree, we heard, from the far end of the garden, not the shrill and assertive alarm bell which assailed and deafened with its ferruginous, interminable, frozen sound any member of the household who set it off on entering "without ringing," but the double tinkle, timid, oval, golden, of the visitors' bell, everyone would at once exclaim "A visitor! Who in the world can it be?" but they knew quite well that it could only be M. Swann. (14)

Proust not only describes the bell that signifies Swann's arrival but also compares the quality of its sound to other familiar bells. Unlike the "ferruginous" sound of the alarm bell, the "double tinkle, timid, oval, golden, of the visitors' bell" announces the arrival of Swann, a figure whom we soon learn will be central to the narrator's self-understanding. Proust likewise furnishes such acoustic detail when he writes about the narrator's habit of reading in the garden on Saturday afternoons when the chimes of the church bells measure the passing hours. The chimes not only parse the hours, but the narrator's sudden awareness that he had missed one indicates the power of his reading to transport him to an entirely different experience of time. On their simplest level, bells and their sounds signal family routines and the comings and goings of characters and acquaint the reader with the social fabric of the novel. As the narrator and, by extension, we, as readers, hear them in all their complex variety – the startling alarm bell, the gentle visitors' bell, domestic bells, church bells – they come to have organic, living qualities as palpable as the narrator's own voice.

So it is with all the senses in Proust's novel, for all prompt him to self-reflection and knowledge. Traveling through the countryside by carriage, when he sees three steeples – the twin steeples of Martinville and that of Vieuxvicq – the visual images awaken him not only to the beauty of the scene and an understanding of changing perspective but, crucially, to his desire to write. The images he has of the steeples shift as surely as the carriage moves, yet they provide something of an anchor for him amid the moving world: "The minutes passed, we were travelling fast, and yet the three steeples were always a long way ahead of us, like three birds perched upon the plain motionless and conspicuous in the sunlight" (198). Noteworthy, too, is how Proust likens the artifacts of the steeples to "birds perched upon the plain," again integrating the human and natural worlds.

While each of the senses opens up the narrator's perception of the world within and beyond himself, Proust prizes smell and taste, above all, for their particular power. When Marcel describes the hawthorns, flowers that hold particular importance for him, it is their fragrance upon which he lingers. Of the hawthorns decorating the altar, Proust's narrator exclaims, "these gusts of fragrance came to me like the murmuring of an intense organic life" (123). He cannot help but ascribe sanctity to them when he comes upon them in the open air: "I found the whole path throbbing with the fragrance of hawthorn-blossom. The hedge resembled a series of chapels, whose walls were no longer visible under the mountains of flowers" (150). Proust describes "smells" as "a deep reservoir of poetry to the stranger who passes through their midst without having lived among them" (53). The fragrance of the hawthorns, like the taste of the famous madeleine that sparks the narrator's memory, and indeed all sense experience constitute this "deep reservoir" that Proust draws from to create his novel, and, as we will see, Stevens does to create his poems.

It is important to bear in mind – as we turn our attention to Stevens – that Proust emphasizes not only the primacy of the senses but also their power in relation to our intellect. The world that Marcel describes – the built environment and nature in all its prismatic manifestations – bears the imprint of layers of human experience and awaits discovery. That discovery, and particularly, for Proust, the discovery of the past, happens exclusively through the senses. He reminds us after the madeleine scene: "It is a labour in vain to attempt to recapture [the past]," for it "is hidden somewhere outside the realm, beyond the reach of the intellect, in some material object (in the sensation which that material object will give us) of which we have no inkling" (47–48). If Proust emphasizes the role our senses play in this discovery, however, this does not mean that our intellectual resources are futile. Toward the end of *Combray*, he reminds us that what he discovers by way of his senses, his retrieval of his past, is due to his "exaltation of mind," a mind that has reflected on and kept alive these memories "through the succession of the years" (200). Of these chance discoveries Stevens would say, "We reason about them with a later reason" (*CPP* 345).

III

"The body is the great poem," Stevens writes in "Adagia" (*CPP* 908), and to create the many lyrics that comprise his "great poem of the earth" (*CPP* 730) Stevens continually draws on sense experience. His many speakers, in a world bereft of traditional forms of belief, seek to discover their relation to the physical world as ever moving and fluctuating as the world that Proust's narrator encounters. Stevens asks probing questions in his work and these often start with how we feel: how do we hear and see, taste, touch, and smell the world within and about us? Are we, as Proust's narrator finally is, part of a world that is an organic whole? Or do we remain tragically separate? Do our sensory – and intellectual – faculties give us the capacity to plumb the depths of memory so that we access "Time" beyond our immediate, present experience? Even a short survey of poems across Stevens's oeuvre can demonstrate how he, like Proust, works through the senses to express their complexity.

Needless to say, Stevens does not present the grand narrative of self-discovery that Proust does in *Remembrance*; yet, the poet's speakers, like Proust's Marcel, often test out their relation to the external world by sensory means, most often in the way they hear and see. The speaker of Stevens's "To the Roaring Wind" is reminiscent of Proust's narrator caught between dreams and sleep: "What syllable are you seeking, / Vocalissimus, / In the distances of sleep? / Speak it" (*CPP* 77). Much as Proust's narrator in Combray awakens in the middle of the night unsure of who and where he is, Stevens gives us a poem consisting only of one question and one imperative sentence in four short lines that produce a similar effect. A disoriented speaker speaks out of the depths of sleep to probe the nature of the mighty sound of which he is barely conscious. That the speaker wonders whether the wind speaks a language that is comprehensible to him is clear from Stevens's choice of the word "syllable" – as if the random sound of the wind might have the same searching spirit as the sleeper/dreamer. That he personifies and names the wind with a formidable Latinate name – "Vocalissimus" – is testament to the speaker's own desire for the wind to speak with human meaning. What initially seems to be a question/answer poem, however, turns out not to be the case, for, rather than receiving an answer from the wind, the speaker's last line simply intensifies the question. The speaker tells the wind to speak as if it were human. "Speak it," he commands.

The sounds of bells ring through Stevens's poems, too, recalling those of Proust: wind chimes, church bells, dinner bells. In the early poem "Indian River," Stevens's speaker searches the sound of the bell-like "jingles" that the wind creates as it moves through the rings of fishnets for what they might say about the coming of spring. In much the same way as Proust likens sounds from one dimension of experience to another, Stevens parallels the "trade-wind jingles" through the "rings in the nets" to the sound of the "jingle of the water among the roots," and to the "jingle of the red-bird." The movement of long lines mimics the movement of the wind, and his repetitions of "jingles" reproduce the sound to which the speaker listens (*CPP* 93). In the late poem "Dinner Bell in the Woods," Stevens not only likens a sound in one domain to that in another, he goes so far as to place the domestic bell – the dinner bell of the title – in a natural setting. As with Proust's alarm bell, the sound seems to pull the speaker out of his reverie and to stimulate the action of the poem: "The picnic of children came running then, // In a burst of shouts," while "The smaller ones // Came tinkling on the grass to the table. . . ." What is most striking here is that Stevens intermingles, as Proust often does, the actual sound with its effect on the listener: "The point of it was the way he heard it, / In the green, outside the door of phantasma" (*CPP* 471).

Just as hawthorns, orchids, lilies, and lilacs fill the pages of Proust's novel, providing visual and olfactory pleasure, so do abundant species of flowers and plants proliferate in Stevens's poems – hibiscuses, larkspur, roses, lilacs, ferns, palms, grape leaves, willows. While in Proust's novel, the images of flowers and their scents hold out the promise of longevity, Stevens's flora does not extend such promise. As beautiful as the flowers are, their bloom is temporary, and they belong to a physical world that eludes us. In "Six Significant Landscapes," the old man who sits "In the shadow of a pine tree" in the first stanza sees "larkspur, / Blue and white, / At the edge of the shadow, / Move in the wind" (*CPP* 58). What he sees lasts only as long as the wind that moves through them. The willow under which Jasmine sits in "Jasmine's Beautiful Thoughts Underneath the Willow" does not stimulate thoughts that transport her outside of the moment, like Proust's narrator's thoughts under the chestnut tree; rather, her "titillations have no foot-notes / And their memorials are the phrases / Of idiosyncratic music" (*CPP* 62). Stevens's lilacs, as Helen Vendler has so poignantly explored, in the later "Things of August" have a "sad smell," and though "one remembered it," it is only "as of an exhumation returned to earth, // The rich earth, of its own self made rich" (*CPP* 419).[2] Even when Stevens basks in the visual richness of the flora of his poems – for instance, the "black reds, / Pink yellows, orange whites" in "Bouquet of Roses in Sunlight" – their beauty evades our efforts to describe them or hold them in the mind: "So sense exceeds all metaphor. // It exceeds the heavy changes of the light. / It is like a flow of meanings with no speech" (*CPP* 370). The reds of "The Red Fern" are so lush – the plants are "red after red," and "dazzling, bulging, brightest" – yet they do not open a gateway to the past, as Proust's hawthorns do: "it is enough in life / To speak of what you see," Stevens writes in the last stanza (*CPP* 316–17).

Stevens, nevertheless, like Proust, still attests to the power of the senses, and like the French novelist, he creates a rivalry between the senses and reason. While Stevens argues in essays and poems for the necessary balance between reason and sensibility, in poem after poem he shows us reason's limitations. As the speaker in the early "In the Clear Season of Grapes" tries to conceptualize the relation of mountains, land, and sea, his reason fails him: "Have I stopped and thought of its point before?" he asks in the first stanza. When he thinks, what comes to mind are not "thoughts" but the sensory associations he has with his "lands": the image of "the house / And the table that holds a platter of pears, / Vermilion smeared over green. . . ."

He longs to penetrate meaning, yet all he can do is exclaim that they mean "more than that" (*CPP* 92). In "Meditation Celestial & Terrestrial," Stevens situates us in the midst of the sumptuous spring world: "The wild warblers are warbling in the jungle / Of life and spring and of the lustrous inundations. . . ." He then contrasts that fertile world with winter, when "We hardened ourselves to live by bluest reason / In a world of wind and frost" (*CPP* 101). His comparisons, however, are not merely seasonal, he suggests at the close of the poem; rather, in the way that he contrasts spring and winter, he poses the culminating rhetorical question: "But what are radiant reason and radiant will / To warblings early in the hilarious trees / Of summer, the drunken mother?" (*CPP* 102).

In his late poems, Stevens often does not pose the rivalry as a question but rather issues statements. In "Pieces," he asserts declaratively, "There are things in a man besides his reason" (*CPP* 306), and in "Saint John and the Back-Ache," he reaffirms such rivalry. Cast as a dialogue between "The Back-Ache" and "Saint John," the latter explains, "The world is presence and not force. / Presence is not mind" (*CPP* 375). Stevens brings us to the threshold of the meaning that Proust's narrator ultimately finds in epiphanic sensory moments, yet such moments in Stevens do not seem to be able to deliver. The voice of the "The Back-Ache" intones at the end of the poem, "It is possible," yet "Presence lies far too deep, for me to know" (*CPP* 376).

Given the value that Stevens places on the senses, then, we may ask whether the senses ever – as the taste and aroma of Proust's madeleine do – grant to Stevens's speakers not only images of the past "in our memory, but . . . their return, their actual, circumjacent, immediately available presence" (89). To close I would like to turn to "A Dish of Peaches in Russia," a poem that seems to put Proust's thesis to the test (*CPP* 206). Its ten unrhymed couplets unfurl in three broad units. In the first (1–3), the speaker, a Russian exile, tastes from a bunch of peaches to a jarring effect. Although it is the taste (the sense, along with smell, in which Proust invests the greatest power) that initially jolts him, one sense follows another until all five senses come into play: "I touch them and smell them," he cries, and he sees them "As a young lover sees the first buds of spring / And as the black Spaniard plays his guitar." Indeed, as the opening words of the poem indicate, he tastes "With [his] whole body. . . ."

So impactful are these peaches that the speaker becomes disoriented. As if he cannot place his own identity, he exclaims, "Who speaks?" and, in the next six stanzas (4–9), Stevens explores how the taste of the peaches displaces the speaker in time and space. To reflect his speaker's confused state, Stevens punctuates the first few lines with questions and pauses: "Who speaks?" he exclaims, as though he does not know who he is. "But it must be that I, / That animal, that Russian, that exile. . . ." Like Marcel when he tastes the madeleine steeped in tea, Stevens's speaker cannot locate himself, and it is almost as if he can hear the sound of the "bells of the chapel" (they "pullulate sounds at / Heart," recalling Proustian bells), which transport him to another time and place. Overcome by the sensation, he describes the peaches again; in the movement from the fifth to the sixth stanza, Stevens frames the description with exclamations, which at once create a pause in the line and emphasize the speaker's wish to linger in this moment in and out of time: "The peaches are large and round, // Ah! and red; and they have peach fuzz, ah! / They are full of juice and the skin is soft."

The tone of the poem markedly changes from exclamatory to calm in the next few stanzas (6–8) as Stevens renders the "presence" of the native land that the taste has brought back to his speaker. Of the peaches, the speaker intones, "They are full of the colors of my village," and, as if to prolong the speaker's imaginative sojourn in his native village, the poet fills these lines with satiate images of "fair weather, summer, dew, peace." Stevens stresses how fragile the speaker's state is and questions its longevity when the speaker says in the penultimate stanza, "Even the drifting of the curtains, / Slight as it is, disturbs me." While "A Dish of Peaches in Russia" approximates Marcel's experience, however much the peaches draw the past into the present for his speaker, it is a Proustian experience with a Stevensian twist. Whereas Proust summons the "vast structure of recollection" that connects all periods of time (51), Stevens cannot help but close his poem on a note of fragmentation: "I did not know // That such ferocities could tear / One self from another, as these peaches do."

Although "A Dish of Peaches" echoes Proust in its theme – the relation between the senses, time, and memory – Stevens nevertheless departs from his predecessor in its resolution. Unlike Proust's narrator, whose sensory experience returns him to a world that is an organic whole, Stevens's speaker's experience, however rich and powerful, leaves him torn, straddling the gulf between past and present. Yet, Stevens's rendering of the Proustian theme in such an explicit way in this poem speaks to the power of the French novelist's resonance. Proust's use of sustained similes throughout *Remembrance* and his exploration of the power of the senses to awaken memory and unleash new modes of understanding dovetail with some of Stevens's own interests as a modern poet. In the sensual richness of his poems, in the rivalry Stevens draws between the senses and reason, and in the way the senses lead us to the threshold of new knowledge and worlds, we hear abundant Proustian echoes.

Notes

1 For a study of Stevens's affinities with Joyce, see Eeckhout.
2 See Vendler.

WORKS CITED

Eeckhout, Bart. "'And yet – and yet!': Connections between Stevens's Poetry and Joyce's *Ulysses*." *The Wallace Stevens Journal*, vol. 42, no. 2, Fall 2018, pp. 143–52.

Proust, Marcel. *Remembrance of Things Past*. Vol. 1, translated by C. K. Scott Moncrieff and Terence Kilmartin, Random House, 1982.

Stevens, Wallace. *Letters of Wallace Stevens*. Edited by Holly Stevens, Alfred A. Knopf, 1966.

   Secretaries of the Moon: The Letters of Wallace Stevens and José Rodríguez Feo. Edited by Beverly Coyle and Alan Filreis, Duke UP, 1986.

   Wallace Stevens: Collected Poetry and Prose. Edited by Frank Kermode and Joan Richardson, Library of America, 1997.

Vendler, Helen. "Wallace Stevens: Memory, Dead and Alive." *The Wallace Stevens Journal*, vol. 28, no. 2, Fall 2004, pp. 247–60.

CHAPTER 14

Poetic Thinking

Charles Altieri

The habit of forming concepts is a habit of the mind by which it probes for an integration.... The philosopher searches for an integration for its own sake ... the poet searches for an integration that shall be ... sufficient for some quality that it possesses, such as its insight, its evocative power or its appearance in the eye of the imagination. (*CPP* 862)

[T]he philosopher's world is intended to be a world, which yet remains to be discovered and ... the poet's world is intended to be a world, which yet remains to be celebrated.... If the philosopher's world is this present world plus thought, then the poet's world is this present world plus imagination. (*CPP* 864)

In one sense, the best this chapter can do is point out how brilliantly Wallace Stevens wrote by the middle of the twentieth century about the differences between philosophical thinking and poetic thinking.[1] But there is much to clarify about why he projects different modes of poetic thinking throughout his career and about what kinds of experience such poetic thinking establish. While the following pages will attempt to clarify the logic informing such changes, space restrictions will confine my efforts at clarification largely to making generalizations and indicating the poems that seem to me best to represent what I am claiming. There will be scant opportunities for the kinds of close reading that would actively display what each model can achieve. And there will be scant opportunities to elaborate how Stevens occasionally explores alternative modes of poetic thinking that either break new ground or return to models he seems to have discarded.

Put simply, four modes of poetic thinking fascinate me in Stevens's work. First, *Harmonium* (1923) affords brilliant positive undoings of the fantasies of sensuous rhetorical argument that were basic to his youthful ambitions as a poet.[2] I think we most fully appreciate *Harmonium* when we can see it entirely reconceiving what poetic thinking can be – from an ideal of cogent masculine argument to the possibility of thinking against generalization. Such thinking offers allegories that fascinate without resolving. And it shifts the sensuality of poetry from an emphasis on referring to sensuous detail to a lyric sensuality that is basic to the forms of concreteness established by the workings of the medium. Second, Stevens turns in *Ideas of Order* (1936) from valuing the eccentric to imagining how poetic thinking can become central to ordinary life. I want to explore how the effort to establish a voice for valuing ordinary experience generates a corollary concern for the heroic figure of "major man" that is capable of giving meaning and value to how the pressures of reality emerge in common life. Third, by the final poems of *Transport to Summer* (1947) Stevens seems to become embarrassed by the rhetoric of the hero and major man. He becomes increasingly concerned with blending the unreal of fiction with the work of realization, a concept strikingly parallel to Paul Cézanne's idea of how art brings force and vitality to nature. For Stevens, "realization" focuses on establishing a sense of wholeness by which the poem enlarges our sense of mutuality between the mind and natural processes. Finally, that theoretical concern for blending fictionality with realization generates in *The Rock* (1954) a mode of poetic thinking inseparable from a sense of self-conscious dwelling that enables us to value the artifice present in even the most elemental of experiences.

I

The first model of poetic thinking in Stevens's *Collected Poems* involves a transformation altering what the young Stevens thought of as the masculine nature of ambitious poetry.[3] He was convinced at an early age that poetry had to ally itself with the efforts at philosophical integration fundamental to all discursive thinking. Yet poetry was not quite discursive thinking, so how could its inner workings modify philosophy to take advantage of its distinctive non-discursive qualities? Stevens's earliest published poems, such as the sonnets "Vita Mea" and "Cathedrals are not built along the sea" (*CPP* 481, 486), responded to this concern by a return to Renaissance ideals of rhetorical generalization sustained by elaborate metaphoric uses of sensuous detail. The second of these sonnets argues by means of a profusion of figures that the sea is a grander object of worship than anything mediated by religious doctrine. The closing couplet offers an elegant emotional figure for how nature provides what religion would disrupt:

Through gaudy windows there would come too soon
The low and splendid rising of the moon. (*CPP* 486)

I think the poems Stevens wrote to and for his future wife, Elsie, a decade
later, in 1908 and 1909, made a major difference in his ideas of self-presentation.
He could not lecture a lover. And he had to find a kind of intimacy that made
poetry a distinctive form of sensibility – important for what it made present
even more than for what it said. After these private attempts, Stevens tried to
establish a poetic thinking in the poems of *Harmonium* that offered two radical,
closely correlated breaks from how he had been fostering his ambitions. In the
place of conventional allegorizing as a mode of poetic thinking, he developed
modes of incomplete or multiply interpretable allegories. Hence the riddling
"Earthy Anecdote" introduces *Harmonium* as Stevens's version of Immanuel
Kant's claim that art creates much thinking that resists any coherent purpose:
the trappings of allegory demand interpretive generalization, but the indefin-
iteness of the relations between the poem's firecat and its bucks calls for
thinking as a tonally deft exploration of possible meanings. Here the mind is
actively engaged in repudiating what seems most natural for a mind to do – to
move fluidly from particulars to generalities. The particulars in "Earthy
Anecdote" (as well as in "Metaphors of a Magnifico" and "Domination of
Black") insist on their force as particulars, not as alternatives to the work of the
mind but as necessary instruments for what can be won from resisting habitual
practices. This is Stevens's plot against the giant – an effort to develop an active
rendering of what a perspective informed by the female can do to and for
inherited priorities in our ways of thinking.

Then the poems have to ask what can be the instrument for poetic
thinking when it refuses traditional models for interpreting particulars.
Stevens's response is to call attention to the constructed intimacy of the
poem as a kind of sensuality that insists on the possible significance of each
linguistic feature for the sensuous structure they establish in relation to
each other. In poems like "The Snow Man," there is reference to an
external winter scene, but the primary sensuous structure is syntax and
sound. Perhaps the richest reallocation of sensual intensity is "Jasmine's
Beautiful Thoughts Underneath the Willow":

> My titillations have no foot-notes
> And their memorials are the phrases
> Of idiosyncratic music.
>
> The love that will not be transported
> In an old, frizzled, flambeaued manner,
> But muses on its eccentricity,

Is like a vivid apprehension
Of bliss beyond the mutes of plaster,
Or paper souvenirs of rapture,

Of bliss submerged beneath appearance,
In an interior ocean's rocking
Of long, capricious fugues and chorals. (*CPP* 62–63)

I cite this poem in its entirety because it makes such a direct statement of thinking that "muses on its eccentricity" and so can insist on embodied titillations as its primary vehicle. The most astonishing element of the poem is the concluding six-line simile that subsumes reference to the world into a reference to its own sensuous features that can claim to define an interior reality in their utter outward visibility. This interior rocking becomes identical with the poem's own marvelous play with "I" and "o" sounds and the cadence they produce.

II

Stevens's subsequent reactions to the kinds of poetic thinking informing *Harmonium* are well known. One summary takes place in his essay "The Noble Rider and the Sound of Words," as Stevens rejects a poetics of the "eccentric" for an ideal of a poetry at the center, in which the poet's "function is to make his imagination theirs" (that is, the audience's), so that the writer "fulfills himself only as he sees his imagination become the light in the minds of others. His role . . . is to help people to live their lives" (*CPP* 660–61). This ambition depends on the conviction "not only that the imagination adheres to reality, but, also, that reality adheres to the imagination and that the interdependence is essential" (*CPP* 663). The interdependence is essential because then poetic thinking can not only engage the truth but also modify the truth by staging its relations to typical human desires and modes of satisfaction. And awareness of that staging comes close to justifying a sense of heroic activity in the forming of fictions that embody our senses of possibility for acting in accord with fundamental desires.

But it is one thing to appreciate Stevens's arguments about the states of nobility made possible by how reality adheres to the imagination, and quite another to engage the passion and precision with which Stevens struggles to arrive at the comfort of such conclusions. It is easy to ignore how passionate and how needy "Farewell to Florida" is in introducing the first volume of Stevens to try for a poetics of the center. The concluding section of the poem starts with two sentences, each utterly overflowing with urgent repetitions of scenic details in which the poet's psyche seems completely removed, except for this strange wish:

> To be free again, to return to the violent mind
> That is their mind, these men, and that will bind
> Me round, carry me, misty deck, carry me
> To the cold, go on, high ship, go on, plunge on. (*CPP* 98)

What kind of freedom is this that traps him in the violent mind of other people, carrying him into the cold and demanding of him this collusion in the ship's plunging on? There is an answer to this question, but it involves a surprising sense that truth is more a trap than a release. Only by entering this totally alienating space, nevertheless, can one escape the seductions of romance provided by Florida. Rarely does poetry so fully capture the physicality of what seems authentic yet inescapably repugnant. Truth for Stevens in the 1930s was no philosopher's honeymoon. In fact, for several years Stevens seems to have felt that he could be sure a thought was true only if it caused pain in the form of disappointment for the imagination.

The conditions of this repugnance suggest why Stevens could treat the marrying of fictions with the real as a heroic enterprise. First let us further explore the causes of the pain. "Sad Strains of a Gay Waltz" powerfully engages the contradictory dimensions of a poetic thinking that entails constraining itself to what goes against all desire for romance. Yet it manages to afford a vision of imaginative adequacy to the real by having the imagination break through to a skeptical music attuned to the forms of disappointment:

> The epic of disbelief
> Blares oftener and soon, will soon be constant.
> Some harmonious skeptic soon in a skeptical music
>
> Will unite these figures of men and their shapes
> Will glisten again with motion, the music
> Will be motion and full of shadows. (*CPP* 101)

Stevens did not quite adapt his poetic thinking to embrace this skepticism. Even in his darkest poems, like "The Man on the Dump," with its hatred for the images that inject desire into the bare real, there is a moment when the speaker feels a "purifying change":

> Everything is shed; and the moon comes up as the moon
> (All its images are in the dump) and you see
> As a man (not like an image of a man),
> You see the moon rise in the empty sky. (*CPP* 185)

The grammatical resources of "as" have the power to make human desire present and vital despite the failure of the mind's capacities for active figuration. And relying on these grammatical resources prepares the way for giving a slightly heroic cast to the final reliance in the poem on the resources of the definite article.

Let me briefly expand this discussion of how poetic thinking turns to the idealization of the poet's capacity to forge what I call "actionable fictions" by turning to the internal logic through which Stevens's poems from about 1934 to 1946 work out what values the fictive makes possible. I can approach this task by working in from the poles. One pole involves the search for a truth capable of engaging the lives of readers by seeking their participation in the poet's capacity to transform pain into the satisfactions of recognition. The other pole develops through the poet's efforts to accommodate fiction to truth as a source of heroism that can provide at least some consolation in times of war, when the political order has manifestly failed.

"The Idea of Order at Key West" presents Stevens's earliest effort to locate and then expand a truth to a situation that actually depends on imagining the reader's taking up what the poetic thinking exemplifies. The first four stanzas of the poem try to understand the spirit of the singer made audible in her activity. Gradually her voice emerges as also "ours," because it establishes some significant contrast to the "meaningless plungings of water and the wind" (*CPP* 105).[4] But even by the end of the fifth stanza, the focus is entirely on the world she made for herself by her singing. Then the situation changes radically with the evocation of Ramon Fernandez that establishes several new elements. It enables the poem to talk of a "we" that expands figuratively into an audience. More importantly, the sense of the singer's making a world for herself morphs into the difference her fiction has produced in what that audience sees of the actual landscape by ultimately "Arranging, deepening, enchanting night" for all those listening to her song (or hearing about it from Stevens) (*CPP* 106).

Finally, there is the poem's moment of absolute self-consciousness about the work fictionality can perform:

> Oh! Blessed rage for order, pale Ramon,
> The maker's rage to order words of the sea,
> Words of the fragrant portals, dimly-starred,
> And of ourselves and of our origins,
> In ghostlier demarcations, keener sounds. (*CPP* 106)

I think readers all too rarely reflect on what is added by the last two lines. Now we have only the ordering power of words of the sea as separate entities, beyond the tasks they perform in ordering the night. What does allusion to that power add to the poem? We are invited not to think of ourselves only as appreciators of the night but as forces in our own right capable of reflection on these origins in "ghostlier demarcations, keener sounds." Ghostlier because the song celebrating the singer's loneliness cannot be absorbed entirely into the landscape that it modifies. There remain the loneliness and the speculation about origins that might interpret this discomfort as an inevitable aspect of the human condition. This is a variation on the constant pain that unvarnished truth produces, even when there are enabling fictions. Then the poem suggests that our awareness of the singer's ordering power affords even keener sounds than those initially articulated by her song. Why "keener"? The sounds occupy a different register now, where the spirit has to confront its own isolation from any transcendental source. And "keener" to my ear produces a pun on "keening." Perhaps the keening results from the fact that the sharper the sense of reality, the sharper also the sense that even this enhanced real cannot be home for the organizing powers of fictive song.

We may detect in this poem the beginnings of Stevens's sense that there is something heroic about what fictions do, even when they exact pain for the self-consciousness absorbed by the work of attaching their form of order to the real. But the more oppressive reality came to seem, especially with the Second World War, the more Stevens began to emphasize the heroic dimension of the powers exercised as the imagination grappled to find a hold within the real. His goal was to celebrate the self-consciousness of particular powers that were capable of establishing values fit for combatting the skeptical music he heard all around him. Yet, at the same time, he had to separate these powers from any image or fixture in marble that would soon be thrown on the dump.

"Montrachet-le-Jardin" and "Examination of the Hero in a Time of War" make the logic of this transition to idealizing the hero strikingly clear. The first poem is remarkable for asking uneasily, "What more is there to love than I have loved?" (*CPP* 234). Characteristically, Stevens does not look outward, for another person, but turns inward, as the answer to his question involves searching his self-consciousness. Thus, he arrives at the possibility of imagining, and finding in that imagining, a way to make the "cell" of isolation into "an heroic world" (*CPP* 235). The key recognition is that imagination is a form of participation in other, often richer, more "capable" lives than what one is leading, with all its self-protective cautions. There are two keys to this transformation. One is to locate the heroic life in one's access to the "auroral creature musing in the mind" (*CPP* 237). Heroism has to be located in what such musing can establish as powers that are significant for how they change not the world but one's ways of being in the world. The other key involves the darker, trivializing sense of what "musing" involves. One has to accept the downside of any values based primarily on states of mind because such interior resolutions have no stable substance. These modes of identification are constructed when and only when our passions give access to them. An awareness of this kind is decidedly not sponsored by theology.

"Examination of the Hero in a Time of War" explores the advantages of that break from theological accounts of what the spirit can establish. This poem seeks a heroism that endures by stabilizing rather than replacing its eccentricity. But it accomplishes this only by fully identifying what might provide substance for an inner life. There is no alternative: "Unless we believe in the hero, what is there / To believe?" (*CPP* 246). However, there has to be significant discrimination if this belief is not to be dismissed as fantasy. A fiction of the hero can resist fantasy by attaching what is heroic to the working of elemental desires and, crucially, by separating the idea of the hero from anything that can be represented as personal traits fixed in marble:

> The marbles are pinchings of an idea,
> Yet there is that idea behind the marbles . . . (*CPP* 246)

Access to this idea demands reading the inner life in the outer life and testing what kind of difference it makes for one's sense that noble ideas are not ridiculous or outmoded but in fact enhance how we can live in skeptical times:

> All his speeches
> Are prodigies in longer phrases.
> His thoughts begotten at clear sources,
> Apparently in air, fall from him
> Like chantering from an abundant
> Poet, as if he thought gladly, being
> Compelled thereto by an innate music. (*CPP* 247)

There remains a sense of potential danger to constructing the hero. But the danger is not in instability so much as in vulnerability, because the terms of heroism are often not available for observation. This idea of heroism cannot defeat skepticism, although perhaps we can replace the ideal of reference to substantial empirical data on which this skepticism is founded. Perhaps we can see reality itself as shifting in what we would now call its "affordances":

> But was the summer false? The hero?
> How did we come to think that autumn

Was the veritable season, that familiar
Man was the veritable man? So
Summer, jangling the savagest diamonds and
Dressed in its azure-doubled crimsons,
May truly bear its heroic fortunes
For the large, the solitary figure. (*CPP* 250)

III

By *The Auroras of Autumn*, Stevens's poems invite replacing a language of self-reflexive efforts to make noble fictions wedded to experience by a language that stresses terms like realization, exemplification, integration, and disclosure. Here is an early instance, from the crucial poem "Chocorua to Its Neighbor," where the heroic imagination is not so much repudiated as quietly reinterpreted:

The air changes, creates and re-creates, like strength,
And to breathe is a fulfilling of desire,
A clearing, a detecting, a completing,
A largeness lived and not conceived, a space
That is an instant nature, brilliantly. (*CPP* 267)

In Stevens's prose, this opening to a different poetics comes more reluctantly because the idea of heroism is difficult to repudiate. But its working out there is clearer, so the prose provides a crucial theater for developing a more elaborate and, I think, effective way of demonstrating how "This endlessly elaborating poem / Displays the theory of poetry, / As the life of poetry" (*CPP* 415). Notice how the following passage from the essay "Imagination as Value" introduces an ontology that opens imaginative paths not consistent with the insistence on heroic images in the concluding half of the sentence: "If the imagination is the faculty by which we import the unreal into what is real, its value is the value of the way of thinking by which we project the idea of God into the idea of man" (*CPP* 735–36). Soon Stevens would realize that a mode of poetic thinking that stresses importing the unreal into the real can be a means of separating the life of poetry entirely from the space of ideas that claim determinate content. Poetry ceases to attempt interpreting life and instead tries to inhabit and sharpen the intricacy of processes fundamental to our experiences of valuing it. Poetry becomes a theater in which self-consciousness focuses on how it can complement the vital movement calling for realization of the powers of the mind. Such powers are not the grounds for heroic self-staging but for becoming "able to see the portal of literature, that is to say: the portal of the imagination, as a scene of normal love and normal beauty." Achieving that normality "is, of itself, a feat of great imagination" (*CPP* 739).

Since I have turned to prose, I want to continue in this domain by citing three passages in which Stevens comes to embrace with confidence his new model of what poetic thinking can accomplish.[5] His elegant directness will save me many words. The first passage is crucial for its use of "exemplify" as an articulation of how the potential for poetry pervades ordinary life because of its capacity to articulate situations rather than imposing affective dimensions on otherwise indifferent facts:

> [P]oetic value is an intrinsic value. It is not the value of knowledge. It is not the value of faith. It is the value of the imagination. The poet tries to exemplify it ... by identifying it with an imaginative activity that diffuses itself throughout our lives. (*CPP* 734–35)

Exemplification is the poet's means of addressing his audience without having to impose meanings. How one's imagination engages a situation can suffice to exemplify ways of relating to the normal that require and reward attention.

The second statement invokes the work of the painter Giorgione as an example of an art that enlarges affective life by embodying qualities for experiencing rather than interpreting it:

> This portrait [of a young man] is an instance of a real object that is at the same time an imaginative object. It has about it an imaginative bigness of diction.... The subject is severe but its embellishment, though no less severe, is big and gay and one feels in the presence of this work that one is also in the presence of an abundant and joyous spirit.... (*CPP* 737)

Then I need a third statement to demonstrate Stevens's awareness of what he seeks to make present by virtue of having ideals of realization and exemplification govern how the lyric imagination displays its force. This is a note on "Les Plus Belles Pages," a poem almost completely unintelligible to me even with the commentary, but the commentary becomes more significant by virtue of that fact:

> What [the poem] really means is that the inter-relation between things is what makes them fecund. Interaction is the source of potency.... But the title also means that les plus belles pages are those in which things do not stand alone but are operative as the result of interaction, interrelation.... The interrelation between reality and the imagination is the basis of the character of literature. The interrelation between reality and the emotions is

the basis of the vitality of literature, between reality and thought the basis of its power. (*CPP* 867)

Now I can turn to poetry and dramatize its capacities of performing linguistic feats probably unavailable to prose. Had I the space for it, I would attend to the section "It Must Change" in "Notes Toward a Supreme Fiction" because I think this section turns the hero into a lover, a role in which idealization is far more intricately concrete than in the previous sections. Just notice the work that the idea of repetition does in the following lines to establish an elemental resonance for poetic thinking:

> Red robin, stop in your preludes, practicing
> Mere repetitions. These things at least comprise
> An occupation, an exercise, a work,
>
> A thing final in itself and, therefore, good:
> One of the vast repetitions final in
> Themselves and, therefore, good, the going round
>
> And round and round, the merely going round,
> Until merely going round is a final good,
> The way wine comes at a table in a wood. (*CPP* 350)

In effect, these lines turn repetition and difference into one expanding whole, the unreal of each establishing the reality of its other. The eccentric is now compatible with the normal: "So that we look at it with pleasure, look // At it spinning its eccentric measure" (*CPP* 350). And poetry finds a home not subject to the vagaries of how the heroic imagination must come and go in its uneasy relation with the facts of our lives. Now simple rhymes speak volumes about the nature of satisfaction:

> Perhaps,
> The man-hero is not the exceptional monster,
> But he that of repetition is most master. (*CPP* 350)

IV

If it were possible, I would now read carefully how the claim "Real and unreal are two in one" (*CPP* 414) is beautifully elaborated in "An Ordinary Evening in New Haven," especially in section 30. But here I can only make a few observations to mark the logic of Stevens's transition to the motif of dwelling in plenitude that is the main concern of *The Rock*. The central motif of section 30 is a realization of how the "barrenness" of an autumn scene "is not part of what is absent, ... / ... a sad hanging on for remembrances." Rather,

> It is a coming on and a coming forth.
> The pines that were fans and fragrances emerge,
> Staked solidly in a gusty grappling with rocks.[6]
> ....
> It is not an empty clearness, a bottomless sight.
> It is a visibility of thought,
> In which hundreds of eyes, in one mind, see at once. (*CPP* 416)

Most of the poems in *The Rock* go beyond this example of what we might call "pictorial plenitude." Their concern is for what is involved in dwelling in an inordinately ordinary life-seeking awareness of the values this commitment to dwelling can make possible. Committed to the idea that "The imagination does not add to reality" (*CPP* 919), the poems explore how the imagination can instead be inseparable from reality – the duller the reality, the greater the feat and satisfaction of the imagination. This is for Stevens the poetics of the normal. Its aim is to project feelings of the normal – not feelings for anything normal so much as feelings for the general condition of normality – perhaps a state as unreal and dependent on the imagination as reality can generate:

> In the statement that we live in concepts of the imagination before the reason has established them, the word "concepts" means concepts of normality. . . . [W]hen we speak of perceiving the normal we have in mind the instinctive integrations which are the reason for living. (*CPP* 738)

On reading this, we almost have to ask, "How can poetic thinking establish and celebrate this normality?" First, thinking and being have to be absolutely one. There cannot be poetic particulars that absorb attention in their own right without calling attention to their comprehensiveness. Every reference seems utterly concrete, yet the sense of totality involved in embracing their reality is as unreal as reality can produce. Speakers have to stage states of feeling that feed on self-limitation as the basis for self-expansiveness. The more the scene remains local, the greater the possible sense that thinking in it can exemplify a moment of complete self-sufficiency. Second, senses of freedom and senses of necessity have to seem identical. In these poems, one is free because one accepts necessity as the only condition in which the will can be totally absorbed (see "The

Plain Sense of Things"). And, finally, the poetry has to seem utterly direct, as if there were no more concise or bare way of stating the speaker's emotional condition. What metaphor there is has to seem in the service of resisting the expansiveness of metaphoric reference so that the expansive seems to depend on total acts of inclusion.

I must choose one poem to represent this magisterial achievement. Among the many virtues of "A Quiet Normal Life" is its brevity:

> His place, as he sat and as he thought, was not
> In anything that he constructed, so frail,
> So barely lit, so shadowed over and naught,
>
> As, for example, a world in which, like snow,
> He became an inhabitant, obedient
> To gallant notions on the part of cold.
>
> It was here. This was the setting and the time
> Of year. Here in his house and in his room,
> In his chair, the most tranquil thought grew peaked
>
> And the oldest and the warmest heart was cut
> By gallant notions on the part of night –
> Both late and alone, above the crickets' chords,
>
> Babbling, each one, the uniqueness of its sound.
> There was no fury in transcendent forms.
> But his actual candle blazed with artifice. (*CPP* 443–44)

Few of us imagine how much artifice it takes for self-consciousness to utter a "here" that attends to all that the expression might refer to. One has to abstract away from material particulars to establish the particular place open to all particulars. Conversely, one has to heighten one's focus on this particular place, so that it is not lost to a variety of particulars. Finally, one has to find a language for pure realization of that level of particularity and that level of abstraction – here largely by denying the temptation to define the referent as something one constructs at an incomplete level of generality. But this denial only clears the way. The ultimate artifice in the poem is its recognizing the work "here" can do in resisting any particular that might bind consciousness to less than what the emotional situation seems to demand.

It is one thing to claim "artifice," another to realize in the poem's activity how artifice and actuality seem ineluctably merged. Stevens begins by calling attention to the work of language with a strange negative use of what readers expect to be positive metaphors. But this transposition makes a significant dramatic point. One cannot fully appreciate what "here" can mean to a person without a comparative base in other positive states. So Stevens has to cast the positive state of becoming "obedient / To gallant notions on the part of cold" as inadequate because such an attitude would define taking one's place in the world as simply accepting necessity rather than willing it as a condition of accord with reality. If one only reconciles oneself to the laws of nature, one is less than fully human, because the will is not everywhere present as a self-reflexive dimension of one's life.

Then, in contrast to the opening, Stevens dramatizes the fullness of "here" as the register of a contrasting level of self-reflection. At first mention, "here" is in the past tense, as if one had to recognize one's own becoming this person before one could fully assert acceptance of that person, as assertion and not just recognition. "This" then changes the speaker's world because he can refer to a quite general situation that perhaps only saying "here" can affirm without descending into particulars. Subsequently, the spirit of repetition takes over for the poem to find emotional identification with the affirmed totality. Notice the inner rhymes that thicken the sense of totality – "here," "year," "here" again – and then the eye-rhyme "heart" as the clinching unification of particular and general. There is also something about the cadence here by which anapestic doublings become themselves indicators of the quality of feeling for particulars that "here" generalizes. Finally, the whole sequence switches in the last two lines to flat generalization, contrasting again the opening lines with the direct assertion of what actuality can be to a self-consciousness absorbed in exploring what "here" can assert.

The inner life that poetry sustains for Stevens cannot be any more intimately connected to the public world that thinking must negotiate than in such compositions.

Notes

1 The claim that poetry differs from philosophy as a mode of integration that celebrates the world is most fully developed in Stevens's essays on "Effects of Analogy" (1948) and "Two or Three Ideas" (1951). Among critics on the topic of poetic thinking from whom I have profited most are Simon Critchley and Edward Ragg.
2 Robert Buttel's classic study makes a significant contribution to our understanding of how *Harmonium* differs from Stevens's earlier work.
3 Among several possible passages from Stevens's journals during his student days at Harvard, this one is most illustrative: "Those who say poetry is now the peculiar province of women say so because ideas about poetry are effeminate. Homer, Dante, Shakespeare, Milton, Keats, Browning, much of Tennyson –

they are your man-poets. Silly verse is always the work of silly men. Poetry itself
is unchanged" (*SP* 40).
4 George Lensing offers an instructive and powerful reading of the poem in
  Making the Poem.
5 I tried to characterize this poetics of interchange in my *Wallace Stevens and the
  Demands of Modernity*, where I argued that Stevens turned from an ideal of
  major man to an emphasis on aspectual thinking. Now I understand that while
  aspectual thinking addresses many of the phenomena involved in this new sense
  of process, the terminology fails to capture the core of what Stevens was after in
  his late work.
6 Stevens sees here the structural principle of Cézanne's *Pines and Rocks* (on
  display at MOMA). What better allusion for realizing what Cézanne's principle
  of realization entails.

WORKS CITED

Altieri, Charles. *Wallace Stevens and the Demands of Modernity: Toward
    a Phenomenology of Value.* Cornell UP, 2013.
Buttel, Robert. *Wallace Stevens: The Making of Harmonium.* Princeton UP, 1967.
Critchley, Simon. *Things Merely Are: Philosophy in the Poetry of Wallace Stevens.*
    Routledge, 2005.
Lensing, George S. *Making the Poem: Stevens' Approaches.* Louisiana State UP,
    2018.
Ragg, Edward. *Wallace Stevens and the Aesthetics of Abstraction.* Cambridge UP,
    2010.
Stevens, Holly. *Souvenirs and Prophecies: The Young Wallace Stevens.* Alfred
    A. Knopf, 1977.
Stevens, Wallace. *Wallace Stevens: Collected Poetry and Prose.* Edited by
    Frank Kermode and Joan Richardson, Library of America, 1997.

CHAPTER 15

Constructive Disorderings

Tom Eyers

When one finds oneself invited to contribute to a volume entitled *The New Wallace Stevens Studies*, an obvious strategy to follow would be to pair Stevens's verse with any number of recent theoretical movements or critical recapitulations – the "new formalism," perhaps, or the "new materialisms." As intriguing as such an experiment might be, I worry that it would betray something central to the thought of Stevens's verse itself, namely its emphatic undermining of the very logic of applying a *theory* to *things*. In Stevens, the implied subject-object, active-passive binaries that attend the notion of testing out a theory (active) on a poem (passive) are inoperative when they are not directly undermined. In consequence, there is, across the breadth of Stevens's poems – early, middle, and late – much that would elude our usual ways of doing literary theory. In what follows, I'll be especially concerned to trace moments in Stevens's verse when temporal expectations are reversed, when what would seem to have come first in fact came later, and when what one would have expected to follow on is shown to have been there all along. This temporal disorientation, I will argue, informs a number of striking intrapoetic claims about literary history, and historical time more generally.

Stevens's constructive disorderings resist collation into a general "theory," and they are the better for it. They are inseparable, too, from the literary techniques that enact them, and they take their distance, I would suggest, from any nostalgic celebration of deconstruction or dismantling as inherently virtuous theoretical presumptions or outcomes. To be clear, this is not to romanticize the literary in Stevens per se, as if literature were somehow a pure aesthetic realm that external theorization or historicization must never pollute. A purely immanent poetic philosophy, untouched by a priori assumptions, would be neither possible nor desirable. But it is my wager that in a space somehow both resolutely inside the domain of poetic materials, and yet outsized in its effects beyond that domain, and therefore in implicit challenge to the very spatial logic of inside and outside, of literary form and historical content, Stevens's poetry often simultaneously announces and ironizes the critical schools or theories with which it has frequently been associated. Put differently, Stevens's poetry enacts a very particular way of invoking, producing, and being constituted by historical time *in toto*, and hegemonic literary history more particularly. I will be interested in the sometimes kitsch quality of Stevens's engagement with what was an already thoroughly literary, which is to say highly mediated, picture of "modernity" as a retrospectively consecrated literary value or aspiration. This is an engagement not entirely exhausted by Stevens's related but distinct relationship to "high modernism" as the angular poeticization of a modernity already framed and produced as retrospective, not only by literary-journalistic canards but also by a then-emerging professional, literary-critical, and academic consensus.

I will demonstrate some of the ways in which Stevens's response to his literary environment issued in the poetic re-temporalization of what had become an ironically *fixed* sense of the US role in modernity as precisely *unfixed* – as untamable, dynamic, and permanent breach in the historical continuum. This latter, and most profound, effect of Stevens's poetic practice will, I hope, allay any fear that I am reserving for his verse some questionably exultant space away from the critical lenses that inevitably construct as much as they parse these poems. Stevens's burden is to be both entirely *of* his time, and therefore of the critical schools that one might still broadly associate with modernism (even as we have usefully pluralized this once narrowly totemic category), and somehow entirely outside it, ironizing his own poetry's multiple claims to literary and historical belonging. The title of the current volume, then, *The New Wallace Stevens Studies*, is quite fitting to both announce and parody a retrospectively canonized modernism's claims to newness, and to point us toward Stevens's particular and implicitly ironical approach to a poetic naming (that of modernism and modernity themselves) that his poetry both assiduously courts and reroutes.

"Of Mere Being"

Given the unexpected temporal scrambling that marks Stevens's particular contribution to a poetic thinking of literary form and historical time, it would be as well to start at the end. "Of Mere Being" is the final poem that Holly Stevens included in her canonizing collection from 1971, *The Palm at the End of the Mind*. Notably, the poem lends the collection its title. Apart from the empirical fact of chronology, Holly Stevens would seem to have put some weight on this short, unassuming poem – four neat tercets, strikingly demure despite the sporadically resplendent, if also rather inert, imagery. The poem was written toward the end of Stevens's life, and this fact has contributed to its critical reception, which has emphasized its reflective quality as well as its stony and resolute authorial voice in the face of mortality. The first tercet reads as follows:

> The palm at the end of the mind,
> Beyond the last thought, rises
> In the bronze decor. . . . (*CPP* 476)

There is much in this poem, I would suggest, that betrays any sentimental reception, given the impersonal, determinedly neutral tenor of these lines. The opening image has been especially associated with the critical canonization of Stevens, not least through the aforementioned collection edited by his daughter. But consider it again, with fresh eyes: "The palm at the end of the mind." The regularity of the beat, the repetition of monosyllabic words, and the quiet incongruity of the "palm" situated at the "end" (but what kind of end: temporal? spatial? both?) of the "mind" – all of this is of a straightforward, unassuming impassivity that would hardly lend itself to post-Romantic encomia to mortality or the afterlife.

The poem begins *in medias res*, so to speak. It is almost as if we were interrupting a private recitation, one that moves rather mechanically in its deployment of one monosyllable after another – a recitation, moreover, that begins without the assignation of a speaker. For these reasons, at least, the lines invite an analysis that does not default to the resolutions of humanist certainty or, indeed, any easily managed pseudo-deconstructive *un*certainty. Rather, I want to suggest, the poem is best understood as an experiment in the presentation of rhetorical, temporal, and spatial logics. These add up to a poetic intervention in, and construction of, historical time, predicated not on any contextual production of immediate historical sense but rather on a constructive withdrawal of the poetic image from any smooth insertion into a historical "message" or narrative. One might even be tempted to suggest that this is an exemplary instance of the signifier uncoupling from the signified, were that beloved old theory-speak not itself too rigid and predetermined to get at what is happening in these lines.

Where to begin in assessing the poem's intervention in, and construction of, historical time? Consider the image of the palm itself. Even as we are told that the palm is "at the end of the mind," this location does little to dial down the sense of isolation that the image carries with it, and that somehow separates it from quite being where we are told it is. Palm trees (for it is clear straight away that we are dealing with a tree) can cluster, it is true, but they remain in some sense totemic, as does the monosyllable that registers the image. Soon we learn that this tree "rises" "Beyond the last thought," although this thought beyond the possibility of that which it announces and the new act of spatial and temporal location are themselves announced with a different temporal logic: the syntax in "Beyond the last thought, rises / In the bronze decor" separates the action – rising – from the object that accomplishes it. Stevens isolates both the palm and its unveiling to sap any residual pathos from his evocation and, more importantly, to show us how poetry can disconnect something – in this case, the palm and its arising in a particular place and time – *even in the act of apparently connecting it*. If we were temporarily to concede that we are dealing here with a poetic thought or claim, and not simply with a semiotic arrangement of images and logics (bearing in mind that such images and logics may well produce the *effect* of thought while not quite being thoughts themselves), we confront the logic of temporal afterwardsness that, I argue, is a particular feature of Stevens's writing.[1] For it is *beyond* the last thought that this impossible thought – of a palm, invoked before we are sure a thought is what is at stake at all – is to be found. And so something, a palm, arises after the possibility of its doing so is, at least from one angle, rendered impossible. It is beyond itself, so to speak, and yet this does nothing to make us doubt its existence, or to consider it in a pseudo-Romantic manner as diaphanous or transcendent.

Stevens would not have us respond to any of this as if it were a revelation – the anonymous presentation of images and ideas forestalls that. It is a broader feature of his writing style that seeming paradoxes, contradictions that might seem startling in the hand of another poet, are presented as quotidian, as if it is their unexceptional everydayness that makes them possible in the first place. In "An Ordinary Evening in New Haven," for example, he will proclaim that "The plainness of plain things is savagery," and that a harmony might be "savage and subtle and simple" all at once (*CPP* 399) – and so what? The arrangement of these features alongside one another negates the very negative or contradictory force we might expect their aggregation to produce. The title of the poem we have begun with alerts us to this curious, undemonstrative effect: it is, after all, "mere" being with which we are dealing.

I wish to resist any hurried appropriation of such Stevensian effects as part of a modernist commitment to poetic impersonality. Stevens by all accounts had little interest in T. S. Eliot's clarion calls for an impersonal surrender to tradition as the means to be modern. But neither do Stevens's poetic effects fit a theory of poetry's "relative autonomy" from its historical conditions, as if the effect of a disconnection occurring within a poetic demonstration of connection is the formal end of the matter, or the opportunity merely for a negative slogan. Given that the effect in question relies in part on the isolation of particular images, beginning with the palm tree itself, we must somehow relate the implications of those images – their radiance of meaning on their own terms – to the temporal and spatial scrambling already described. When philosophers approach these lines, they tend to consider the paradox of the palm "Beyond the last thought" above all else, worrying at its potential eschatological, certainly death-infused, senses.[2] But this is to ignore the manner in which the isolation of the palm as an image, foregrounded at the beginning but also beyond the last thought, at the edge of things, must have us confront its various and singular associations. And these associations, when folded into the literary-critical and historical senses that we have of Stevens as a poet and cultural avatar, are nothing if not historically meaningful, albeit perhaps not in the sense that we have become accustomed to seek in our post-theory, hege-monically historicist-contextualist, present.

How are we to understand the poem's historicity, then? I would argue that the very disconnection of the palm from any easily recoverable narra-tive context is precisely what allows it to make a claim to historical-temporal, and geographical, specificity. For what is called forth is an image as American as can be. Think, in particular, of the pastoral shades of Florida, so beloved by Stevens, but also of related if distinct hues of meaning: a certain stillness and repose that we might associate with the ideology of leisure, of stepping aside from things, a whole set of senses around postwar accumulation and consumer spending that then add their own layer to the text. One might even write of a distinctly *Floridian modernism* in Stevens that has almost but not quite become kitsch, a modernism already wary, in a distinctly American way, of being too self-serious – even, and perhaps especially, in its self-serious innocence – a modernism of palm trees and a certain form of idling and dissipation.

And so we might talk of an image that locates, and I would argue also ironizes, this poem's position in America, such locational specificity func-tioning as an ironic reframing of the superficial whiff of incipient eternity to which the poem is so easily conscripted. This sense of location emerges, arguably, in a symbol associated, through the ideological evocation of leisure, with the very *negation* of history's onward movement. The implicit image of Florida, through the palm tree and our knowledge of Stevens's broader poetic attention to the state, amounts here to a withdrawal from the usual temporal-historical run of things. And, yet despite this, or perhaps because of it, it is one of the principal material realities that allows us to situate the poem's abstractions that helps to bring them down to the earth, so to speak. In this sense, Florida becomes abstractly allegorical for a very particular kind of historicization, one that is irreducible to any of the more narrative-driven, humanistic modes of reading that the various historicisms have made their own.

That this is an act of poetic historicization deployed in an image of temporal interregnum and expressed in the very medium of leisure – that we encounter here, that is to say, the simultaneity of temporal slowing down ("The palm stands on the edge of space. / The wind moves slowly in the branches" [*CPP* 477]) and of historical activation – all of this allies this curious literary-historical logic with the aforementioned repeated occurrence in Stevens of a temporal-historical afterwardsness. And it does so in the same breath as it refuses the too-easy appeal of contextualization. It is, above all, a kind of specifically poetic abstraction that is at issue here, I think, one that is revealed in those moments in Stevens's poetry when the before is later than the after, when a connection emerges after those things being connected have already arisen under the sign of their having been ripped asunder.

It would seem to be important that this historicization-in-negation is quickly removed from the possibility of any recuperation under the sign of the human:

> A gold-feathered bird
> Sings in the palm, without human meaning,
> Without human feeling, a foreign song.
>
> You know then that it is not the reason
> That makes us happy or unhappy.
> The bird sings. Its feathers shine. (*CPP* 476–77)

Those attached to a reading of this poem couched in the existential dramatics of mortality, of a Romantic-ironic attempt to express the ineffable, would surely claim that the non-humanity of the bird's song is just another sign of us being situated somewhere at the inevitable endpoint of life and of mindedness, on the cusp of something entirely other. But for all the reasons already given, I think something very different is at work.

These lines prevent the central images of the poem – not only the palm but also the gold-feathered bird, an ambiguous image of luxury that runs together the artificial and the natural – from sinking back into a Romantic ideology that Stevens, in my view, was always out to parry.[3] The golden bird, incidentally, seems to be related to W. B. Yeats's bird of "hammered gold" in "Sailing to Byzantium," a bird whose song sings "Of what is past, or passing, or to come" (194) – the very temporal markers that it is Stevens's habit to both acknowledge and productively redirect. Meanwhile, the much-remarked implicit pun on the bird as phoenix (the date palm's Latin appellation being *Phoenix dactylifera*) directs us inward, back to language again, to the determinately linguistic and ultimately extra-, if not entirely non-, metaphysical tenor of these lines.

As a poem concerned to stage a particular account of the interlacing of verbal form and historical time, "Of Mere Being" in the previously quoted lines seems to me primarily to suggest the fundamentally non-human quality of both literary form and time, their capacity at once to enable us but also to remain fundamentally "foreign" to us, to use the poem's own term – their capacity, in other words, to be ultimately indifferent to our all-too-human desire to assume that language and time are always passively subjected to our will. The bird's song is "without human meaning," and where one might expect a mellifluousness pleasurable to the ear, the song is instead "Without human feeling," pure enunciation outside sense. One is reminded of any number of Paul de Man's epigrammatic statements on the machine-like inhumanity of language, of what in his late work he would ambiguously label "materiality," although practitioners of deconstruction rather too often underplayed the enabling or constructive dimension of this inhumanity.[4] For this reason, aspects of Stevens's poetics may mark an advance, *avant la lettre*, beyond some of those critical movements that emerged in his poetry's wake, new historicisms and deconstructions among them. In doing so, it offers another instance of the curious afterwardsness – here in the mode of useful anachronism – we have already noted. We are, at any rate, far from critical modes that would rely, no matter how tacitly, on dichotomies of text and context, or even form and content.

It seems appropriate that "Of Mere Being" ends with a line that arrives at something like a pure present, achieved through sheer alliterative verve and repetition: "The bird's fire-fangled feathers dangle down" (*CPP* 477). It is as if the poem, having rehearsed and rotated a number of temporal-historical-linguistic logics for our inspection, has chosen finally to cancel them out in favor of one final possibility, that of the pure present of poetic enunciation itself. Earlier the golden bird brought to mind Yeats's metaphysical feathered apparition, if only to underline the contrast with the distinctly non-Yeatsian mereness on display in "Of Mere Being." The inescapable contrast here is with Gerard Manley Hopkins, whose poems are filled with similarly spiky, punctuated repetitions. "[F]ire-fangled feathers dangle down" has about it such a monotonous and yet insistent rhythm that the moderate dialectical sensitivity of the poem's earlier rhythms whites out in a rather more concussive series of spondees and trochees. Repetition here turns the mind away from sense and to the mere – the word from the title won't leave us alone – articulation of sound, of material insistence before or beyond its being graced with meaning. And so if there is a "beyond" in question in this poem, I would wager that it is less the beyond of death conceived in a late-Romantic, emphatically (post)metaphysical sense but rather the deathliness of the linguistic itself. The latter rhymes with, and in part makes possible, the different ways (retrospective, projective, in the pure present, and so on) in which historical time marches onward, or, just as likely at this poem's end, marches on the spot.

"The Idea of Order at Key West"

We would do well to test some of these ideas, and in particular the curious Stevensian conjunction of uncanny temporal-historical disorderings with a materialist emphasis on the primacy of the linguistic imprint, with one of the better-known, lengthier, and much earlier poems. That this would be, usefully enough, one of the Florida verses, "The Idea of Order at Key West" of 1934, should further help us cement the sense of historical-geographical specificity that, I am arguing, helps Stevens ironize his poetry's already complicated relationship with canonical (especially English) poetic modernisms. But I want immediately to claim that the central, overarching, and animating tension of this poem is the abstraction of its principal subject – the woman who "sang beyond the genius of the sea" – from the specificity of location as indicated by the poem's very title, a specificity that, in fact, largely remains tethered *to* that title, and that is never recognizably realized in the body of the poem. The first stanza reads as follows:

> She sang beyond the genius of the sea.
> The water never formed to mind or voice,
> Like a body wholly body, fluttering
> Its empty sleeves; and yet its mimic motion
> Made constant cry, caused constantly a cry,

That was not ours although we understood,
Inhuman, of the veritable ocean. (*CPP* 105)

In his invaluable monograph on Stevens, Harold Bloom quotes two moments from Stevens's letters when the poet reflects on the "order" in question in this poem: "If poetry introduces order, . . . and if order means peace, even though that particular peace is an illusion, is it any less an illusion than a good many other things that everyone high and low now-a-days concedes to be no longer of any account?" And: "In 'The Idea of Order at Key West' life has ceased to be a matter of chance. It may be that every man introduces his own order into the life about him and that the idea of order in general is simply what Bishop Berkeley might have called a fortuitous concourse of personal orders" (*L* 293; qtd. in Bloom 93). This, for Bloom, is unhelpful since he is after a Stevens steeped in a very American, and so markedly belated, brand of Romanticism. As a result, he finds in the poem a yearning for transcendence, albeit one that is ultimately frustrated because it cannot be specified or pinned down. Yet I would give greater credit than Bloom to Stevens's self-reflection, at least to a point. There is here, as there was in "Of Mere Being," a subtle interaction between structure – pure order, so to speak – and meaning, history, purpose.

I think it possible to read Romanticism into this verse only in the mode of parody, and the parody is less of Romantic poetry itself than of the critical romance about the Romantic that Bloom, among others, advanced so doggedly. This is another instance of the metapoetic, reflexive impulsive in Stevens – a kind of retrospective self-canonization undertaken under the heavy spell of irony – that we also found at work in "Of Mere Being." For both M. H. Abrams and the broadly deconstructive American critics who ostensibly opposed him (Bloom, of course, but also the early Geoffrey Hartman), Romanticism concerns itself above all with apocalypticism, with the dramatic coming apart, and potential future coming back together, of Nature and the Subject. (That Bloom's 1977 book on Stevens significantly postdates the poem that parodies in advance the former's amplification of an extant romance about romance would be another example of Stevens's reversing our usual expectation of temporal-historical linearity, even if, in this case, it is so only in my own framing of it.) And yet, the stark parallels between "The Order at Key West" and "Of Mere Being" take us away from such metaphysical portentousness and back to the curious temporal-historical rearrangements and insistences beyond or before sense that define the later poem.

It is of some importance that this poem, like "Of Mere Being," begins with a "beyond": the after, what is over the horizon, once again comes first in Stevens. To sing beyond the "genius" of the sea is both to shrug off the aforementioned Romantic ideology (while inevitably invoking it in the mask of parody) and to situate the poem not so much at the cusp of things but in an unknowable space, once again beyond mindedness and meaning. This is so even as we putatively know, from the title, from which location this poem speaks. In "Of Mere Being," principally through the image of the palm, Florida was palpably part of the poetry's thought production, even if in the mode of a certain temporal-historical stilling. Here, by contrast, that stilling is radicalized in the mode of an absolute absence, that of the woman singing beyond the genius of the sea – although this absence is confronted from the beginning by a presence ("Key West") that is in fact radically more particular than anything encountered in "Of Mere Being."

This is the abstract dialectic mentioned at the beginning of this section, between the disappeared "she" who is denied form by the sea ("The water never formed to mind or voice") and the nomination-without-referent ("Key West") – without referent to the extent that it is a location not further brought into focus in the poem itself – that gives the title of the poem its color. With my comments on form and historicization in "Of Mere Being" in mind, I want to suggest that "Key West," qua locational specificity, stands in here for something like directed purpose, perhaps even history's movement. At the same time, the varying kinds of absence – the lack of mindedness and bodiedness that one finds rehearsed in the poem itself – are to be understood as order per se, the mere imposition of form as such, the most minimal structuration imaginable, indifferent to meaning-history-purpose, but without which those things would be impossible.

The water, Stevens tells us, is "Like a body wholly body," which is to say mere form, structuration reduced to itself: this is not a sea that will capitulate to any pseudo-Romantic spiritualization of nature. The "cry" that such a pure form makes cannot be anything but "Inhuman," if "human" is to mean directedness, teleological sense making, and so on. Intriguingly, the cry ("Made constant cry, caused constantly a cry") is set within an experiment around cause and effect, one not unrelated to the principle of afterwardsness that has been our focus. "Made constant cry" places us in the present of a presumed (but not here directly named) agent (the sea), but the following clause distances that agent, who can now be said only to have "caused constantly a cry": the security of causation attaching to an agent stutters here, and absence interposes itself again.

A challenge to the certainty of ascribing a cause to a cause-agent may be understood as a species of the temporal scrambling that, I have argued, is one of the most powerful constructive disorderings of Stevens's verse.

One might think, when one thinks of a pure cry, of Jacques Lacan's theory of the "unary trait," the smallest possible material unit of sense that can be imagined, or that speck of nonsense that might allow for sense – Lacan compares it to the notches on wood early humans may have made to count their success in hunting (see Lacan). I think this is something similar to what Stevens means by "order." In the first previously quoted letter, the poet refers to order as something imposed, something even that brings peace, but the poetry itself stubbornly resists any such humanist recuperation. Instead, we're closer to the logic of the second quotation from *Letters*, where he writes of life ceasing to be a matter of chance, becoming a question, rather, of the imposition of order or form. Stevens becomes almost a critic of Paul de Man *avant la lettre* here. Where de Man argued that the "auto-impositional" force of language is a species of randomness, that it gives the lie to any expectation of a before or after, a beginning or an end, Stevens understands the order of form here as that which intervenes *upon* randomness, just as it also allows for the uncanny temporalities and ambiguous causalities that have been my quarry in this chapter. A certain articulation of space and time, even, is enabled by these minimal structurings: as the poem's penultimate stanza makes clear, the lights of boats – pinpricks of form and order in the inky darkness – "Mastered the night and portioned out the sea, / Fixing emblazoned zones and fiery poles, / Arranging, deepening, enchanting night" (*CPP* 106). A temporal designation, the night, is given extraordinary spatial breadth and depth here, all of it issuing, not from the now-massified sea, but from the merest prick of light.

The logic of the constitutively minimal imprint, no less than the upending of temporal expectation, is why one of the poem's strongest images doesn't appear in the least unexpected or contradictory: "It was her voice that made / The sky acutest at its vanishing" (*CPP* 106). Usually, we would expect the sky, or other natural features, to be at their most acute when in full view, but in this instance it is only upon the sky's disappearance that its full power may be registered. I can think of no better metaphor for the eerie power of Stevens's formal choices, the curious effect that his disorderings have. By enforcing a disconnection or a vanishing, they paradoxically promote the activation of historical specificity. Doing so, they quietly challenge our habitual assumptions about form, historical time, and the geographical-historical specificities of modernism.

Notes

1 In using the term "afterwardsness," I hope to evoke the capacious psychoanalytic reimagining of temporality found in the work of Jean Laplanche, who uses
the term as a somewhat free translation of Freud's *Nachträglichkeit*. See
Laplanche.
2 An exemplary and excellent instance is Bates, but see also the superb Critchley.
3 I defend this claim at length in my "Alain Badiou, Wallace Stevens and the
Paradoxical Productivity of Poetic Form."
4 See especially the essays and lectures posthumously collected in de Man.

WORKS CITED

Bates, Jennifer. "Stevens, Hegel, and the Palm at the End of the Mind." *The Wallace Stevens Journal*, vol. 23, no. 2, Fall 1999, pp. 152–66.
Bloom, Harold. *Wallace Stevens: The Poems of Our Climate*. Cornell UP, 1977.
Critchley, Simon. *Things Merely Are: Philosophy in the Poetry of Wallace Stevens*. Routledge, 2005.
de Man, Paul. *The Resistance to Theory*. U of Minnesota P, 1986.
Eyers, Tom. "Alain Badiou, Wallace Stevens and the Paradoxical Productivity of Poetic Form." *Textual Practice*, vol. 30, no. 5, 2016, pp. 835–55.
Lacan, Jacques. *Séminaire 1961–62: L'Identification*. Unpublished transcript.
Laplanche, Jean. *Essays on Otherness*. Translated by John Fletcher, Routledge, 1999.
Stevens, Wallace. *Letters of Wallace Stevens*. Edited by Holly Stevens, U of California P, 1996.
The Palm at the End of the Mind: Selected Poems and a Play by Wallace Stevens. Edited by Holly Stevens, Alfred A. Knopf, 1971.
Wallace Stevens: Collected Poetry and Prose. Edited by Frank Kermode and Joan Richardson, Library of America, 1997.
Yeats, W. B. *The Collected Poems of W. B. Yeats*. Edited by Richard J. Finneran, Simon & Schuster, 1996.

CHAPTER 16

Manner and Manners

Zachary Finch

When considering stylistic and rhetorical features in the poetry of Wallace Stevens, one finds oneself returning to a question that occupied the very first Stevens critics. *Harmonium* (1923) was obviously a significant accomplishment, yet its verbal artifice contradicted what a new generation of critics was celebrating – the emergence of what Warner Berthoff called "the voice of the natural man, speaking from direct personal experience and the self's inmost conviction, as the right basis for style" (7). This sentiment was part of the mission of many of the little magazines of the 1920s, such as *The Seven Arts*, whose editors stated, "We have no tradition to continue; we have no school of style to build up. What we ask of the writer is simply self-expression" ("Editorial" 53). What's more, this celebration of self-expression was part of a national, ideological project, in which American writers were encouraged to write in a way befitting of a still young country finding its natural voice.

Harmonium did not fit into this project. Critics found its language to be highly mannered, infatuated with artifice, elitist in its fashion. Harriet Monroe believed that Stevens, whose tastes descend from a "haughty . . . lineage," was sensitive to "color-subtleties and sound-vibrations which most of us do not detect" (qtd. in Doyle 59, 61). The poems' "exquisite tact" led critics to suspect that Stevens was insufficiently democratic, was "born, say, for the grand piano," supposed Paul Rosenfeld (qtd. in Doyle 77, 74), a sentiment echoed by Gorham Munson's assessment that the "correctness and elegance" of Stevens's manners, and the "material ease" of his language, smacked of "the America that owns baronial estates" (qtd. in Doyle 78, 81–82). Anticipating Stevens's later analogy that "Money is a kind of poetry" (*CPP* 905), Marianne Moore thought that the "verbal security" of *Harmonium*, combined with the exorbitant "gorgeousness" of its language, "recalls Balzac's reputed attitude to money, to which he was indifferent unless he could have it 'in heaps or by the ton'" (qtd. in Doyle 52, 49). In Stevens, readers found a poet whispering "Heavenly labials in a word of gutturals" as a strategy for taming the Calibanesque monster in "The Plot Against the Giant" (*CPP* 6), and who converted the raw power of the ocean into the slender wrists of a young female courtier in "Infanta Marina," where we read of "The rumpling of the plumes / Of this creature of the evening" and "the roamings of her fan" (*CPP* 6) – imagery that recalls Diego Velázquez's mid-seventeenth-century Mannerist portrait of the Infanta Maria Theresa of Spain, the folds of her elaborate white handkerchief an unlikely equivalent for the pounding surf.

In this chapter, I argue that what these critics confronted, and what we encounter today when reading Stevens, is a poet for whom questions of manner and manners were paramount. While critics have usually analyzed Stevens's language in terms of its style, the concept of manner, I believe, more accurately captures the social registers of his poems and speaks to Stevens's cultural and economic conditions. Moreover, Stevens's characteristic "manner" – sometimes repeated to the pitch of mannerism – distinguishes him from other major modernist poets. Fredric Jameson once noted that the "peculiarly unmodern" quality of Stevens's language stemmed from the fact that he did not pursue the disruptive heroisms of style ("*style* being above all the ambiguous and historical category in which, in high modernism, the specificity of the individual subject is expressed, manifested and preserved" [213]). As opposed to poets like William Carlos Williams or Gertrude Stein, there is "no stammering" or "awkwardness" in his poetry. Reading Stevens one experiences primarily verbal ease, fluency, *sprezzatura*. "One of the key features of the modernist will to style is lost" in Stevens's rhetoric, Jameson believes, "the necessity for its violent birth, for a painful conquest of the private voice over against the universal alienation of public speech" (208). This is not to say that in Stevens there are never any signs of aesthetic labor, and it is certainly not to suggest that he didn't engage with the alienating effects of public speech. It's just to agree that Stevens is more exiled Prospero than postcolonial Caliban: his way with words unfolds as a practice of mastery rather than being situated at a contested site of strife, difficulty, dissent.

Giorgio Agamben has suggested that manner should be viewed as the dialectical opposite of style. Manner implies "expropriation and nonidentity" because its "exaggerated adhesion to a usage or model" eclipses the writer's uniqueness with a set of behaviors made visible through excessive repetition (97, 99). Expressed through the social guise of tone, gesture, comportment, decorum, and bearing, the impersonality of manner (singular) is related to the concept of manners (plural) in ways that have a long genealogy. First appearing in the French courtly literature of the thirteenth through fifteenth centuries, writing on social manners was popularized by Baldassare Castiglione's *The Book of the Courtier*. The elegance most highly prized by this literature – the virtues of *grazia*, *facilità*, and *sprezzatura* – would soon get grafted into the concept of *maniera* that cinquecento art critics used to describe the complex changes in the arts of the late Renaissance. *Maniera* resulted from artists "constantly copying the most beautiful objects" from previous masters, as Giorgio Vasari put it in *Lives of the Painters* (28). The European genealogy of manner, in other words, is concerned with the transmission and acquisition, the refinement and repetition of traditional cultural codes, tropes, poses, and ritualized gestures rather than with the irruption of unruly forms of natural expression. According to this formulation, manner arrives with a rather highborn cultural pedigree, whereas style is the disruptive realm of the organic, the personal.

"Manner" was one of Stevens's favorite words, and it appears regularly throughout his poetry in connection with the social posture and operation of poetry. It "does not mean style," he writes in "The Irrational Element in Poetry" (*CPP* 784). Rather, it defines "the attitude of the writer, his bearing rather than his point of view" (*CPP* 784–85). Here "bearing" refers to physical and rhetorical "pose." Stevens was never settled on the proper carriage of poetry. He believed deeply, of course, that poetry's social bearing should indicate its cultural standing, its noble heritage. Writing "On the bearing of the poet" in the "Adagia," Stevens linked bearing with prestige: "1. The prestige of the poet is part of the prestige of poetry. 2. The prestige of poetry is essential to the prestige of the poet" (*CPP* 912). But since the prestige of poetry could no longer be taken for granted in the twentieth century ("the idea of nobility exists in art today only in degenerate forms" [*CPP* 649]), its particular manner was an open, dynamic, perhaps insoluble question. "The manner of it is, in fact, its difficulty," he admitted in his essay "The Noble Rider and the Sound of Words," "which each man must feel each day differently, for himself" (*CPP* 664).

His earliest poems show Stevens wondering openly, and performatively, about aesthetic manner, as a matter of public import. It forms the whole subject of "Of the Manner of Addressing Clouds," in which the speaker, as if posed at a lectern, presses his interlocutors to consider the best way to renew "the still sustaining pomps / Of speech" (*CPP* 44). The poem's pentameter language ranges from the antic (the audience addressed as "Gloomy grammarians in golden gowns") to the more reserved and stately ("So speech of your processionals returns / In the casual evocations of your tread") (*CPP* 44). The same question of how a "dull scholar" might compose a "great hymn" forms the subject of "Le Monocle de Mon Oncle" as well, in which the speaker "quiz[zes] all sounds . . . For the music and manner of the paladins / To make oblation fit" (*CPP* 13). And in a similar vein, "Architecture" asks the question "What manner of building shall we build?" in the first-person plural, suggesting that manner is indeed a collective concern (*CPP* 66). Building an analogy between public architecture and the social construction of poetry, the speaker wonders,

> In this house, what manner of utterance shall there be?
> What heavenly dithyramb
> And cantilene?
> What niggling forms of gargoyle patter?
> Of what shall the speech be,
> In that splay of marble
> And of obedient pillars? (*CPP* 66)

This imagined edifice would appear to be patently mannerist in the extravagant variety of its admixture – "dithyramb" conjuring Greek hymns to Dionysus; "cantilene" evoking European medieval song; and "patter" suggesting a more contemporary, perhaps racially marked, if not actually racist, jazz vernacular. The building might become a "kremlin of kermess," Stevens says later (*CPP* 67), again colliding distinct cultural traditions ("kremlin" referring to a Russian citadel, "kermess" a Dutch term associated with festivals). The ornamental pastiche suggests a transcultural heteroglossia of the sort that Harris Feinsod has recently studied in his analysis of Stevens's inter-American "aesthetics of fluency" (107), but it also sounds elitist in its fashion, written in the voice of an architect who wants to "Keep the laborers shouldering plinths" and pledges to "set guardians in the grounds" so that only the right people will gain admission (*CPP* 66–67).

This tension, between the inclusive and the exclusive character of poetic language, is imbricated in the concept of manner, particularly when viewed through a sociological lens. For Pierre Bourdieu, for instance, manners display the class-based inequities of a given culture. In *Distinction: A Social Critique of the Judgement of Taste*, he shows how "'manner' is a symbolic manifestation" of processes by which people acquire special kinds of cultural fluencies, such as "the competence of the 'connoisseur'" and that "ease which is the touchstone of excellence" (66). And in fact, when the word "manner" crops up in Stevens's work, it frequently refers to figures of nobility. "An age is a manner collected from a queen," proposes "Description Without Place" (*CPP* 297); in "Sunday Morning," Jove makes "Large-mannered motions" (*CPP* 54); the fictive "major man" of

"Notes Toward a Supreme Fiction" is more legible "in the manner of his hand" than through acts of intellectual cognition (*CPP* 335); even the nationalistic heliotrope, the "blue sun in his red cockade" in "The News and the Weather," possesses a manner that devolves upon the striking auto workers: "His manner took what it could find, // In the greenish greens he flung behind / And the sound of pianos in his mind" (*CPP* 237–38); and in "The Man with the Blue Guitar," the poetic speaker wonders whether he can sound "A million people on one string? / And all their manner in the thing?" (*CPP* 136). In other words, Stevens often employs the word when considering how an Emersonian representative – a god, a queen, a priest, or a sun – may confer a sense of unity on the scattered plurality of other voices. Stevens may have thought that manner risked sounding "portent-ous or demoded" (*CPP* 664) – "It is manner that becomes stale," he noted in "Adagia" (*CPP* 909) – but he was always certain that, whatever its timbre or pitch, poetry should strive to express its noble cultural and spiritual heritage, less through the assertion of any specific content or stated ideol-ogy, and more through its manner.

What, then, especially characterizes the sound of Stevens's manner? The question is, of course, a large one, as demonstrated by the range of approaches taken by critics in special issues of *The Wallace Stevens Journal* devoted to sound in fall 1991 (edited by Jacqueline Vaught Brogan) and spring 2009 (edited by Natalie Gerber). Both issues contained essays that thoroughly undermine the assumption that to study the sound of Stevens's language is to surrender to "mere aestheticism," as Gerber put it (4), or to court "dead-end mannerism," as Al Filreis wrote (15). Although the constraints of the current chapter don't permit a full-length investiga-tion of the relation between sound and manner (an investigation I began in an essay on that topic in the fall 2012 issue of *The Wallace Stevens Journal*), I'd like to refer briefly to an excerpt from "Extracts from Addresses to the Academy of Fine Ideas." This is yet another poem in which a Stevens speaker is formally addressing an assembled group. Defying Jean-Jacques Rousseau's claim that "All that is needed for quickly rendering a language cold is to establish academies among the people who speak it" (qtd. in von Hallberg 73), Stevens's speaker is energized by the artificial public setting (he ironically refers to his homogeneous-seeming audience as "My beards") as he considers the challenges of an atomized world in which "all men are priests":

> They preach and they are preaching in a land
> To be described. They are preaching in a time

To be described. Evangelists of what?
If they could gather their theses into one,
Collect their thoughts together into one,
Into a single thought, thus: into a queen,
An intercessor by innate rapport,
Or into a dark-blue king, *un roi tonnerre*,
Whose merely being was his valiance,
Panjandrum and central heart and mind of minds. . . . (*CPP* 229)

At the level of prosody, Stevens's most characteristic manner is founded upon repetition. Note how frequently the word "into" is repeated in this stanza. Stevens wants to invite readers into the folds of the language. Language is a kind of infinitely extendable, foldable fabric in Stevens, a form of social materiality that one can inhabit. The phrasal repetitions and syntactical plies, so characteristic of Stevens's serialized mode of writing, are indispensable to creating a sense of the extravagance, largesse, and stamina of language, which ideally functions as a sort of social "intercessor." I say "ideally" because this poem also believes the reverse may be true, that perhaps "the multitude of thoughts, / Like insects in the depths of the mind," can "kill / The single thought . . . the single man" (*CPP* 229).

Gilles Deleuze has named the fold the central trait of Mannerist and Baroque aesthetics, the way its language "twists and turns," "unfurls all the way to infinity" (3). In describing Gian Lorenzo Bernini's famous sculpture of Saint Teresa, for instance, he notes how "In every instance folds of clothing acquire an autonomy and a fullness *that are not simply decorative effects*" (122). This describes the acoustic fabrications draped amply across the armature of line breaks throughout so much of Stevens's *oeuvre* as well. As early as "The Curtains in the House of the Metaphysician," Stevens was equating motion and sound within a framework that suffused natural description with a sense of cultural aristocracy:

It comes about that the drifting of these curtains
Is full of long motions; as the ponderous
Deflations of distance; or as clouds
Inseparable from their afternoons;
Or the changing of light, the dropping
Of the silence, wide sleep and solitude
Of night, in which all motion
Is beyond us, as the firmament,
Up-rising and down-falling, bares
The last largeness, bold to see. (*CPP* 49)

It may seem odd to suggest that this poem invokes a form of sociality, for it stages such a solitary, entirely unpopulated scene, reminiscent of Hugh Kenner's often repeated claim that there are no people in Stevens's poems. But perhaps the poem's repetitions are exactly what create the sense that language is a medium to be inhabited, at least by those with whom it shares "innate rapport" (*CPP* 229). It's not any transcendental signified that unifies readers – the "last largeness" that looms above us. Rather, it's the material scrim or curtain of language, a haptic textile that gathers listeners into its folds.

It so happens that the word Stevens is supposed to have repeated on his deathbed, when discussing religion with Reverend Arthur Hanley, was "the fold." "I think I ought to be in the fold," he confessed when considering whether to accept Catholic rites (qtd. in Brazeau 294). "He called for me," Hanley recalls, "and he said, 'I'd better get in the fold now.' And then I baptized him, and the next day I brought him Communion" (295). (Stevens supposedly also told Hanley that he hoped to write a poem about Pope Pius X, and that one of its possible titles was "The Tailor" [294].) Indeed, "fold" has several harmonic resonances for Stevens. It names a group of people enclosed by a common belief, as well as an aesthetic device that synesthetically conflates sound, image, touch. Repetition creates a sense of exorbitant excess, a verbal surfeit that elaborates the freedom of perpetual open-endedness within the comforts of enclosure.

It is worth noting how closely Stevens's manner resembles that of Henry James in this regard – that most famous American mannerist – in whose later work especially the elongated sentences combine verbal virtuosity and social grace under the auspices of an almost supreme sense of civility, and a demanding care for the "tone-standard" of "sound . . . the touchstone of manners," as he wrote in "The Question of Our Speech" (45). Stevens's most cherished sentence by James, the one he called most "precious," and which he frequently quoted to friends, reveals repetition as motor:

> To live *in* the world of creation – to get into it and stay in it – to frequent it and haunt it – to *think* intensely and fruitfully – to woo combinations and inspirations into being by a depth and continuity of attention and meditation – this is the only thing. (*L* 506)

While this sentence may seem to promote an experience of private interiority, we must not forget that James was extremely outspoken on the sociality of speech, particularly when it came to the crudeness of the "*vox Americana*" (51). In "The Manners of American Women," for instance,

James urges his audience to tend carefully to "articulation and utterance," to "measure[s] of social grace," to the "saving salt of a felt proportion in things" (94–95). James spoke of language as "the very hinge of the relation of man to man" (47); it creates an inhabitable "margin" connecting people, a "small structure of civility" that is most successfully erected "in communities where the general question of manners has an importance, by the *form*, so to speak, that clothes the naked fact" (84). Importantly, both writers derive their authority, their tone standards, from their associations with privileged social classes, a status they perform through the fluency and ease with which a labyrinthine distance is elongated between the verbal and the real, creating a suspended temporality. "Patterns of speech allude to social orders," critic Robert von Hallberg has written about the poetics of civility (89). The vatic locomotion in both Stevens and James is symptomatic of their longing for a stable social order that they both saw as disappearing, and in need of saving.

One of the most palpable examples of Stevens's mature manner is "The Owl in the Sarcophagus," the elegy for Henry Church that has the explicitly social function of conferring peace not just upon the departed but also upon the dead's survivors. Here Stevens weaves a text that imagines "the whole spirit sparkling in its cloth, // Generations of the imagination piled / In the manner of its stitchings" (*CPP* 373). The third section opens as follows:

> There he saw well the foldings in the height
> Of sleep, the whiteness folded into less,
> Like many robings, as moving masses are,
>
> As a moving mountain is, moving through day
> And night, colored from distances, central
> Where luminous agitations come to rest,
>
> In an ever-changing, calmest unity,
> The unique composure, harshest streakings joined
> In a vanishing-vanished violet that wraps round
>
> The giant body the meanings of its folds,
> The weaving and the crinkling and the vex. . . . (*CPP* 372)

The poem's "meanings" are conveyed in the "moving masses" of sound itself. These sounds are not completely liberated from the substance of the poem, but wrap around the ineffable content of the body, like some surplus artifice ("Manner is an additional element," Stevens once wrote [*CPP* 902]). In so doing, the language resembles the movement "implied by garments," as Deleuze sees it: the Mannerist garment tries to "free its own folds from its usual subordination to the finite body it covers" (121). Deleuze's account of the repetitions in Mannerist and Baroque music involves the notion of a harmonic "accord." "*I produce an accord*," he explains, "each time I can establish in a sum of infinitely tiny things differential relations that will make possible an integration of the sum" (130–31). This integration engenders "a pleasure that can be continued, prolonged, renewed, multiplied" (131).

We know that one of the basic intentions of Stevens's manner is that "It Must Give Pleasure," as declared by "Notes Toward a Supreme Fiction" (*CPP* 344). But beyond a ritualistic description of the acoustics of the poem there remains the question endemic to the sociology of manners: with whom is this pleasure being shared, and who might feel excluded? If Stevens is a social poet, who gets collected within his fold? The answer to this question reveals why the literary society devoted to Stevens's legacy in the Hartford area is called "Friends & Enemies of Wallace Stevens," because readers have long been of many minds on the question of the actual sociality of Stevens's music. For poet Louise Glück, "Stevens's meditative poems are not addressed outward," making her feel "superfluous, part of some marginal throng" (115). She does not feel part of the fold. By contrast, poet Jack Spicer remembers rejecting Stevens's poetry because he was so keenly wary of the fold who already claimed and revered him (mainly "everybody in English Departments" of the 1950s and 1960s) (72). More recently, critics such as Lisa M. Steinman and Rachel Galvin have considered the complicated reception (often non-reception) of Stevens among nonwhite readers. The problem isn't just a function of the poetry's sound, according to Galvin, but of an implicit racism embedded in the vocabulary and concepts of traditional literary criticism and the "socio-political system that facilitated [his poetry's] production and dissemination" (232).

By introducing "manner" into our critical vocabulary, we can connect the aesthetic, formalist study of Stevens's poetry with a deeper interrogation of the cultural dynamic wherein Stevens's work often feels as exclusive as it feels inclusive. The two "Nudity" poems, for example, from *Ideas of Order*, model manners in a way that affirms, in Galvin's words, "the ideology of empire that clusters around the idea of imitation" (240):

Nudity at the Capital

But nakedness, woolen massa, concerns an innermost atom.
If that remains concealed, what does the bottom matter?

Nudity in the Colonies

Black man, bright nouveautés leave one, at best, pseudonymous.
Thus one is most disclosed when one is most anonymous. (*CPP* 117)

When giving a philosophical justification for baring his backside in the capital, this "Black man" emulates politeness, wit, and decorum; however, the supposed joke is that he is only imitating – unsuccessfully – the discourses of both manners and logic. By contrast, when the second "master" speaker renders his decision on the question of clothing versus nakedness, his authority comes through his distant tone, his employment of the French "nouveautés" (against the slang dialectic of "woolen massa") as well as the equipoise of the final sentence's syntax, whose sonic closure, sealed by the four-syllable rhyme, is designed to appear irrefutable. Anonymity, not self-expression, has the last laugh.

In his own gloss of the "Nudity" poems in a letter to Hi Simons, Stevens explained the intended meaning of the second couplet: "What I wear disguises me, gives me another self, and if I wore enough I should have no self at all" (*L* 347). Of course, anonymity, pursued here through the art of dress, is itself culturally coded: anonymity, the condition of being unmarked, whether by race or class or gender, is only imaginable by members of a dominant group. Bourdieu underscores this dynamic when writing that "the 'parvenus' who presume to join the group of legitimate, i.e., hereditary, possessors of the legitimate manner . . . are trapped . . . in a choice between . . . the conformity of an 'assumed' behavior whose very correctness or hyper-correctness betrays an imitation, or the ostentatious assertion of difference." Members of a dominant group, on the other hand, possess both "the privilege of indifference to their own manner (so they never have to *put on* a manner)" plus "the power to define the value of manners" themselves (95). Perhaps the "impersonal" poetics pursued by modernists like Stevens is not a neutral cultural value, but one available only to poets of privilege.

To read Stevens through the lens of manner rather than style relates to Henry Adams's image of the writer as a "tailor." Comparing his own approach to memoir with the naked sincerity attempted by Jean-Jacques Rousseau's *Confessions*, Adams says he wants to model the social, cultural, economic, and educational experiences that formed him, rather than trying to divest himself of those inheritances. In *The Education of Henry Adams*, "the object of study is the garment, not the figure" (722). In just this fashion, by studying the metaphorical (and often literal) garments of Stevens's poetry, we are not thinking of a social artifice that needs to be taken off to reveal the real meaning underneath. Language is not "the dress of thought" according to an eighteenth-century idea of rhetoric, the notion that led American oratory to imagine a plain, personal style stripped of all plumage and brocade. Rather, in Stevens, the garment – the rhetorical manner, whether "scrawny" or "colossal" – is very often the thing itself (*CPP* 452).

On this note, I'd like to end by pointing out a particularly telling metaphor from Stevens's essay "Imagination as Value." It's the metaphor that he cites from the *Pensées* of Blaise Pascal, the magisterial "red robes" worn by court magistrates in seventeenth-century France (*CPP* 724). For Pascal, these robes are evidence of the falseness and deceptiveness of the imagination. "If they possessed true justice," the judges would not need such "vain devices," he protests (11). But for Stevens, the magistrates' regalia, "their ermines in which they swathe themselves, like furry cats, the palaces in which they sit in judgment, the fleurs-de-lis, and the whole necessary, august apparatus" may be "a potent good" – if, that is, they prove effective in bringing "vast populations . . . to live peacefully in their homes and to lie down at night with a sense of security and to get up in the morning confident that the great machine of organized society is ready to carry them on" (*CPP* 724–25). This is the social power of the imagination's artifice. For Stevens, it is not a revolutionary or unsettling power. He was, after all, an upper-middle-class corporate executive who valued security, who liked to envision "a world in which insurance has been made perfect" (*CPP* 795), and who imagined that money and poetry were similar, for if people possessed both in abundance, they would be able to sleep more easily at night. The question for Stevens the poet, separate from Stevens the insurance executive, was how to write in a way that sustained the "nobility" of the imagination but was also "potent" enough for people to believe in it.

That this is a problem of manner, or manners, implies that it is never just an aesthetic question. As Lionel Trilling once wrote, in "Manners, Morals and the Novel," manners are just the visible, audible index to cultural values and ideologies that do not often get stated directly. Manners are "that part of a culture which is made up of half-uttered or unuttered or unutterable expressions of value." For Trilling, the politics of manners are, or should become, paramount for both artists and critics. This is imperative because, for "any complex culture" where "there is not a single system of manners but a conflicting variety of manners," the work of that culture becomes "the adjustment of this conflict" (201). In the modern novel, Trilling suggests, "the problem of appearance and reality" is actually not a philosophical problem; it is the problem of "the shifting and conflict of social classes" (203). Perhaps the same problem holds true for a "new"

Stevens criticism trying to integrate the aesthetic, the cultural, and the political dimensions of his poetry.

WORKS CITED

Adams, Henry. *Henry Adams: Novels, Mont Saint Michel, The Education.* Edited by Jayne Samuels and Ernest Samuels, Library of America, 1983.

Agamben, Giorgio. *The End of the Poem: Studies in Poetics.* Translated by Daniel Heller-Roazen, Stanford UP, 1999.

Berthoff, Warner. *The Ferment of Realism: American Literature, 1884–1919.* Free P, 1965.

Brazeau, Peter. *Parts of a World: Wallace Stevens Remembered; An Oral Biography.* Random House, 1983.

Brogan, Jacqueline V., editor. *Stevens and Structures of Sound.* Special issue of *The Wallace Stevens Journal,* vol. 15, no. 2, Fall 1991, pp. 107–241.

Bourdieu, Pierre. *Distinction: A Social Critique of the Judgement of Taste.* Translated by Richard Nice, Harvard UP, 1984.

Deleuze, Gilles. *The Fold: Leibniz and the Baroque.* Translated by Tom Conley, U of Minnesota P, 1993.

Doyle, Charles, editor. *Wallace Stevens: The Critical Heritage.* Routledge & Kegan Paul, 1985.

Editorial. *The Seven Arts,* vol. 1, no. 1, Nov. 1926, pp. 52–53.

Feinsod, Harris. *The Poetry of the Americas: From Good Neighbors to Countercultures.* Oxford UP, 2017.

Filreis, Alan. "Sound at an Impasse." *The Wallace Stevens Journal,* vol. 33, no. 1, Spring 2009, pp. 15–23.

Finch, D. Zachary. "'He That of Repetition Is Most Master': Stevens and the Poetics of Mannerism." *The Wallace Stevens Journal,* vol. 36, no. 2, Fall 2012, pp. 194–205.

Galvin, Rachel. "'This Song Is for My Foe': Olive Senior and Terrance Hayes Rewrite Stevens." *Poetry and Poetics after Wallace Stevens,* edited by Bart Eeckhout and Lisa Goldfarb, Bloomsbury, 2017, pp. 229–43.

Gerber, Natalie. Introduction. *Wallace Stevens and "The Less Legible Meanings of Sounds,"* edited by Gerber, special issue of *The Wallace Stevens Journal,* vol. 33, no. 1, Spring 2009, pp. 3–14.

Glück, Louise. *Proofs & Theories: Essays on Poetry.* Ecco P, 1994.

James, Henry. *Henry James on Culture: Collected Essays on Politics and the American Social Scene.* Edited by Pierre A. Walker, U of Nebraska P, 1999.

Jameson, Fredric. *The Modernist Papers.* Verso, 2016.

Pascal, Blaise. *Pensées.* Translated by A. J. Krailsheimer, Penguin, 1995.

Spicer, Jack. *The House That Jack Built: The Collected Lectures of Jack Spicer.* Edited by Peter Gizzi, UP of New England, 1998.

Steinman, Lisa M. "Unanticipated Readers." *Poetry and Poetics after Wallace Stevens,* edited by Bart Eeckhout and Lisa Goldfarb, Bloomsbury, 2017, pp. 217–28.

Stevens, Wallace. *Letters of Wallace Stevens*. Edited by Holly Stevens, U of California P, 1996.

Wallace Stevens: Collected Poetry and Prose. Edited by Frank Kermode and Joan Richardson, Library of America, 1997.

Trilling, Lionel. *The Liberal Imagination: Essays on Literature and Society*. Macmillan, 1950.

Vasari, Giorgio. "Preface to the Third Part." *Readings in Italian Mannerism*, edited by Liana De Girolami Cheney, Peter Lang, 2004, pp. 27–34.

von Hallberg, Robert. *Lyric Powers*. U of Chicago P, 2008.

CHAPTER 17

Lyrical Ethics

Johanna Skibsrud

"The eye's plain version is a thing apart, / The vulgate of experience,"
writes Wallace Stevens in "An Ordinary Evening in New Haven" (*CPP*
397) – a late poem included in his penultimate collection, *The Auroras of
Autumn* (1950). Here, as in many instances throughout his career, Stevens
celebrates the disjunction between language and experience by establishing
both the affordances and restrictions of the individual subject's point of
view. What we see "plainly," he posits, is not the world – or even an image
of the world – but our own particular version, or invention, of that world:
"a thing apart." The inherent solipsism of this perspective forms the basis
of our experience. It provides a seemingly natural and inevitable language
for our understanding and expression of what we feel and see at the same
time that it delimits that understanding and the possibilities of expression.
The poem as a whole radiates from this seeming paradox, the limits of
perspective serving, on the one hand, as an exemption from and, on the
other, as the foundation for, reality. Of this paradox, Stevens says, "A few
words, an and yet, and yet, and yet – " (*CPP* 397). The poem, Stevens
suggests, offers a way of deferring definition. It extends itself as a slow
unraveling of rational thought, a series of articulations that move *away*
from the central paradox of being – certainly from the possibility of
"getting to the bottom of it." Neither question nor answer, and resisting
both summary and conclusive response, a poem can only be furthered by
the reader "As part of the never-ending meditation, / Part of the question
that is a giant himself" (*CPP* 397).

In this concluding chapter, I offer my own "and yet" to the "never-
ending meditation" Stevens initiates. I argue that Stevens's intricate poetic
"evasions" and "endless" elaborations (*CPP* 415) demonstrate the capacity
for lyric poetry to express the immanent relation between subjectivity and
objectivity, knowledge and truth, self and other. Although committed to
expressing the complexities and paradoxes within moments of being,
Stevens successfully "evades" a fundamentalist approach to ontology –

one that, like Heidegger's, cannot progress or is deemed invalid if the thinker has not *"previously clarified the meaning of Being sufficiently and grasped this clarification as its fundamental task"* (10). Stevens is far too interested in, and faithful to, fleeting sensations and plays of light – and far too pragmatic – to spend much time pondering the fundamental "meaning of Being." The goal for Stevens is, as he suggests in "The Man with the Blue Guitar," to elaborate a space in which the necessarily limited and illusory aspects of experience are united with a larger reality he conceives of beyond the circumscribed framework of a subjective perspective. His poetry moves – haltingly, uncertainly – toward the representation neither of the "dream" of existence nor of a conception of a fixed, material "reality" from which the dream is drawn but instead toward "A dream no longer a dream, a thing" – toward an expression "Of things as they are" (*CPP* 143).

For Stevens, despite his reputation for abstraction, the ideal expression of "things as they are" is found in the interface between subjectivity and objectivity. He is wary of dwelling within the circuitries of an endlessly refractive "inner" space, but he is also too aware of the pervasive role of the imagination – even in establishing the distinction between "inside" and "out" – to trust in any description of the physical world as final or absolute. Alain Badiou's "radical thesis" that "ontology . . . is nothing other than mathematics itself" (xiii) – that certain patterns and properties exist regardless if there is someone to perceive them – would have been suspect, and ultimately not very interesting, to Stevens. What he finds compelling is the movement and relation between different perspectives and supposedly disparate modes of interpreting the world. His poetry is committed neither to a metaphysical nor to a physical expression of reality; it strives to be neither subjective nor objective, neither abstract nor concrete. By exposing the limits of the subject as an open border with what is unseen, unspoken, and unknown, he stages a lyric encounter that hinges not on the possibility of response (either imagined or real) from a projected "other" – whether that be a narrative "you" or the reader of the poem – but on the play between the known parameters of selfhood and what exceeds those parameters. Lyric poetry, for Stevens, *is* this play: the performance of "A tune beyond us, yet ourselves" (*CPP* 135) that invites lived moments of encounter with the immanent relation between "inside" and "out."[1] The ethics implicit within Stevens's poetry is thus an ethics of sensual discontinuity and rupture rather than of abstract, projected contact. Stevens encourages us to *feel into* the gaps he presents between self and other, language and meaning, idea and thing, to arrive at a felt rather than rational awareness of the way this gap is never quite bridged due precisely to the fact that we – our very subject positions – are blocking the way.

I am indebted to Derek Attridge, William Waters, Rachel Cole, Mara Scanlon, and others who have argued persuasively that rather than a demonstration of "solipsistic exclusivity" (Cole 383), the lyric is instead an invitation toward participation and ethical response. Here I want to push this thinking further and suggest that if we take this ethical possibility afforded by the lyric as a *starting point* and at the same time seriously confronting the impasse of subjective perception, we may find ourselves in a position to read the lyric as an actual extension of selfhood beyond a linear, narrative frame. Rather than reading Stevens's poems as poetic resources to be mined for meaning, my aim is to activate them as generative sites of meaning-making. The following pages are therefore a performance of sorts, the aim of which is to demonstrate both the limits and possibilities of my own language and imagination. But this performance will also, I hope, act as both testament to and argument for the capacity of lyric poetry to access and express what is ultimately beyond language and individual perspective (both Stevens's and my own).

From the memorable moment in Stevens's first collection, *Harmonium*, in which from the perspective of "The Snow Man" – "nothing himself" (*CPP* 8) – we encounter two different kinds of nothing, to Stevens's final collection, *The Rock*, where we are reminded that "the absence of the imagination had / Itself to be imagined" (*CPP* 428), Stevens creates vantage points from which to perceive the partial and constructed nature of perception.[2] Clarified through this process is the unavoidable limit of the human imagination. Stevens writes both in celebration of the imagination's power to extend subjective experience beyond selfhood and in passionate resistance to a reduction of the world to its subjective interpretation. What results is a sometimes disorienting movement between multiple perspectives and shifting points of contact and relation between subjects and objects, as well as between the "peculiar and general" (*CPP* 343).[3]

"The greenhouse never so badly needed paint," he writes, for example, in "The Plain Sense of Things," a late poem included in *The Rock*. "The chimney is fifty years old and slants to one side. / A fantastic effort has failed, a repetition / In a repetitiousness of men and flies" (*CPP* 428). Here, we're propelled swiftly from a close-up view of a crumbling garden to a panned-out vision of the cyclical nature of life and death. By the time we reach the "repetitiousness of men and flies," we are no longer in a position to distinguish between the "fantastic effort" (think both "immense" and "fantastical/illusory") of constructing a chimney and the "fantastic effort" it takes just to live. Within this dizzying juxtaposition we sense the intrinsic relation between birth and death, between creative intention and its eventual, necessary disintegration. From the specific and the time-bound, we are spun out toward a sweepingly inclusive perspective that seems to take in "the whole." But before we can rest too comfortably within the seeming inclusivity or "holism" of this perspective, we are reminded that even it is produced through the finite imagination and depends upon a version of reality that remains inaccessible.

"The Plain Sense of Things" exists, in other words, both utterly beyond thought and language and as absolutely necessary to it. Stevens directs our attention toward this seeming dichotomy, exposing the simultaneity of what exists at the foundation of human perspective and knowledge and what is forever beyond it. The "plain sense" of the world, he suggests, is an expression of "silence" – but not silence in the ordinary sense of the word, which would imply an opposition to what is heard (from a particular, human perspective) as sound or noise. The silence produced by the "plain sense of things" is described as "silence // Of a sort," because Stevens specifically wants us to imagine a resonance that, while virtually exceeding the human imagination, is actually dependent on it: "silence of a rat come out to see, / The great pond and its waste of the lilies, all this / Had to be imagined as an inevitable knowledge, / Required, as a necessity requires." Though we are here asked to adopt the perspective of a rat, we are also encouraged to recognize that our experience of that perspective can only be imaginative – not, therefore, the rat's, but our own. Stevens does not aim merely to point to the limits and inadequacies of the human imagination; the drive of the poem is ultimately beyond a subjective framework. Stevens reminds us that we do not exempt ourselves from a reality that includes the perspective of a rat just because we fail to imagine it. We may, the poem suggests, be necessarily blind to, and therefore be forced to talk "around," the true nature of things, but that truth is nonetheless "inevitable" – unavoidable (*CPP* 428). As Stevens writes in "The Man with the Blue Guitar," it exists "beyond us, yet ourselves" (*CPP* 135) – an inextricable if inexpressible part of our own highly subjective experience of the world.

Though his entire career was spent, more or less explicitly, making "Notes Toward a Supreme Fiction," and he persuasively announced, "It Must Be Abstract," Stevens was ultimately committed to engaging deeply and specifically with the facts of the world beyond subjective interpretation by promoting a sense of the integral connection between our limited perceptions and the larger structure of which they are a blurred but "necessary" part. The space of the lyric thus becomes not a private space of reflection or absorption with a narrativized version of either subject or object, self or other, but – through the process of reading and interpretation – a space of encounter with what exists beyond, and therefore delineates, selfhood.

Stevens emphasizes the poem as a site of active interpretation. Rather than a form or a genre, poetry is, for him, an act, a possibility, one that promotes the possibility of, but in no way guarantees, an expanded awareness of what already – without our seeing or knowing it – *is*. The poem, in other words, as Stevens writes in "An Ordinary Evening in New Haven," is always "the cry of its occasion, / Part of the res itself and not about it," neither a description nor a thing (a "res"), but an exclamation – an outburst of sound and meaning brought about through its encounter with a moving body. "The poet speaks the poem as it is, // Not as it was," Stevens writes, emphasizing that it is the embodied act of *speaking* that allows the poem to transition from "thing" – imagined as somehow separate from a lived experience of time – to "Part of the res itself." Although for the poet "There is no / Tomorrow," it is not because he has exempted himself from linear temporality but because he can articulate his essential engagement with a nonlinear structure of time. The narrative opposition between self and other, self and world, is abandoned; the imagined fixity of the lyric "I" is shattered by unexpected shifts in grammar and logic – blown about, like the "marble statues" Stevens describes, "like newspapers blown by the wind." The poet "speaks // By sight and insight" at once here – and suggests that the "words of the world" exist not as separate, indicative signs but as integral parts of "the life of the world." In the same way, the objects represented in the poem are evoked as active expressions of the "whirlings" that gave rise to their seemingly unified and particular form (*CPP* 404).

Crucially, the poetic process for Stevens is sensual, not theoretical, ideational, or textual. It is not enough for him that we think or write poetry, that we think or write alterity and otherness. Even as it is being employed, lyric poetry's virtual "other" or abstract "you" is also being questioned, disassociated from, and overturned. This is, perhaps, why Stevens's work has for so long been read as solipsistic: we come to understand, through Stevens's treatment of the lyric encounter, that there is no one to address, no narrative figure to speak to, or – even potentially – take up the poet's call. This is precisely Stevens's point. For him, lyric poetry is a way of exposing the limitations of our personal, narrative perspectives to engage with a broader, nonlinear experience of being and time. His poetics can, in this way, be understood to align with some of the most innovative developments in contemporary physics. For Stevens, poetry affords an opportunity to extend perception beyond pre-conceived limits of selfhood and language, but it does so by inducing both a sensual and cognitive awareness of the material parameters and entangle-ments of perception. Similarly, the contemporary Italian physicist Carlo Rovelli defines poetry as "the capacity to see beyond the visible" and suggests it as one of science's "deepest roots" (21). In *The Order of Time*, Rovelli sketches out some of the "unexpected and disconcerting" features modern physics has revealed about the nature of time, including the idea that the binary distinctions we have for so long presumed to exist between past and future, cause and effect – and therefore between "memory and hope, between regret and intention" – do not actually exist (20). "[T]he difference between the past and the future," he writes,

> refers only to *our own* blurred vision of the world. It's a conclusion that leaves us flabbergasted: is it really possible that a perception so vivid, basic, existential – my perception of the passage of time – depends on the fact that I cannot apprehend the world in all of its minute detail? (31)

Rovelli's poetic account of the physics of time explodes our ingrained conception of a necessarily linear temporality, but it also endeavors to explain how and why we have come to conceive time that way. It is, he informs us, all a matter of perspective, of scale. Like Stevens, Rovelli stresses the importance of acknowledging the situatedness of individual perspective and its narrative possibilities within – and therefore as a potential point of access to – a larger non-narrative structure. Our limited perspectival framework is essential to our understanding of the world, but it is important, Rovelli warns us, not to confuse the structures "that belong to the world 'as seen from the outside' with the aspects of the world that we observe and which depend on our being part of it, on our being situated within it" (134). Stevens likewise refuses any physical model of the world as "seen from the outside," although he does invite us, through the process of reading and poetic interpretation, to attend closely to our situatedness "within a mind, a brain, a position in space, a moment in time" (Rovelli 134) – and to *sense* (based on this heightened awareness of and proximity to what exists "beyond" our finite, narrative frameworks) what we cannot see, or know, "from the outside."

Take the poem titled "A Postcard from the Volcano," from *Ideas of Order*. At the start, we are introduced to a moment in the projected future when we, the poem's present readers, will be long gone, barely imaginable in our current form: "Children picking up our bones / Will never know that these were once / As quick as foxes on the hill … " The poem suggests a confluence between the present – the "cry" of the poem's occasion – and a far distant future, the immanent connection between the two seemingly disparate realities preserved and made visible through the image of "our bones." Stevens ultimately addresses not only an audience of potential readers – imagined as contemporaries – but also a generation of readers in the far future: children who, presumably in the course of innocent play, will chance upon the traces we have left and be invited to read those traces (though not – it is suggested – in the way that we imagine or intend). The children, Stevens writes, will never "know" and "least will guess that with our bones / We left much more, left what still is / The look of things, left what we felt // At what we saw" (*CPP* 128). Through this evocation of the absolute limit point of perception, we are invited to encounter ourselves "from the outside," to read ourselves from the perspective of future generations – as children, oblivious to the meanings we take for granted within and as our own (literal) articulations: our joints and bones.

Rather than seeking to exempt itself from linear temporal flow or make contact with what exceeds the singular speaker, this imagined encounter asks us to engage with the limits of individual identity and our *perception*, from that limited vantage point, of temporal flow. What results is an evocation of a broader, non-narrative structure that both exceeds and gives rise to our specific, situated conceptions of selfhood and our "blurred" temporal perceptions. We "left what still is / The look of things," Stevens writes – suggesting that, ultimately, the narrative elements of our experiences are *not* lost (*CPP* 128). Although "Children, / Still weaving budded aureoles, / Will speak our speech and never know," this projected ignorance neither infringes upon nor relativizes the irrefutable reality of the present. By the same token, our irrefutable ignorance of the experience of others – now, in the past, or in the unimaginable future – neither infringes upon nor relativizes those experiences, or the connection those experiences have with our own seemingly discrete subjective moments. As a haunted house in the poem's concluding line is "Smeared with the gold of the opulent sun," we may sense the way our own moment spills over the imagined bounds of both knowledge and the present; we may sense the haunted nature of every moment, the existence of a greater "spirit storming in blank walls" (*CPP* 129). Ultimately, it is our exclusion from a greater knowledge and reality that allows for brief, shadowed glimpses of our connection to it.

Juxtaposed against the serene, already belated imagery of children sensing our extinguished presence in the form of old foundations and

scattered bones, the poem's final image of a haunted, sunlit house emphasizes the sometimes hidden, always potent and protean power of the life-
giving – and light-giving – sun at the root of all our experiences of being
and time. The sun illuminates, these lines suggest – but it also blinds. It is
the source of what "still is / The look of things," but it is also indifferent to
"what we felt // At what we saw" (*CPP* 128). In this poem, Stevens's images
often have an ambivalent relationship to material form: bones, haunted
houses, the rays of the sun. What interests him is the material reality of
what only appears abstract. The declarative section heading "It Must Be
Abstract" from "Notes Toward a Supreme Fiction" – and indeed the long
poem as a whole – is a reminder not of the immaterial or relative nature of
the world but rather of the way that our language, and our modes of
observing and addressing the world, must encompass and confront what
appears abstract.

"[T]he world is nothing but change," writes Rovelli (85), seeming to echo
Stevens's poetic pronouncement from three-quarters of a century ago –
another section heading from "Notes": "It Must Change." Rovelli writes
that the contemporary dissolution of the notion of time as singular, linear,
and continuous allows us to see the world, instead, as "a network of events."
As a result, we are able to confront "the simple fact that nothing is: that
things happen instead" (85). In "The Man with the Blue Guitar," Stevens's
repeated testing of the phrase "things as they are" similarly invites us to
confront this phenomenon. Meaning and indeed reality itself are presented
in this poem as a continuous "happening" rather than a fixed (even if
hidden) code. "So that's life, then: things as they are? / It picks its way on
the blue guitar" begins the first sentence of the poem's fourth section. Only
six lines later, the section concludes by repeating this phrase, with
a difference: "And that's life, then: things as they are, / This buzzing of the
blue guitar" (*CPP* 136). In the space of this transition, from question to
seemingly definitive response, the buzzing of multiple directions for thought
may be heard – including the evocation of such seeming binaries as self and
other, reality and the imagination. The question at the beginning of the
section suggests an alignment between "things as they are" and our finite
subjective interpretation of them. "A million people on one string?" begins
to upset this alignment, however. It asks us to attend to the unseen, unheard
reverberations of what we might otherwise conceive of as a unified object,
a single voice, a whole. The final statement in this section, though declarative, points to a still broader and even more unknown structure: "And that's
life, then: things as they are, / This buzzing of the blue guitar" arrives at
a pronouncement of life not as a series of things to be "seen" and understood

separately, but instead as a network of events connected through the erratic, chance-based, and ultimately nonlinear process of active voicing and subjective interpretation. Insofar as poetry is understood as a vehicle for both, it is proposed as a mode of expressing life's non-narrative complexity.

Stevens further emphasizes poetry as an active approach to reading rather than as a fixed form or genre to be read in the next section when he begins, "Do not speak to us of the greatness of poetry, / Of the torches wisping in the underground, // Of the structure of vaults upon a point of light." Once again, the relationship between "inner" truths and an "outside" reality is explored through the evocation of different images, and perspectives, of light. "There are no shadows in our sun," writes Stevens. And a little later: "The earth, for us, is flat and bare. / There are no shadows" (*CPP* 136). We perceive and invent the world for ourselves from individual points of view, Stevens suggests through this poem, but the true nature of that world, while *including* the situatedness of those perspectives, remains ultimately aloof from them. We will always dwell in reflected light – will always live and dream in and among shadows. It is for this reason that Stevens emphasizes both our proximity to and distance from the sun.

As in "A Postcard from the Volcano," the sun represents the singular, indifferent source of everything we see – emphasizing that source as both integral to us and utterly unknowable, "beyond us as we are" (*CPP* 137). The forms that arise and retreat within the poem are as they can only be: "described but difficult." They emerge, like the form of the blue guitar itself, as shadowy figures, difficult to see let alone grasp. And yet it is because they are so difficult to see, touch, and know that they allow us to glimpse our own shadowy forms: "And I am merely a shadow hunched // Above the arrowy, still strings, / The maker of a thing yet to be made" (*CPP* 138). "There are no shadows anywhere," we were told in section five of the poem. Here, though, only a few short sections later, we are asked to identify with a "mere" shadow. We are asked to dwell with this shadowy figure within the poignant space "Above the arrowy, still strings" – to pause here, within the *potential* of communicated perspective, even as we definitively arrive (from our shifting and limited perspectives) at the *particular* meaning of Stevens's poem. What we have arrived at is this: the ethical problem that exists at the root of every expression of self and other, and therefore at the root of every lyric poem. "Where / Do I begin and end?" Stevens asks. "And where, // As I strum the thing, do I pick up / That which momentously declares // Itself not to be I and yet / Must be" (*CPP* 140). Although Stevens has hitherto explored the problem of perspective by concentrating on the theme of sight, at this point he shifts to a confrontation with the problem as it manifests itself in our experience of time. "Throw away the lights," he challenges us in the penultimate section of the poem. "Nothing must stand // Between you and the shapes you take / When the crust of shape has been destroyed." Relieved of the shifting light of individual perspective, which has up until this point afforded us the impression of encountering both ourselves and the things of the world as discrete and separate entities, we confront not space but "Time in its final block" (*CPP* 150). Is Stevens suggesting that there exists a larger, ultimate shape to being and time – a sort of absolute, geometric reality? Or is this "final block" an abstract expressionist demonstration that shape need no longer be connected with any "thing" at all? My guess is both and neither.

We are left, finally, not with "truth" or "reality," but with "a wrangling of two dreams." On the one hand, we confront the illusory aspect of singular perspective and any equation between things as they appear from that perspective and "things as they are." On the other hand, we experience a sense of proximity with what exists beyond knowledge, language, and selfhood. The "wrangling" of these two approaches to reality is expressed in temporal terms as a fundamental incompatibility between our finite and limited "now" (a sense of "things as they are" or appear to be) and a projected, unapparent temporal framework (unmoored from sequentiality and the visible appearance of things) suggested by the "time to come." Though seemingly abstract, it is this "time to come" that proves most solid and sustaining in the end: "Here is the bread of time to come," Stevens writes. "Here is its actual stone. The bread / Will be our bread, the stone will be // Our bed" (*CPP* 151). Here, we are invited to acknowledge that what appears to us as abstract, projected, and unknowable is in fact deeply connected both to the material structure of the world and to our sensual and emotional experiences of human being. Although the poem gestures toward an oppositional relationship between "bare" reality and the reflective imagination, between the pure source of the sun and the refracted light of the moon, Stevens successfully evades such a dualistic conception. What results is not an abstract representation of either "subjective" or "objective" reality within the absorptive and absorbing space of private reflection, but a sense of the immanent connection between what makes up and what exceeds the experience of the private body and mind. We experience this connection through the act of reading. Stevens's evasive grammar – its frequent shifts, especially in possessive pronouns, its endless qualifiers, and loops and swerves of logic – frustrates every attempt to solidify a rational concept, express a singular identity, or sustain a direct line of thought. "The poem must resist the intelligence / Almost successfully," he posits in "Man Carrying Thing" (*CPP* 306).

Wallace Stevens's oeuvre can be read as an illustration of this imperative: a resistance to singular intelligence that – crucially – never quite succeeds in disabling or overwhelming the lyric "I." The singularity and situatedness of individual perspective are evoked by Stevens as a point of departure, not as a stopping point. Through the often befuddling process of reading his poems, we are reminded that the borders of language and selfhood are real, but that they are also immersive and open. Ultimately, he confounds us. His "intricate evasions" elaborate neither a theory of poetry nor one of life. Instead, they provide an opportunity for encounter, through the active process of reading and listening, with the limits of rational thought and narrative selfhood – as well as with the nonlinear, fundamentally poetic nature of our relation both to being and time.

Notes

1 "The major abstraction is the idea of man / And major man is its exponent, abler / In the abstract than in his singular," Stevens writes in "Notes Toward a Supreme Fiction" (*CPP* 336).
2 "The Snow Man" ends with "the listener, who listens in the snow, / And, nothing himself, beholds / Nothing that is not there and the nothing that is" (*CPP* 8).
3 "Is the poem both peculiar and general?" Stevens wonders in "Notes Toward a Supreme Fiction," adding, "There's a meditation there, in which there seems // To be an evasion, a thing not apprehended or / Not apprehended well. Does the poet / Evade us, as in a senseless element?" (*CPP* 343).

WORKS CITED

Badiou, Alain. *Being and Event*. Translated by Oliver Feltham, Continuum, 2006.
Cole, Rachel. "Rethinking the Value of Lyric Closure: Giorgio Agamben, Wallace Stevens, and the Ethics of Satisfaction." *PMLA*, vol. 126, no. 2, March 2011, pp. 383–97.
Heidegger, Martin. *Being and Time*. Translated by Joan Stambaugh, SUNY P, 2010.
Rovelli, Carlo. *The Order of Time*. Translated by Erica Segre and Simon Carnell, Penguin, 2018.
Stevens, Wallace. *Wallace Stevens: Collected Poetry and Prose*. Edited by Frank Kermode and Joan Richardson, Library of America, 1997.

Index

Abelove, Henry, 123
Abrams, M. H., 209
Abstract Expressionism, 164, 166
Abstraction, 9, 22, 33, 44, 46, 52, 64–65, 78, 100,
  109, 114, 120, 163, 167, 168, 198, 206, 208,
  210, 227, 229, 233, 235
Achebe, Chinua, 21
Adams, Henry, 222
Adichie, Chimamanda Ngozi, 88
Adorno, Theodor W., 31
Aeschylus, 88
Aestheticism, 124, 125, 127
Aesthetics, 4, 7, 27, 44, 45, 63, 67, 77, 88, 90–91,
  92, 120, 124–25, 127, 132, 133, 163, 165, 168,
  170, 174, 201, 216, 218, 219, 224
aesthete, 9, 163
aesthetic autonomy. *See* Autonomy
aesthetic experience, 77, 148–49, 152, 155
aesthetic form, 8, 12, 73, 93, 148, 154–56,
  210–11, 234
aesthetic labor, 214
aesthetic manner, 11, 215, 221
aesthetic play, 65–69
aesthetic pleasure, 12, 105, 148–51, 154–57,
  182, 221
and cognition, 8, 148–52
and politics. *See* Politics
and urbanization, 7, 112–15, 116, 120
beauty, 111, 114, 145, 166, 169, 179, 182, 195
local aesthetic, 71, 74, 76, 82
transnational aesthetic, 74–75, 81–82
Affirmation, 30, 41, 58, 60, 63–65
Africa, 17, 21, 23, 24–26, 32, 42
Afterwardsness, 11, 204, 206, 207, 210
Agamben, Giorgio, 11, 102, 214
Ali, Agha Shahid, 6, 91–92, 93
Ali, Kazim, 91
Allegory, 20, 22, 63, 75, 76, 129, 187, 188, 206
Allen, Donald, 161–62
Altieri, Charles, 10–11, 27, 70, 171
Ames, Adelbert, 108

Amherst College, 132
Anderson, Benedict, 138
Andrews-Hanna, J. R., 152
Anedda, Antonella, 95
Anjou, France, 79
Anthropocentrism, 100, 107
Anthropology, 5, 63–65
Anthropomorphism, 58, 63–64, 66
Apollinaire, Guillaume, 168
Architecture, 1, 7, 75, 112, 116, 117, 118–19, 155,
  176, 216
Armstrong, Tim, 156
Asad, Talal, 69
Ashbery, John, 131, 161, 162, 163–65, 166–68, 170
Asia, 71, 74, 82, 89–90
Attridge, Derek, 12, 228
Auden, W. H., 52, 132, 164, 166, 170
Audience, 3, 4–5, 6, 12, 44, 45, 48, 50, 52, 53, 95,
  119, 144, 189, 191, 195, 215, 217, 219–20, 232
Augustine, Saint, 115, 116
Austin, A. Everett, Jr., 126
Autonomy, 5, 6, 31, 53, 59, 62, 66–67, 88, 92–93,
  205, 218
Avant-garde, 9, 161–64, 166, 169–70

Bacigalupo, Massimo, 95–96
Badiou, Alain, 212, 227
Baer, William, 91
Bai, Fei, 90
Balthaser, Benjamin, 27
Balzac, Honoré de, 213
Bashwiner, David M., 152
Bassnett, Susan, 90
Bates, Jennifer, 212
Bates, Milton J., 90
Bateson, Gregory, 107–9
Baudelaire, Charles, 95, 166
Baxter, Charles, 48
Beardsley, Aubrey, 125
Beat poetry, 161
Beauty. *See* Aesthetics; beauty

Bechdel, Alison, 131
Beijing, China, 91
Belfi, Amy M., , 155, 157
Bell, Clive, 155
Bellamy, Edward, 29, 32
Béranger, Pierre-Jean de, 166
Berkeley, Bishop, 209
Berman, Jessica, 72, 73
Bernini, Gian Lorenzo, 218
Berrigan, Ted, 163, 169–70
Berthoff, Warner, 213
Bevis, William W., 89–90
Bishop, Elizabeth, 49, 131, 162
Black Mountain School poetry, 161
Blackmur, R. P., 50
Blanco, Richard, 145
Blasing, Mutlu Konuk, 55
Bloom, Harold, 103, 165, 171, 209
Bordeaux, France, 75
Borges, Jorge Luis, 21
Boston Review, The, 136
Boston, Massachusetts, 89, 115–16, 118
Botteghe Oscure, 95
Bourdieu, Pierre, 11, 216, 222
Brazeau, Peter, 123, 129–30, 219
Brazil, 75, 80
Breiner, Laurence, 91
Brielmann, Aenne A., 152
Brodkey, Harold, 165
Brogan, Jacqueline Vaught, 34, 142, 217
Brooks, Gwendolyn, 144
Browning, Robert, 199
Buddhism, 73, 89, 91
Bulgaria, 46
Burke, Kenneth, 68
Burnshaw, Stanley, 46, 119
Burt, Stephanie, 18, 48–49, 74, 83, 115
Bussell, Mirle Rabinowitz, 121
Butler, Judith, 126
Buttel, Robert, 199
Bynner, Witter, 126, 131

Cairo, Egypt, 21
Calhoun, Lucy Monroe, 90
Calhoun, William, 90
Campo, Rafael, 131, 145
Canada, 89, 94
Canton, China, 17, 26
Carbado, Devon W., 138
Caribbean, The, 71, 75, 90
Carolinas. *See* North Carolina; South Carolina
Carthage, 115
Carver, Charles, 155
Casanova, Pascale, 6, 88, 91, 92, 94, 97

Castiglione, Baldassare, 215
Castro, Fidel, 129
Cather, Willa, 174–75
Central America, 75
Ceylon. *See* Sri Lanka
Cézanne, Paul, 11, 187, 200
Chauncey, George, 125
Chicago, Illinois, 115
China, 20, 23, 75, 88, 89–91
Church, Barbara, 48, 78
Church, Henry, 81, 129, 175, 220
City Beautiful Movement, 119
Clarke, Austin, 96
Class, 8, 11, 30, 34, 112, 119, 136, 138, 139, 141–42, 216, 222, 223
Classes, 220
Cleghorn, Angus, 17, 24
Clune, Michael, 152
Cognitive perspectives, 8, 148
    and aesthetics. *See* Aesthetics
cognition, 6, 49, 128, 148, 152, 217, 231
cognitive literary studies, 6, 8, 148
cognitive process, 152
cognitive psychology, 154
Cold War, 6, 38, 72, 81, 96, 130
Cole, Rachel, 12, 228
Coleridge, Samuel Taylor, 155
Collectivity. *See* Community
Collins, Patricia Hill, 137
Colombo, Sri Lanka, 91
Colonialism, 3, 12, 17–21, 22–23, 25–26, 73, 75–76, 77, 214
Coltrane, John, 149
Combray, France, 178, 181
Commodity, 19–20, 24, 25–26, 73, 91, 137
Community, 3, 4, 7, 12, 44–55, 112, 113, 120, 145, 220
Connecticut, 23, 50, 77, 78, 91
Conrad, Joseph, 21
Constable, Marianne, 137
Cook, Eleanor, 55, 65, 78, 87, 142
Cosmopolitanism, 73, 82, 87
Costello, Bonnie, 27, 45, 51–52, 55, 79, 83, 121
Coyle, Beverly, 95, 128–29
Crane, Hart, 123, 131
Creeley, Robert, 162, 163
Crenshaw, Kimberlé Williams, 136–37, 139
Critchley, Simon, 104, 106, 199, 212
Cuba, 89, 91, 94–95, 126, 129–31, 176
Cubism, 164
Cullen, Countee, 144
Culleton, Claire, 90
Cummings, E. E., 117
Cunningham, Michael, 131

Dada, 164
Damrosch, David, 87
Daniel, Julia E., 7
Dante Alighieri, 199
de Man, Paul, 207, 211
de Vignemont, Frédérique, 152
Defamiliarization, 130
Delany, Samuel R., 123
Deleuze, Gilles, 102, 218, 221
Denmark, 47
Denver Post, The, 136
Dialectic, 27, 61, 100, 104, 208, 210, 214, 222
Dickinson, Emily, 124
Diogenes, 143
Donne, John, 154
Doty, Mark, 131
Doyle, Charles, 213
Doyle, Laura, 73
Du Bois, W. E. B., 32
Duncan, Robert, 131
DuPlessis, Rachel Blau, 93, 94, 141, 142, 144
DuRose, Lisa, 138, 141–42, 144

Eatough, Matt, 73
Eckermann, Johann Peter, 87
Ecocriticism. *See* Ecological poetics
Ecological poetics, 6, 100, 102–5, 106
    and ecological systems, 107–8
    ecological environment, 6, 102–4, 105, 107
    ecological space, 103
Edelman, Lee, 125
Eeckhout, Bart, 7, 30, 74, 114, 117, 165, 170, 171, 185
Egypt, 21
Elegy, 50, 220
Eliot, T. S., 29, 30, 34, 52, 73, 88, 96, 124, 161–62, 163, 165, 205
Elizabeth Park, Hartford, 48, 111, 115, 120
Ellison, Ralph, 145
Emerson, Ralph Waldo, 55, 70, 217
Empson, William, 125
Engels, Friedrich, 87
England, 46, 78, 79, 208
Environment, 6, 12, 48, 76, 102–4, 105, 107, 112, 114, 115, 118–19, 127, 149, 177, 180
Epimenides, 107
Epstein, Andrew, 9, 134, 170
Ethics, 9, 11, 21, 130, 227–28, 234
Ethiopia, 3, 18, 23, 25, 27, 42
Europe, 23, 24, 26, 42, 71, 74, 96, 118, 121, 164, 215, 216
Exile, 23, 38, 68, 79, 82, 91, 183–84, 214
Exoticism, 17, 20, 21, 50, 72, 73, 74, 80, 105, 141–43

Eyers, Tom, 11
Eysteinsson, Astradur, 88

Faulkner, William, 175
Feinsod, Harris, 50, 74, 81, 216
Femininity, 2, 8, 80, 120, 140–41
Fenollosa, Ernest, 89
Feo, José Rodríguez. *See* Rodríguez Feo, José
Fernandez, Ramon, 52, 120, 191
Feuerbach, Ludwig, 64
Filreis, Alan, 18, 31, 34, 74, 78, 95, 128–29, 139, 163, 170, 171, 217
Finch, Zachary, 11
Firbank, Ronald, 125
First World War, 20
Flaubert, Gustave, 175
Florida, 120, 130, 189–90, 205–6, 208, 210
France, 22, 78, 79, 80, 93, 163–64, 168, 214, 222, 223
Frankfurt School, 40
Fredericks, Claude, 134
Fredrickson, Barbara L., 155
Freud, Sigmund, 63, 125, 212
Friedman, Susan Stanford, 72, 96

Gage, Sybil, 123
Galvin, Rachel, 74, 144–45, 221
García Lorca, Federico, 168
Gardner, Sebastian, 100
Gascoyne, David, 96
Gates, Henry Louis, Jr., 145
Gender, 8, 126, 128, 136, 138, 139–42, 144, 222
Geneva, Switzerland, 38
Gerber, Natalie, 217
Germany, 21, 26, 32, 37, 79, 80, 113
Ghalib, 93
Ghazal, 92–94
Giannoni, Roberto, 95
Gide, André, 175
Gilbert, Roger, 55, 105
Gilbert, Sandra, 140
Gilman, Charlotte Perkins, 32
Ginsberg, Allen, 123, 162
Giorgione, 195
Giscombe, C. S., 145
Glissant, Édouard, 90
Globalization, 6, 20, 23, 27, 71–76, 82, 94, 95
    and world literature. *See* World Literature
    global imaginary, 71, 74, 75–76, 77, 80–81, 96
    global marketplace, 6, 26, 90, 92
    global reception of Stevens, 6, 90, 95, 96
    global South, 88
    lingua franca, 50, 71, 81–82
Glück, Louise, 44, 221
Goethe, Johann Wolfgang von, 87

Goldfarb, Lisa, 10, 114, 121, 165, 170, 171
Golding, Alan, 162, 170
Gooch, Brad, 165, 167, 171
Graham, Jorie, 162
Great Britain, 77, 96, 121, 125
Greece, 88, 216
Guatemala, 77
Guattari, Félix, 102
Gubar, Susan, 140
Guest, Barbara, 161, 163, 167–68

H.D. (Hilda Doolittle), 88
Hafez, 94
Haft, Lloyd, 90
Haglund, David, 83
Halliday, Mark, 44, 53, 55
Halperin, David M., 127
Hammer, Langdon, 131–32
Hammond, Mac, 105
Han, Gül Bilge, 5–6, 17, 22, 45, 56
Hanley, Reverend Arthur, 219
Hardt, Michael, 46
Harris, Cheryl I., 138
Harrison, Ruth, 89
Hartford Accident and Indemnity Company,
    137, 139
Hartford Times, The, 18
Hartford, Connecticut, 21, 23, 25, 48–49, 83, 111,
    114, 115, 120, 129, 221
Hartman, Geoffrey, 209
Harvard Law Review, 138
Harvard University, 89, 94, 95, 126, 127, 128, 140,
    164, 165, 199
Harvey, Giles, 165
Havana, Cuba, 75, 129–30
Hayes, Terrance, 45, 144–45
Hayot, Eric, 73
Heaney, Seamus, 96
Heidegger, Martin, 226
Hemingway, Ernest, 174–75
Herd, David, 171
Hero, 24, 27, 39, 41, 54, 60, 61–62, 75, 125, 187,
    189–91, 192–95, 196, 214
Herring, Scott, 134
Holland. *See* Netherlands, The
Hollander, John, 162
Homer, 200
Hong Kong, 91
Hopkins, Gerard Manley, 208
Howard, Richard, 7, 131, 132–33
Howe, Irving, 30, 38
Howe, Susan, 163, 170
Hughes, Langston, 144
Huizinga, Johan, 66

Humanism, 31, 52, 59, 107, 203, 206, 211
Huxley, Aldous, 32

Iceland, 22, 77
Ideology. *See* Politics
Imagination and reality, 4, 29, 39, 113, 115, 132,
    189, 197, 229, 235
Imagist poetry, 162
Imperialism, 3–4, 12, 17–21, 22–27, 73, 75, 78, 90,
    92, 96, 221
Impersonality, 5, 44, 46, 53, 55, 63, 65, 164, 203,
    205, 214, 222
India, 17
Inhuman/non-human, 5, 51, 53, 58, 61–62, 63, 65,
    107, 206–7, 210
Intentionality, 108
Intersectionality, 6, 8, 12, 136–41, 144–45
    intersectional studies, 8, 136, 138, 139–40, 142, 145
Inventario, 95
Iran, 26, 92–94
Ireland, 91, 96, 126
Irish Times, The, 96
Irony, 32, 61, 65, 150, 157, 202, 205, 206,
    208–9, 217
Italy, 18, 23, 24, 25, 27, 32, 46, 95–96

Jackson, David, 132
Jackson, Major, 144–45
Jackson, Virginia Walker, 154
James, Henry, 11, 124, 125, 128, 129, 174, 219–20
James, William, 58, 128
Jameson, Fredric, 17, 30, 214
Janssen, Lesley, 171
Japan, 73, 89
Jarraway, David R., 127–28, 134, 167–68, 171
Jarrell, Randall, 44, 53
Java, Indonesia, 91
Jenkins, Lee M., 6
Johnson, Barbara, 141
Joseph, Lawrence, 137
Joyce, James, 73, 175

Kalliney, Peter, 73
Kant, Immanuel, 68, 188
Kantorowicz, Hermann, 34
Kashmir, 91–92
Keats, John, 171, 199
Keenaghan, Eric, 74, 81, 130
Keller, Lynn, 171
Kenner, Hugh, 44, 53, 74, 88, 162, 219
Key West, Florida, 52, 115, 120, 210
Kinsella, Thomas, 96
Kleinberg-Levin, Richard, 31
Kleinzahler, August, 48

Knopf, Alfred A., 131
Koch, Kenneth, 161, 163, 164, 168–69
Konstantinov, Fyodor Vasilevich, 38, 39
Korea, 89
Kotin, Joshua, 27, 31, 42, 45, 47
Kringelbach, Morten L., 149

Lacan, Jacques, 211
Ladkin, Sam, 171
Lake Geneva, Switzerland, 38
Language poetry, 162, 170
Laplanche, Jean, 212
Latimer, Ronald Lane, 23, 89, 126
Latin America, 75
Law, 36, 41, 66, 78, 88, 126, 136–37, 138
Le, Brenda, 94
Lee, Peter H., 89
Lehman, David, 168, 171
Lenin, Vladimir, 38–39
Lensing, George S., 101, 114, 121, 200
Lentricchia, Frank, 17, 30, 31, 90–91, 92–93, 139,
    140, 141–42
Lerner, Max, 4, 34–35
Levinson, Marjorie, 109
Lewis, F. D., 93
Lezama Lima, José, 81, 131
Locke, Alain, 142
Longenbach, James, 17, 27, 30, 31, 34, 134, 139
Lorca, Federico García. *See* García Lorca,
    Federico
Louvre Museum, Paris, 27
Lowell, Robert, 161
Luhan, Mable Dodge, 125
Lyric, 11–12, 45, 51, 53, 55, 89, 101, 154, 163, 187, 195,
    226–28, 230–31, 236

Macdonald, D. L., 38
Macksey, Richard, 101–2
MacLeod, Glen, 2, 124–25, 134, 170
MacNeice, Louis, 166
Maeder, Beverly, 105–6
Magrelli, Valerio, 6, 96
Mahon, Derek, 96
Maine, 17, 26
Mani, B. Venkat, 88
Manner, 11, 213–18, 219–23
Mannheim, Karl, 4, 33–36, 40–42
Mao, Douglas, 4, 72
Marchand, Jean, 78
Marchand, South Africa, 78
Marcus, Harold G., 23
Marx, Edward, 17, 21, 22
Marx, Karl, 87
Marxism, 87, 119

Masculinity, 24, 80, 120, 186
Matterson, Stephen, 27, 76
Matthiessen, F. O., 165
Maturana, Humberto, 7, 103, 104
Mazzoni, Guido, 95
McGarrity, Maria, 90
McGreevy, Thomas, 91, 96, 126
McKendrick, Jamie, 95
Memory, 10, 79, 174, 178, 180, 183, 184, 231
Merrill, James, 7, 131–33, 162
Merwin, W. S., 93
Metaphysics, 29, 59–62, 64, 66, 69, 207–8, 209,
    218, 227
Mexico, 22, 75
Migration, 22, 46, 54, 72, 75, 76, 89, 92, 118–19
Miller, J. Hillis, 45, 47, 101
Milton, John, 24, 199
Modernism, 11, 17, 30–31, 45, 48, 52, 71, 76, 88, 92,
    93, 112–14, 130, 162, 168, 170, 174, 202, 205,
    208, 211, 214, 222
    American modernism, 74, 88, 205
    global modernism, 5, 71
    high modernism, 30, 31, 202, 214
    modernist fiction, 9, 174
    new modernist studies, 7, 72–73, 82, 124
    planetary modernisms, 96
    transnational modernism, 71–74, 82, 90
Modernity, 5, 19, 24, 25, 49, 58–59, 60, 62, 64, 66,
    73, 74, 111, 115, 202
Monacell, Peter, 115
Monroe, Harriet, 90–91, 213
Moody, David A., 71
Moore, Marianne, 31, 52, 161, 164, 213
Moore, Nicholas, 96
More, Thomas, 29, 32
Moretti, Franco, 88
Moss, Thylias, 145
Motokiyo, Zeami, 89
Muñoz, José Esteban, 130
Munson, Gorham, 213
Murry, John Middleton, 34
Museum of Fine Arts, Boston, 89
Museum of Modern Art, New York City, 200
Mussolini, Benito, 3, 18, 23–25, 26–27, 42
Mutter, Matthew, 5
Myklebust, Nicholas, 149–50, 152
Myth, 35, 39, 47, 49, 63, 69, 76, 101, 112, 115,
    118, 120

Nancy, Jean-Luc, 47
Narayanan, Vivek, 145
Nation, 5, 8, 12, 23, 55, 71, 73–74, 76–77, 78,
    81–82, 87–88, 92, 94, 118, 138, 213, 217
Native Americans, 23

Nature, 6–7, 17, 19, 50, 58–59, 68, 75, 92, 102, 103, 105, 106, 111, 115, 116, 120, 148, 150, 155, 176–78, 179–80, 181, 187, 199, 209, 210–11
Negation, 1, 46, 60, 205–6
Negri, Antonio, 46
Nesme, Axel, 114
Netherlands, The, 216
New American poetry, 161–62, 170
New Criticism, 161, 163
New Republic, 34, 39
New York City, New York, 7, 25, 77, 93, 113–15, 116, 117, 123, 125, 132, 166
New York School poetry, 9, 131, 161–70
New York Times, The, 18
Newcomb, John Timberman, 30
Newness, 1, 18–19, 30, 41, 60–61, 63, 68, 77, 80–81, 101, 112, 148, 152, 162, 184–85, 195, 201, 202, 223
Nickels, Joel, 46
Niebuhr, Reinhold, 34
Nielsen, Aldon Lynn, 17, 25, 27, 141–42
Nietzsche, Friedrich, 38, 59
Noë, Alva, 102
North Carolina, 22, 75, 76
Nostalgia, 46, 51, 59, 60, 79, 201

O'Hara, Frank, 123, 131, 161, 162, 163, 164–68, 169–70
Objectivist poetry, 162
Olson, Charles, 162
Ontario, Canada, 17, 26
Ordinary, 9, 11, 20, 30–31, 38–39, 49, 81, 100, 163, 168, 187, 195, 197, 204
Orientalism, 6, 72, 73, 78, 89–90
Orígenes, 94
Osvaldini, 134

Pacific Islands, 26
Paris, France, 133
Pascal, Blaise, 62, 223
Passaic, New Jersey, 116
Pater, Walter, 124
Pearce, Roy Harvey, 94, 106–7
Pelli, Denis G., 152
Pennsylvania, 91
Performativity, 76, 105–6, 215
Perloff, Marjorie, 55, 162, 164, 166, 171
Phelps, Lyon, 171
Philadelphia, Pennsylvania, 94
Phillips, Carl, 145
Phillips, Siobhan, 169, 171
Philosophy, 2, 10, 18, 52, 95, 102, 107–8, 112, 114, 119, 121, 222, 223
  and poetry, 6, 9, 10, 12, 100, 163, 164, 167, 170, 186, 187, 201
  deconstruction, 10, 201, 203, 207, 209

empiricist philosophy, 63
epistemology, 58–59, 61, 102, 104, 109, 170
immanence, 5, 58, 63, 67–69
ontology, 25, 58–59, 65, 105, 194, 226–27
phenomenology, 10, 102, 104, 107, 108, 150
philosopher, 127, 153, 186, 190, 205
political philosophy, 4, 45–46
pragmatism, 10, 70
transcendence, 5, 31, 42, 67–69, 204, 209
Pike, Burton, 112
Pius X, Pope, 219
Place, 2, 4, 18, 20, 22, 25, 45, 48, 101, 111, 113, 114, 116, 153, 168, 184, 198, 204
  and locality, 50, 75, 76–77, 79, 82, 120, 197
  foreign places, 71, 77, 78–79, 82
  placelessness, 118
  place-names, 50, 78, 79, 92, 94
  provincialism, 71
Planck, Max, 62
Plato, 29, 66, 68, 127, 129, 130
Poersken, Bernhard, 104
Poetic form. *See* Aesthetics; aesthetic form
Poetic thinking, 10, 186–88, 189–91, 195, 196, 197, 202
Poetics, 3, 7, 9, 22, 27, 63, 71, 72, 74–77, 82, 100, 102, 104–5, 106, 121, 124, 128, 130, 139–40, 162, 163–64, 168, 189, 194, 197, 207, 220, 222, 231
Poetry, 89, 90, 140
Poggioli, Renato, 95–96
Poiesis, 104, 106
Politics, 4–5, 12, 19, 21, 23, 26–27, 45–46, 52, 54, 72, 73, 80–81, 119, 129, 132, 137, 191, 223
  and aesthetics, 4, 6, 11, 88, 91, 94, 120
  and utopia, 12, 29–31, 33–37, 40
  communism, 32, 34, 38, 87
  democracy, 34, 48, 213
  fascism, 24–25, 32, 76
  political satire, 22, 24–25
Posnock, Ross, 128
Pound, Ezra, 9, 29, 30, 40, 71, 73, 82, 88–89, 124, 161–62, 170
Princeton University, 129, 138, 175
Prokofiev, Sergei, 171
Prospect Park, New York City, 119, 121
Proust, Marcel, 10, 125, 174–85
Puskar, Jason, 45, 46

Qian, Zhaoming, 74, 82, 90
Queerness, 12, 47, 124–28, 130–31, 132–33
  queer genealogy, 124–26
  queer studies, 6, 7, 124, 126, 128
  queer temporality, 133
Quinn, Justin, 45, 55

Race, 8, 11, 17, 21, 32, 34, 50, 53–55, 136–40, 141–45, 216, 221–22
Ragg, Edward, 27, 74, 82, 89, 166, 171, 199
Raichle, Marcus E., 152
Ramazani, Jahan, 50, 72–73, 80, 82, 89, 90
Realism, 59, 63, 103, 109, 167, 168, 175
Redding, Patrick, 27
Religion, 5, 58–60, 61–62, 63–68, 101, 187, 219
Revista de Avance, 94
Rhetoric, 9, 11, 69, 76, 79, 81, 93, 105, 106, 137, 150, 154, 183, 187, 203, 213, 214–15, 223
Rich, Adrienne, 48, 93, 131
Richards, I. A., 70
Richardson, Joan, 70, 144, 170
Ricoeur, Paul, 63
Rieke, Alison, 80
Rilke, Rainer Maria, 168
Rimbaud, Arthur, 124
Robertson, Eleanor, 136–37
Rodríguez Feo, José, 7, 81, 91, 94–95, 126, 127, 128–31, 174–76
Rodríguez, Mariano, 95
Roethke, Theodore, 162
Roffman, Karin, 165, 171
Romanticism, 2, 39, 87, 107, 115, 162–63, 165, 204, 206–7, 208, 209–10
Roosevelt, Franklin Delano, 32
Rosenfeld, Paul, 213
Rotella, Carlo, 113
Rousseau, Jean-Jacques, 222
Rovelli, Carlo, 231, 233
Rowe, John Carlos, 17, 26, 27, 82
Russia, 38, 79, 83, 164, 183–84, 216
Rutherford, New Jersey, 116

Said, Edward, 17
Salibra, Elena, 95
Samarkand, Uzbekistan, 92
Sanborn, Pitts, 126
Santayana, George, 7, 126, 127–28, 130, 134, 153
Sapiro, Gisèle, 90
Saurat, Denis, 176
Scanlon, Mara, 12, 228
Schaum, Melita, 140–41
Schiller, Friedrich, 66
Schjeldahl, Peter, 72
Schuyler, George, 32
Schuyler, James, 131, 161, 163, 168
Science, 6, 62, 64, 67, 102, 137, 148, 231
biology, 6, 102–5, 107–9, 148
neuroscience, 8, 149
Sebastian, Saint, 134
Second World War, 32, 79, 81, 142, 192
Secularism, 3, 5, 49, 58–69, 95, 118
Sedarat, Roger T., 6, 92–94

Sedgwick, Eve Kosofsky, 126
Selassie, Haile, 23
Selinger, Eric Murphy, 55
Senior, Olive, 144
Serio, John N., 2, 55, 170
Seven Arts, The, 213
Sexuality, 7, 67, 124–30, 131–33, 139, 140, 142
Shakespeare, William, 96, 143–44, 169, 199
Shams, Anahita, 94
Shapiro, David, 171
Shelley, Percy, 171
Shepherd, Reginald, 145
Shiraz, Iran, 92–94
Shoptaw, John, 171
Shostakovich, Dmitri, 171
Siam. *See* Thailand
Silverberg, Mark, 171
Simmel, Georg, 113–14, 116, 118
Simons, Hi, 45, 53, 222
Siraganian, Lisa, 3–4
Skepticism, 4, 9, 10, 39, 41, 46, 60, 63, 128, 163, 190, 192, 193
Skibsrud, Johanna, 11–12
Skinner, B. F., 32
Socrates, 127
Solipsism, 45, 53, 109, 226, 228, 230
South Africa, 77–78
South America, 75
South Carolina, 22, 75, 76
Soviet Union, 32, 79
Spaide, Christopher, 4–5
Spain, 32, 75, 79, 80, 183, 214
Spenser, Edmund, 170
Spicer, Jack, 171
Spivak, Gayatri Chakravorty, 88
Sri Lanka, 22, 77–78, 91
St. Louis, Missouri, 136
St. Nicholas Society, 126
Stafford, William, 93
Starr, G. Gabrielle, 8–9, 151, 155
Stein, Gertrude, 164, 214
Steinman, Lisa M., 8, 137, 141, 145, 221
Stendhal (Marie-Henri Beyle), 31, 175
Stevens, Elsie, 113, 118, 123, 188
Stevens, Holly, 123, 202
Stevens, Wallace
    "Academic Discourse at Havana," 94
    "Adagia," 45, 52, 133, 150, 178, 180, 215, 217
    "Anecdote of the Jar," 3, 18, 19–20, 92–93
    "Architecture," 216
    "Arrival at the Waldorf," 77
    "Auroras of Autumn, The," 31, 46–47, 55, 151, 167
    "Banjo Boomer," 155–57
    "Bantams in Pine-Woods," 80, 169
    "Blue Buildings in the Summer Air, The," 39

Stevens, Wallace (cont.)
 "Bouquet of Roses in Sunlight," 150–51, 154, 182
 "Cathedrals are not built along the sea," 187
 "Chocorua to Its Neighbor," 69, 165, 194
 "Comedian as the Letter C, The," 18, 22–23, 74–77, 81, 82, 149, 169
 "Common Life, The," 117
 "Connoisseur of Chaos," 77–79
 "Course of a Particular, The," 42
 "Credences of Summer," 68, 103, 104
 "Curtains in the House of the Metaphysician, The," 218
 "Description Without Place," 38–39, 65, 216
 "Dinner Bell in the Woods," 181
 "Dish of Peaches in Russia, A," 79, 183–85
 "Domination of Black," 188
 "Earthy Anecdote," 87, 188
 "Effects of Analogy," 199
 "Esthétique du Mal," 38, 59–60, 65, 68
 "Examination of the Hero in a Time of War," 192–94
 "Exposition of the Contents of a Cab," 141
 "Extracts from Addresses to the Academy of Fine Ideas," 35–36, 37, 39, 41, 217–18
 "Farewell to Florida," 189–90
 "Final Soliloquy of the Interior Paramour," 152
 "Hermitage at the Center, The," 48
 "High-Toned Old Christian Woman, A," 66
 "Holiday in Reality," 80
 "How to Live. What to Do," 59, 61–62
 "Idea of Order at Key West, The," 52, 53, 103, 119–20, 191–92, 208–11
 "Idiom of the Hero," 27
 "Imagination as Value," 64, 194, 223
 "In the Clear Season of Grapes," 182
 "Indian River," 181
 "Infanta Marina," 214
 "Irrational Element in Poetry, The," 215
 "Jasmine's Beautiful Thoughts Underneath the Willow," 182, 188–89
 "July Mountain," 49–50
 "Landscape with Boat," 30, 62
 "Large Red Man Reading," 51
 "Le Monocle de Mon Oncle," 124, 169, 216
 "Les Plus Belles Pages," 195
 "Life Is Motion," 167
 "Life on a Battleship," 3, 24
 "Loneliness in Jersey City," 118
 "Lytton Strachey, Also, Enters into Heaven," 39
 "Man Carrying Thing," 235
 "Man on the Dump, The," 190
 "Man Whose Pharynx Was Bad, The," 117

"Man with the Blue Guitar, The," 31, 36–38, 41, 54, 80, 95, 104, 106, 108, 168, 217, 227, 229, 233–35
 "Martial Cadenza," 79
 "Meditation Celestial & Terrestrial," 183
 "Metamorphosis," 117
 "Metaphors of a Magnifico," 103, 188
 "Montrachet-le-Jardin," 192–93
 "Mythology reflects its region, A," 49
 "New England Verses," 118
 "News and the Weather, The," 217
 "Noble Rider and the Sound of Words, The," 19, 21–22, 63, 132, 138, 139, 189, 215
 "Not Ideas About the Thing but the Thing Itself," 90, 106
 "Notes Toward a Supreme Fiction," 37, 39, 53, 54, 55, 64–65, 67–68, 80–82, 120, 132, 196, 217, 221, 229, 233, 236
 "Novel, The," 94, 130
 "Nudity at the Capital," 221–22
 "Nudity in the Colonies," 221–22
 "Nuns Painting Water-Lilies," 48, 120
 "Of Hartford in a Purple Light," 120
 "Of Mere Being," 106, 202–8, 209–10
 "Of Modern Poetry," 20, 21, 60
 "Of the Manner of Addressing Clouds," 215
 "On the Road Home," 106
 "Ordinary Evening in New Haven, An," 30–31, 196, 204, 226
 "Owl in the Sarcophagus, The," 51, 220
 "Owl's Clover," 3, 17, 18, 24–27, 30, 32–33, 34, 39, 42, 46, 76, 119, 121, 141
 "Parochial Theme," 26
 "Pastor Caballero, The," 65
 "Pieces," 183
 "Plain Sense of Things, The," 48, 62, 100, 197, 228–29
 "Planet on the Table, The," 71, 87, 96, 106
 "Plot Against the Giant, The," 214
 "Postcard from the Volcano, A," 51, 54, 91–92, 139, 231–33, 234
 "Prelude to Objects," 27
 "Prologues to What Is Possible," 80, 81
 "Pure Good of Theory, The," 63
 "Quiet Normal Life, A," 198–99
 "Reality Is an Activity of the Most August Imagination," 109
 "Red Fern, The," 182
 "Region November, The," 106–7
 "Relations Between Poetry and Painting, The," 176
 "River of Rivers in Connecticut, The," 49
 "Rock, The," 51, 95
 "Sad Strains of a Gay Waltz," 39, 40–41, 190
 "Saint John and the Back-Ache," 60, 183

"Sea Surface Full of Clouds," 65, 169
"Sense of the Sleight-of-Hand Man, The," 69
"Sick Man, The," 54–55
"Six Significant Landscapes," 89, 116, 120, 182
"Sketch of the Ultimate Politician," 80
"Snow Man, The," 55, 89, 90, 92, 95, 103, 117, 188, 228
"Someone Puts a Pineapple Together," 94, 169
"St. Armorer's Church from the Outside," 1
"Sunday Morning," 29, 32, 33, 53, 104, 139, 140, 153, 168, 171, 216
"Table Talk," 51, 133
"Tea," 120
"Things of August," 153, 182
"Thirteen Ways of Looking at a Blackbird," 89, 90
"This Solitude of Cataracts," 95
"Thought Revolved, A," 116
"Three Academic Pieces," 94
"To an Old Philosopher in Rome," 121, 127, 128, 153
"To the Roaring Wind," 181
"Two or Three Ideas," 64, 199
"Vacancy in the Park," 120
"Virgin Carrying a Lantern, The," 8, 142–45
"Vita Mea," 187
"Weak Mind in the Mountains, A," 3, 18, 22, 77
"Word with José Rodríguez-Feo, A," 94, 130
"Worms at Heaven's Gate, The," 51
"Yellow Afternoon," 165
Auroras of Autumn, The, 44, 194, 226
Carlos Among the Candles, 89, 117
Collected Poems, The, 87, 90, 94, 96, 105, 106, 131, 187
Harmonium, 8, 10, 50, 51, 71, 87, 89, 91, 101, 106, 140, 142, 165, 186, 188, 189, 213, 228
Ideas of Order, 11, 187, 221, 231
Mattino Domenicale ed Altre Poesie, 95
Palm at the End of the Mind, The, 202
Parts of a World, 77–78, 82, 165
Rock, The, 11, 71, 101, 187, 197, 228
Three Travelers Watch a Sunrise, 89
Transport to Summer, 187
Tutte le Poesie, 95
Stewart, Kathleen, 49–50
Strachey, Lytton, 39
Strand, Mark, 93, 162
Summers, Claude J., 134
Surrealism, 164, 168
Sweden, 46
Switzerland, 38
Symbolism, 124, 162, 163

Tartakovsky, Roi, 157
Taylor, Charles, 61, 69
Teasdale, Sara, 117
Technology, 27, 49, 106, 112, 116
Temporality, 11, 41, 72, 79, 88, 103, 107–8, 133, 177, 201–4, 205–7, 208, 209–11, 220, 230, 231–32, 235
Tennessee, 19–20, 92–93, 94
Tennyson, Lord Alfred, 199
Teresa, Saint, 218
Thailand, 91
Tillich, Paul, 34
Tomlinson, John, 17
Towle, Tony, 166
Tragedy, 60, 118, 180
Translation, 33, 63, 87, 89–90, 94–97
Transnationalism, 3, 5, 6, 12, 71–73, 74–82, 90, 97, 128, 130
Trilling, Lionel, 11, 223–24
Tsur, Reuven, 149

Universality, 23, 51–53, 64–65, 78, 94, 155, 214
University of Chicago Legal Forum, 139
University of Pennsylvania Museum, Philadelphia, 94
Urbanization, 7, 113, 116, 121
urban studies, 111–13
urbanism, 7, 25, 48, 111–12, 115, 117, 118, 119–20
urbanization of mind, 113, 114
Utard, Juliette, 114
Utopia, 3–4, 12, 29–42, 112, 119

Valéry, Paul, 95
van Geyzel, Leonard C., 78, 91, 175
Van Vechten, Carl, 124, 125–26, 132
Varela, Francisco, 7, 103
Vasari, Giorgio, 215
Velázquez, Diego, 214
Vendler, Helen, 11, 51, 55, 73, 105, 106, 144, 182
Verlaine, Paul, 124
Vermont, 49–50
Vessel, Edward A., 155, 157
Vico, Giambattista, 63–64, 69
Vienna, Austria, 17, 109
Vita, Carlo, 95
von Hallberg, Robert, 217, 220
von Uexküll, Jakob, 102
Vox, 136

Wadsworth Atheneum, Hartford, 126
Walcott, Derek, 91
Walkowitz, Rebecca L., 72, 73
Wallace Stevens Journal, The, 2, 125, 217
Wallerstein, Immanuel, 88
Ward, Geoff, 171

Waters, William, 12, 228
Weinstein, Arnold, 113
Werner, Craig Hansen, 93
Whitman, Walt, 104, 124, 125, 164
Wilbur, Richard, 162
Wilde, Oscar, 124–25, 132, 133
Williams, Tennessee, 131
Williams, William Carlos, 76, 82, 96, 116, 161–62, 164, 167, 168, 169, 214
Winkiel, Laura, 73
Winks, Christopher, 81
Wolfe, Cary, 6–7, 109
Wollaeger, Mark, 73

Woolf, Virginia, 73
World Literature, 6, 12, 87–88, 92, 96–97
World War I. *See* First World War
World War II. *See* Second World War

Yan, Zhuang, 90
Yeats, William Butler, 38, 40, 52, 124, 207
Yiheng, Zhao, 90
Yucatan, Mexico, 75

Zimbabwe, 26
Zukofsky, Louis, 163
Zurich, Switzerland, 17

Lightning Source UK Ltd.
Milton Keynes UK
UKHW041350300621
386382UK00002BA/9